PING

PING

The Secrets of Successful
Virtual Communication

ANDREW BRODSKY, PHD

Simon Acumen

New York Amsterdam/Antwerp London Toronto Sydney New Delhi

SIMON
ACUMEN

An Imprint of Simon & Schuster, LLC
1230 Avenue of the Americas
New York, NY 10020

First Simon Acumen/Simon Element hardcover edition February 2025

SIMON ELEMENT is a trademark of Simon & Schuster, LLC

For information about special discounts for bulk purchases, please contact Simon &
Schuster Special Sales at 1-866-506-1949 or business@simonandschuster.com.

The Simon & Schuster Speakers Bureau can bring authors to your live event.
For more information or to book an event, contact the Simon & Schuster Speakers
Bureau at 1-866-248-3049 or visit our website at www.simonspeakers.com.

Interior design by Silverglass

Manufactured in the United States of America

1 3 5 7 9 10 8 6 4 2

Library of Congress Cataloging-in-Publication Data has been applied for.

ISBN 978-1-6680-5524-3
ISBN 978-1-6680-5526-7 (ebook)

To my wife and muse, Stephanie. Your unwavering love and support made this book a reality.

CONTENTS

1

The PING Approach

Once a new technology rolls over you, if you're not part
of the steamroller, you're part of the road.
—Stewart Brand, *The Media Lab: Inventing the Future at MIT*

"You have cancer."

Can you imagine words that are harder to hear—or deliver?

I was sixteen years old, sitting in the emergency room with my parents beside me. I had been admitted because of a fever that wouldn't break. The three of us had been slumped on hard plastic chairs in the waiting room for hours, the monotony punctuated by a variety of tests, followed by more waiting.

I had been feeling under the weather for a couple of weeks—unable to stay awake long enough to get through the day, losing my appetite, feverish . . . I thought I had a bad case of the flu. Certainly nothing life-threatening. I was a fit, healthy teenager outside of this momentary blip, and on top of the world (or at least my high school's debate club). My two-year plan featured applying to college and working up the nerve to ask my crush to prom. It definitely didn't involve hospitals, or chemotherapy, or radiation, or—

"I'm so sorry to be the bearer of this news," said a grim-faced physician. "But you have cancer."

Cancer. Amid all the other medical jargon that followed, that one word stood out.

Impossible, my inner voice insisted. *I'm only sixteen. Only old people get cancer. I couldn't be* that *sick. Maybe this is all just a bad dream . . .*

As my parents and I sat in a sterile office dazed and mute, the doctor went on to explain that I had a rare form of leukemia and would need a bone marrow transplant. My prognosis wasn't good.

Likely as a coping mechanism, I started to wonder about my doctor. A core part of her job was figuring out how to communicate life-threatening diagnoses to patients. What was it like for her to have to tell a sixteen-year-old he might die? How does someone even *do* that?

The doctor handed my mother a tissue when she started crying. When my father dropped a pen because his hands were shaking, the doctor retrieved it while gently assuring my parents their reactions were completely normal and that she would do everything in her power to help get us through this difficult time.

When we left her office, the doctor gave each of us a hug.

As you might have already guessed from the fact that I'm writing this book, thanks to an extraordinary team of doctors, I survived. My interaction with that doctor in the ER was the first of many difficult conversations my parents and I had over the course of my two-year-long treatment. From that day on, my interest in how people communicate as part of their professions began to take shape. Through my jobs and conversations with professionals in various fields, I became fascinated by the topic of how we adapt our communication practices to an increasingly digital world.

The question of how technology alters our communication practices was the basis of my PhD research at Harvard Business School, and now as a professor at The University of Texas at Austin and founder of Ping Group, where I've consulted for and trained employees in organizations from startups to Fortune 100 companies like Dell and Amazon. I have studied more than 100,000 people in their work engaging in different types of communications—from executives attempting to inspire employees through video calls, to teachers in Vietnam needing to tell parents that their child failed a course via email.

Beyond my research expertise, I also have a unique relationship with virtual communication. Because of a lifelong immune deficiency resulting from my cancer treatment, I've often found myself only able to interact with others from a distance. As a result, I understand the good and bad of virtual communication in a very personal way, which is why I've made this topic my life's work.

Before we go any further, I need to define virtual communication. Simply put, it's any communication that occurs via electronic means, which includes video (e.g., Zoom, Microsoft Teams, Google Meet, and Webex), audio (e.g., webcam-off conferences and telephone calls), and text communication (e.g., email, instant messaging, and text messaging).

Virtual communication doesn't just diverge from in-person interactions in terms of its mode—it also necessitates a different approach both to how it's used and received. To illustrate what I mean, let's return to my cancer diagnosis story I shared earlier. I'm going to tell this story again, except this time the scenario will be slightly modified. Picture another family with one difference: the meeting doesn't happen in person. Instead, because the family doesn't live near the cancer center, this doctor's appointment takes place as a video visit.

As the minutes tick by, the family finds themselves staring at their reflection on their laptop video display while waiting for the doctor to arrive. Once the doctor joins the meeting, ten minutes after the appointment was scheduled, there are several false starts due to sound issues. Then there's an echo that takes long minutes to resolve.

There is no way for the doctor to know the father's hands are shaking, and when the mother ducks away from the screen to hide the fact that she's crying, the doctor doesn't see it. There are no hugs.

On the whole, it sounds like an inferior experience, right?

The takeaway seems to be that, whenever difficult conversations need to be had, in-person is best. But is that necessarily true?

A benefit to this hypothetical video appointment is that the family doesn't receive dire news in a sterile hospital setting. They don't have to leave the comfort of their house, which is especially convenient since the child is so nauseous and dizzy he can't even walk to the car. And after the call ends, there's no need to converse with front-office staff to deliver health insurance information, all while trying to come to terms with a life-altering diagnosis. Instead, they can do that in the privacy of their home without strangers watching.

Whereas the old way of thinking was that in-person communication is always better, newer research has now demonstrated that isn't always the case. There are often trade-offs to communicating in person, and in many situations, video calls, phone calls, email, and even text messages have been shown to be the superior mode of communication.

The Times They Are a-Changin'

I can imagine what you're thinking at this point: most of us won't ever have to tell someone else they have cancer. However, we all face communication challenges in our daily lives. You may need to explain to your boss why the new initiative they're excited about isn't going to work. You might have to tell a customer that the loan they desperately need wasn't approved. Or maybe you're compelled to express congratulations to a coworker who got the promotion you felt you deserved.

And then there are the communications that are less memorable but can be even more important because they occur so regularly. For example, you might be giving your boss an update about the work you accomplished during the past week. Or you're trying to convince a customer to sign up for your service. Or you're just reaching out to a coworker to see how their weekend was.

Whether monumental or mundane, modern workplace conversations are complicated by the fact that many of them are conducted virtually.

Let's face it: the ways we interact at work today aren't the same as they were ten—or even five—years ago. And virtual communication isn't going away. With ongoing innovations in artificial intelligence and augmented reality, the pace of change in our communication options is poised to accelerate. In the immortal words of Bob Dylan, "the times they are a-changin'." And we need to adapt.

By one estimate, the average worker spends five hours a day on email and ninety minutes instant messaging. That's six and a half hours—a serious chunk of your waking hours—spent on text communication. And that doesn't even begin to cover the tremendous amount of time now spent in audio and video calls on platforms like Zoom, Microsoft Teams, Google Meet, or Webex.

Even for those who do work in an office 100 percent of the time, it is commonplace to use instant messaging and email to communicate with people who are only a cubicle away. Given the ease of interacting via communication technologies, people often avoid physically going to a colleague's office to ask them a question. Unless you've scheduled a meeting in advance, barging in unannounced can (rightfully so) be perceived as an interruption.

I'm not just talking about employees working at desk jobs. Tradespeople who don't use a computer for their primary work functions are facing these same challenges. Plumbers and landscapers use email, text messages, and online platforms like Nextdoor, Facebook, and Yelp to communicate with customers. Grocery store cashiers and fast-food workers regularly text managers about schedules and receive emails from corporate headquarters about new procedures.

The new landscape of communication technology has changed the calculus for how we interact with each other. The debate is no longer about what is lost when communicating through technology. It has become: How can we leverage technology to improve our interactions even more?

Paradoxically, the number of communication technologies now at our disposal can make it harder to connect with each other. Here are just a few of the questions I've gotten in recent years, and which I'm going to answer throughout this book:

"Should I turn my camera on or off during meetings?"

"How can I show I'm a high performer through something as bare as an email?"

"Does using emojis help or hurt?"

"I am losing my mind from communication overload; how can I improve my work productivity and well-being?"

And, of course, the age-old question: *"Could this meeting have been an email?"* (Hint: The answer to this one is *it depends on the situation*, but there are strategies you can use to evaluate each communication on a case-by-case basis. More on that to come.)

In this book, I'm going to give you a blueprint to navigate these virtual communication modes.

To Remote or Not to Remote. That Is NOT the Question.

Let me be clear: this isn't another book on the pros versus cons of remote work. There's already been a lot written on the topic. Let me briefly summarize those findings so we can move forward. Simply put, there are both costs and benefits to remote work, and finding the best solution depends on the organization. For some companies, having access to a broader and more diverse talent pool, which remote work enables, is most important. Others prioritize an in-person culture that allows for more spontaneous interactions between employees. Hybrid work isn't always an optimal solution either. In many cases, a hybrid model just makes everyone unhappy: workers who prefer to be remote end up being dissatisfied that they are being forced to commute to the office, despite not feeling any more productive on those days, and employees who prefer to be in the office find their days at home to be isolating and demoralizing.

I also caution you from overinterpreting headlines on remote work research, as it is a multi-piece puzzle, and we currently only have some of the pieces. For instance, if you read a headline that remote work improves/decreases productivity by X percent, remember that productivity is only one of many factors that lead to organizational success. There are other elements that are just as important, such as employee creativity, job satisfaction, diversity, and retention. Let me give you a simple illustrative example. If a company's employees are split so that half are randomly assigned to work remotely, and those remote employees are found to be 2 percent less productive, then people will begin drawing conclusions from an incomplete picture. But this experimental design only utilizes existing employees. What about the impact of recruiting? If posting a job as remote allows the company to recruit workers who are on average 10 percent more talented (as you're drawing from a larger talent pool), that means the net productivity would likely be higher with remote work (as the 10 percent recruiting improvement would outweigh the 2 percent remote work decrement). Additionally, recent research findings don't account for the fact that humanity has had thousands of years of experience with in-person work, but remote work has only become mainstream in the past few years. It is likely that innovations gained through more experience with remote work will change the in-office versus remote-work equation. Honestly, research aside, unless you are a CEO, there often isn't anything actionable you can do to select your ideal work context, aside from quitting your current job and applying to organizations that are remote/in-person.

Now that you know what this book isn't about, let's get to the good part. This book *is* about how to strategically use virtual communication to achieve your goals—whether those tools are email, video, instant messaging, audio calls, text messaging, or (as is so often the case) some combination thereof. In the current world of work, it isn't only remote workers who are using these tools; it's everyone. Whereas only a sub-segment of the workforce is remote, we are all virtual communicators.

Let me say it again. We are all virtual communicators.

I want to emphasize this point because, too often, I encounter the incorrect assumption that virtual communication is only relevant to remote workers. That couldn't be further from the truth. Remote employees are individuals who work outside of a specified office, usually from home. Virtual communication is any communication that occurs electronically; for instance, even if the person you are instant-messaging is only sitting one desk away, you're still communicating virtually. From construction workers to office employees, many of our most important interactions with customers and colleagues now take place via technology. For this reason, much of my research over the past fifteen years has focused on communication strategies for everyone, ranging from those who use virtual communication tools—such as email or video calls—for a small part of their everyday work to those who rely on virtual communication as their sole means of interacting at work.

Many people were thrust into remote work unexpectedly in 2020 due to the COVID-19 pandemic. However, the vast majority of workers were using technology to communicate, with mixed success, long before then. But the limited advice I've seen broadly distributed beyond academia has been rather anecdotal—based only on stories from individuals about what they feel has worked best for them. Yet there has been a great deal of scientific research on virtual communication (some of it by yours truly). Unfortunately, scientists who study virtual communication don't always have a clear channel for sharing their findings outside of academic circles. As a result, only a fraction of this research tends to find its way into the public's hands. This book will help bring everyone in on these conversations, so you'll be able to make better (and data-driven) decisions about how to best approach virtual communication.

My goal is to help people communicate more effectively, full stop. There is a better way than white-knuckling it and hoping for the best or going on "intuition." A CEO who laid off nearly a thousand people on a video call did that, and it wasn't pretty (more on that in a bit). There are countless instances of people thoughtlessly misusing communication tools in ways that change their lives (and not for the better). Yet, when used well, technology can help us thrive in the workplace, build valuable connections with others, and innovate like never before.

The science-based strategies I'll introduce in this book will generally take one of two approaches. The first will provide insight into which types of communication modes are optimal in different situations. How do you choose the appropriate mode to appear most authentic or empathetic, to best showcase your work performance, or to improve your own well-being (or all of the above)? And, maybe more prominent in people's minds, how do you avoid choosing a mode and method that will backfire? As I'll be discussing, there is no single "best" mode across every situation, but there are best choices for each individual situation. And making the wrong choice in high-stakes settings can lead to dire outcomes. That's why it's well worth learning how to make the best decision possible based on the context, rather than just defaulting to habit.

The second approach will provide recommendations for how, once you've selected your communication mode, to best leverage it. I'll cover topics including how to avoid emotional pitfalls in email, how to build trust through video calls, and how something as basic as text messaging can be used to increase team cohesion. By intermixing these tools with captivating stories and surprising research studies, this book is intended to serve as an actionable guide that will transform you into a communication technology pro.

When Things Go Wrong

You've likely heard of at least a few shudder-inducing moments when someone on a video call, unaware that their camera was on, did something embarrassing. A colleague used the toilet mid-call . . . in front of everyone in the meeting. Or your dog decided the bird outside your window was a threat to humanity while you were trying to negotiate with your boss for a promotion. Or someone's child raced in front of the camera shrieking "Baby Shark" lyrics at the top of their lungs during a work presentation.

Okay, that last one is admittedly cute, but still not ideal.

At this point, most of us have figured out how to avoid the most humiliating of those virtual communication blunders. But there is another type of error, one that is much subtler but equally problematic, that hasn't garnered nearly enough attention. I'm talking about the failure to be deliberate in choosing how and over which medium to communicate a message.

We have numerous options at our fingertips, yet people thoughtlessly select whichever mode of communication seems easiest or is directly in front of them. Many workers go about their day completing tasks and utilizing whichever communication mode is most readily available. Or they select a given mode because it's the one they've always used. Or just because "that's the way it's always been done" . . . without questioning whether it's the right (or best) choice for the given situation. They aren't thoughtful or strategic about it. And this passive approach to virtual communication can have irrevocable consequences.

In 1999, GlaxoSmithKline (GSK), a subsidiary of pharmaceutical giant SmithKline Beecham, developed a drug called Avandia. Avandia was meant to control blood sugar for patients with type 2 diabetes.

The problem?

SmithKline Beecham had conducted a secret study to compare Avandia to a competing drug. And the results were less than favorable. Not only did Avandia perform worse than their competitor, but their data showed that their drug resulted in a 30 percent increased risk of heart attacks.

Not good. Especially since diabetes patients are already at increased risk of heart attacks.

By 2007, the Senate Finance Committee had started an investigation of GSK and other pharmaceutical companies. One of the critical pieces of evidence in the investigation? An internal email sent by a GSK executive:

> Per Sr. Mgmt request, these data should not see the light of day to anyone outside of GSK.

Yikes.

As you might expect, this investigation was accompanied by a media storm. The *New York Times* and major news networks covered the story in great detail. And most of the reports included those damning words emailed by one of GSK's own executives.

The ongoing investigation resulted in a black-box warning label being placed on Avandia in 2007. In 2012, GlaxoSmithKline paid $3 billion in settlement fines for failing to report information they'd obtained about the drug's safety. However, after the Food and Drug Administration (FDA) did a three-year review of clinical trial data in 2013, they determined that Avandia did *not* show an increased risk of heart attack compared to standard type 2 diabetes medicines.

By withholding information in an attempt to save themselves a warning label on the drug—which generally wouldn't attract much, if any, media coverage—GlaxoSmithKline ended up with a whole lot of extra negative publicity . . . plus a $3 billion fine.

Obviously, it is both unethical and illegal for a pharmaceutical company to hide data. But for the moment, let's ignore the ethics and just consider that an executive decided to communicate that they would be hiding data over *email*. The executive responsible took the same approach that so many people do in their daily communication—they didn't think about it at all. If they had been more thoughtful about their form of communication, they might have decided a less permanent mode would better suit their unethical needs.

So, why didn't they choose their mode more carefully? The short answer is they probably didn't really think about it. Email was there, and it was what everyone else involved in the conversation was using.

There are countless other examples of communication blunders with disastrous results—from a Sony executive emailing racist comments about Barack Obama, to Spirit Airlines' CEO accidentally replying-all to a customer, "we owe him nothing as far as I'm concerned. Let him tell the world how bad we are. . . ." I could keep going, but you get the picture.

At this point, you might be thinking, *I'm not covering up fraud or saying something racist, so I have nothing to worry about.* But here's the thing. If highly successful executives are so thoughtless in their communication choices when doing something obviously in the wrong, then think about how little consideration most of us are putting into our interactions when we aren't worried about our messages sending us to jail.

Although you may not be communicating something that feels like it's high stakes, all your workplace interactions are still meaningful, especially when you consider their effect over the course of your career. If time and time again you're not actively considering how your messages might be coming across to others, then you're going to miss out on crucial opportunities—like connecting with a new coworker or showing your boss how hard you're working—that build up over time and can make the difference between whether you're promoted or fired.

All of this is not to say you should avoid email, because as you'll find out in the chapters ahead, other modes can backfire just as spectacularly. And in some cases, email actually is the best choice. What I'm arguing here is that there is no comprehensively right or wrong mode of communication; the important part is making an informed choice based on the situation. Defaulting to a particular approach out of habit will keep you from fully thriving at work. At best you'll miss out on opportunities and fail to grow work relationships to their full potential. And at worst, as you saw in the Sony, Avandia, and Spirit

Airlines examples, the consequences of thoughtlessly making communication choices could haunt you for years to come.

When approaching virtual communication, it is vital to be strategic in ways that are unnecessary when communicating in person. Whereas we can take many aspects of in-person communication for granted (for example, that no one is likely to be recording us), that isn't the case with communication technologies. Many crucial nuances aren't communicated virtually, such as facial expressions when conversing via email or body language when engaging in a video call. When treating virtual communication the same way we would an in-person interaction, important cues are missed, and consequently misinterpretations and conflicts can run rampant.

Many virtual communicators undermine their own messages simply by failing to engage in deliberate decision-making about how they communicate. Throughout this book, you'll learn how to avoid falling prey to that passive mentality, and all the negative consequences that come with it.

When Things Go Right

Here's where the advice in this book runs counter to a lot of the woe-is-technology pieces that pop up on our social media feeds. There are countless advantages to communication technologies. Being able to show off your impressive bookshelves to anyone with whom you have a meeting allows colleagues to get to know you in a way they never could have before. Workers can introduce their cuddly dogs over video. People bond over their shared interests, and can forge new connections, sometimes even more quickly than in person. Many of us have been engaged in this type of virtual community-building for years in hobby-related chat rooms, online forums, and more. Now we're doing the same at work.

We're all acutely aware of what it looks like when virtual communication goes wrong, but what about the flip side . . . when things go right?

As part of a research study I was conducting, I interviewed an accountant—let's call her Leigh. I asked Leigh how often she needed to use multiple virtual communication platforms during a single meeting. Laughing, she told me that this was basically her "entire day in a nutshell."

Leigh launched into a story about a recent meeting she had with a client to discuss some urgent financial statements. Several minutes before logging into the video meeting, she noticed an error in a spreadsheet that would change everything she and her colleagues had prepared. So, in order to quickly alert her team members, she sent them an instant message to provide the updated information. Meanwhile, she used her personal cell phone to send a text message to her supervisor, who was working in the office next door fifteen steps away. After the meeting, Leigh sent a follow-up email to the client and her colleagues to review everything they discussed and outline next steps.

"It felt like a lot of communication for a one-hour meeting," Leigh told me. "But it's a situation tons of us find ourselves in all the time, and if you don't pick the right technology at any given moment, things can fall apart."

Sound familiar?

I've heard so many employees express their frustration at the magnitude of communication tools available . . . and the lack of clarity over which one (or *ones*, as is so often the case) is best in any given scenario. And choosing the right mode is only half the battle. The other is using it most effectively to achieve your goals.

The question is no longer simply how we act appropriately within the setting of a virtual conversation. It has transformed and opened a whole new can of [virtual] worms, encompassing everything from how we select the appropriate medium to how to effectively juggle multiple conversations on various platforms simultaneously.

As Leigh and I delved deeper into her reasoning for the various forms of communication she selected during that one-hour meeting, a trend emerged: Leigh thoughtfully used all of the platforms to achieve a specific goal. Instant messaging was the quickest way to reach her colleagues before the meeting. Leigh chose to alert her supervisor via text, since that was the only way he liked to be contacted outside of scheduled meeting times (and it also prevented Leigh from needing to leave her office when a video meeting was about to begin). Writing an email after the meeting created a written record that could easily be found and referenced at a later date.

These are the actions—digitally speaking—of a virtual communication pro. Leigh's teammates agreed. In a separate interview, her supervisor noted that Leigh was "the best communicator we have on the team. I can always count on her to get information to the right people at the right time."

There are so many conversations we initiate throughout the course of a day that necessitate the use of technology. We promote, we fire, we onboard at new jobs, we meet for the first time, we deliver good news and bad . . . all from our smartphones and laptops. These conversations can determine whether we succeed or fail in our jobs, and drive interpersonal relationships to thrive or crumble. Getting off on the wrong foot with these conversations can wreak havoc on our mental health and can be the cause of quitting—"quiet" or loud.

À la Mode

To tackle the question of which modes of communication are best and how to use them, it's first important to classify them so we can come up with a kind of "ordering." Although there are many dimensions that can be used to classify communication technologies, the two main areas scientists have continually found to be most important are:

1. The variety of cues (e.g., can you see facial expressions or hear tone of voice?)
2. Synchronicity (i.e., does the communication occur more in real time like videoconferencing, or is it delayed like email?)

These two dimensions combine to determine how "rich," or how similar to face-to-face interactions, a mode of communication is.

The chart below illustrates how a number of common interaction modes tend to fall within these dimensions, with the richest communication modes appearing in the top right of the chart and the least rich appearing on the bottom left. As an important note, I intentionally used the word *tend* to describe the location of these technologies, since depending on the user, these characteristics can vary. For example, although rarer, some people respond to emails more quickly than text messages.

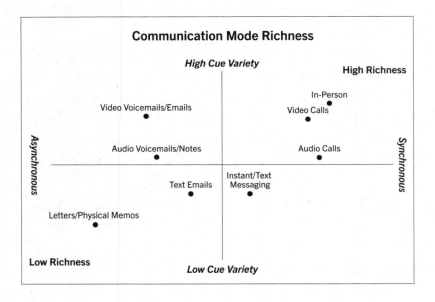

A key point about this chart is that even small differences within these dimensions can be meaningful. Video calls (e.g., Zoom, Microsoft Teams, Google Meet, and Webex) are lower on the graph than in-person interactions, since webcams generally don't capture your whole body and video calls are not in perfect resolution, and thus do not include—or make it harder to detect—all the nonverbal cues that in-person interactions might have. Similarly, in terms of synchronicity, audio and video calls are slightly less synchronous than in-person interactions. Due to small lags driven by data transfer speeds, your conversation might not be happening with the exact 1:1 speed you'd encounter during an in-person conversation.

Some of these nuances may seem pedantic, but even small differences in cue variety or synchronicity can alter the outcome of your interactions. For instance, research has shown that tiny lags of less than a second in video calls can cause interruptions and difficulty with conversational turn-taking. The spoof news website *The Onion* humorously described this problem with the headline "Coworkers on Zoom Trapped in Infinite Loop of Telling Each Other 'Oh Sorry, No, Go Ahead.'"

Identifying the dimensions on which communication technologies can vary is fundamental in understanding why things go right (or can go massively wrong) when interacting with others virtually. That's only one part of the equation, however. The other, of course, is figuring out how to employ your chosen mode and make the most of it. The combination of these two—identifying and implementing—is the key to becoming a true virtual communication expert.

The PING Approach

To bring all the lessons in this book together into an actionable plan, I've developed a framework that will help you navigate all your virtual communication, from mode choice to message framing. Whether it's video, audio, or text, this tool will give you a template to ensure success in every aspect of your virtual communication. The strategies in each chapter will fit into this broader framework, enabling you to tackle any communication challenges that come your way.

The best part is, it'll be easy to remember. It's called—wait for it—PING, which stands for **p**erspective taking, **i**nitiative, **n**onverbal, and **g**oals.

Perspective taking. When we approach our virtual communication—especially when the person isn't standing right in front of us—we tend to be more self-focused, often without realizing how our decisions will impact others. Even when people are other-focused, they can still fall short of comprehending how their messages will be perceived by its recipients.

Throughout this book, I'll highlight how people often think they're making improvements to their messages, such as adding emojis to indicate excitement, and yet these seemingly innocuous choices can have an unintended backlash. I'll also look at how CEOs, who take what they believe is the caring path to announce hard decisions like layoffs via video, may be undermining their own goals.

In the chapters to come, I'll show you how to more effectively take your virtual interaction partner's perspective and craft your messages so they're worded in a more impactful way. When done correctly, integrating perspective taking into your virtual communication strategy can ensure that miscommunication becomes a thing of the past.

Initiative. Much of what happens in face-to-face interactions— like introducing ourselves, self-disclosing personal information, and building rapport—doesn't occur as naturally in virtual interactions. As a result, we need to be more mindful about what's missing and how we can fill those gaps. And this challenge applies to everyone, even for those who are still in the office five days a week. After all, it might get you some weird looks if you walked up three floors to talk to someone in another department rather than simply sending an email or instant message.

Despite the fact that we all use technology for the majority of our communication needs, there's still a shocking amount of hesitation when it comes to virtual communication. Many people believe that using virtual communication to cold-contact someone they'd like to meet feels unnatural, and they avoid doing so because they worry social cues will be missed if they're not interacting face-to-face. Similarly, when it comes to existing relationships, people often incorrectly assume they don't need to take the initiative to reach out. However, this misconception underestimates the power of something as simple as sending a text. Later, you'll learn how a star NBA player strengthens relationships with his teammates through a quick virtual gesture, and how taking even the smallest initiative with virtual communication can make all the difference.

Understanding how to properly initiate and cultivate relationships via virtual communication is a skill you'll learn to hone. Not only will you become a master of employing various modes, but you'll get better at achieving your communication goals. And taking the initiative is an essential first step.

Nonverbal. One of the biggest virtual communication fallacies is that people mistakenly believe virtual communication contains less nonverbal language than in-person, especially for modes like email. The truth of the matter is that, even though virtual communication lacks the breadth of cues of in-person communication (e.g., voice and hand gestures), there are many signals you're sending through your virtual messages—intentionally or inadvertently—even beyond those that are possible face-to-face.

I'm going to share what science has shown regarding the impact of cues that people don't even realize they're conveying—like what time of day your message is sent, your choice of mode, and even your email signature. For example, in the chapters ahead, we'll debunk the common advice to block out a single part of your day for emails to avoid work interruptions. As you'll see, that oft-cited best practice may send unintentional signals that can undermine your goals.

Once you become an expert in understanding nonverbal cues in interactions—something most people don't consider in virtual contexts—you'll be able to utilize these cues more strategically.

Goals. One of the questions I'm consistently asked by both students and executives is *what's the best way to communicate virtually* . . . and they're disheartened to know that the answer to that all-important question is *it depends*.

This book would be a lot shorter if there were "one mode to rule them all," but alas, the right answer depends on what is most important to you in a given situation. When it comes to virtual communication, there are often conflicting goals, such as the optimal mode for being viewed by your manager as a high performer versus the best mode for increasing your own well-being. Without first being mindful and identifying what you hope to gain from an interaction, and then understanding what the best approach is for achieving that outcome, you are likely to fall short on all your goals.

I'm going to give you the tools to decide, for any given situation, which mode to use and how to most effectively leverage it.

Where We're Heading

In this book, I'm going to tackle the core components of how to more effectively navigate communication and technology challenges in modern workplaces. To do so, I'll be sharing fascinating stories, as well as the outcomes of hundreds of studies that have been conducted on virtual communication. Through this approach, I'll reveal science-based secrets about the most effective strategies for communicating in a technologically complex world so that you'll be prepared to tackle any workplace interaction. Lest you think your every digital interaction will soon be filled with only unicorns and perfectly worded messages, let me divest you of that misperception. There will always be new and unexpected communication challenges to tackle. With the right toolkit, however, you'll be able to confidently overcome any virtual communication challenge.

As the first tool in your kit, I suggest that after finishing this chapter, you pause reading and head to the Appendix to complete the *Virtual Communication Styles Tool*. This is a practically focused tool that I often use in my consulting and training to help people begin to mindfully identify some of their core virtual communication strengths and weaknesses. Better understanding yourself and how others might differ in their approach to virtual communication is the first step to becoming a virtual communication expert.

This book will provide you with research-based virtual communication strategies in three core, overarching domains of workplace interactions relevant to any communicator. The first part of this book will deal with how to use communication technologies to get ahead in your job. From optimizing your communication schedule to your choice of communication mode, I'll highlight how to actually become more productive via your virtual communication. As in-person work interactions have decreased (even in office environments, where managers now spend more time behind computers rather than physically walking around overseeing their employees' productivity), employees are now being heavily evaluated based on how they present themselves digitally. Yet, in spite of the fact that many work interactions are now occurring virtually, the old methods of performance evaluation—based on how many hours a worker is "seen" working at their desk—predominates. Thus, employees are often faced with the challenge of demonstrating to their managers that they're diligent and high performing via emails and instant messages. Being perceived as a star performer in increasingly technology-mediated workplaces isn't necessarily just about the work you do, but rather how you communicate about it, too. In the next few chapters, I'll offer strategies to show you how to use different communication technologies to manage other people's perceptions of you.

The second part of this book will broadly deal with how to build and strengthen relationships via virtual communication tools. In this section, I'll identify the central challenges to forming strong relationships virtually and offer tools for overcoming them. Further, once your relationship is established, there arises a question about how to virtually build trust in an authentic way. I'll cover communication strategies from both CEOs and employees across industries, and describe how their attempts to appear more likable have led to either great success or scandal. For instance, you'll discover how Arianna Huffington was able to allay employees' concerns regarding Uber's toxic culture via a communication mode as low-richness as email. We'll look at what research has to offer about how to initially spark and later strengthen key relationships with coworkers, superiors, and mentors—without ever needing to be in the same room.

The third and final part of the book is going to address interactions that are especially challenging in a virtual context. I'm sure we've all had an email or phone conversation that went completely off the rails, and we internally shrivel at the mere memory of how uncomfortable it was. I know I do. Dealing with challenging and tense situations was already hard enough in person. How are we supposed to do it via video or email? This section of the book will deal with how even simple mistakes in tense situations can ruin careers and companies—a hard lesson for HSBC Bank to learn after a misinterpretation cost them over $10 million—and how to avert them. You'll learn how to avoid emotional pitfalls and reach optimal negotiation agreements, as well as mitigate racial, cultural, disability, and gender stereotypes in a virtual context. Perhaps most important of all, you'll find yourself armed with the knowledge of how to emotionally thrive in a world of communication overload.

My goal is that you'll gain a new toolkit of practical communication strategies you'll be able to implement as soon as you put this book down. You'll be able to easily transition from in-person to email to video, select the best technology to fit the task, and craft messages in a way that will strengthen your work relationships, professional trajectory, and team success. As technology becomes more central to our personal and professional lives, we need to adapt our communication practices. And this book will enable you to do just that.

KEY LESSONS

✦ Remote work ≠ virtual communication. Whether you are in
the office or not, virtual communication tools are an essential
(and unavoidable) part of our work. Thus, we are all virtual
communicators. In order to thrive in the modern work
environment, it's impossible to avoid being a virtual communicator.

✦ There is no single best mode of communication. The optimal mode
is contextually dependent, and so it is vital to understand the
strengths and weaknesses of each.

✦ Many people use virtual communication without thinking about
the consequences of their mode and messaging decisions. Virtual
communication experts are deliberate in their decisions and
consider how their communication goals shape their choice of
mode and messaging.

✦ Knowing where on the "Communication Mode Richness" chart
a technology falls can help you understand the characteristics of
communication modes (and, subsequently, how to begin to avoid
virtual communication pitfalls).

✦ PING: Perspective Taking, Initiative, Nonverbal, and Goals. You'll
be able to refer to this framework again and again as you become a
virtual communication pro.

2

To Meet or Not to Meet . . . That Is the Question

How to Communicate More Productively

Meetings handled well reduce email. Email handled well reduces meetings.
—DAVID ALLEN, AUTHOR OF *GETTING THINGS DONE*

What happened during the War of 1812? How many songs did the Beatles record? What's the technical term for a group of cats? (The answer, in case you are curious, is a clowder.) *Is it possible to die from laughing?* (Apparently yes. Talk about a mood killer.)

What do all of these questions have in common?

They can be answered on Wikipedia.

While it's easy to focus on the ways in which a seemingly endless flow of emails, instant messages, and meetings undermine productivity, a strategic approach can transform virtual communication from a time sink into a productivity amplifier. To dispel the myth that virtual communication has made us less efficient, let's examine one of the most noteworthy cases of virtual communication being used to enhance productivity.

For over two hundred years, the only way for encyclopedia publishers to get content from experts was to interact with them individually, often requiring them to work locally in the publisher's headquarters. As you can imagine, that was quite a slow process that resulted in narrowly focused encyclopedias. But that changed in January 2001, when Wikipedia, the free online encyclopedia written by an online community of volunteers, officially went live. To understand how this massive project came to fruition, it's necessary to go back to the technology that initially made Wikipedia possible.

In 1995, a programmer named Ward Cunningham discovered an ingenious method of creating links to pages that didn't yet exist. Building on Apple's HyperCard program, which gave users the ability to create virtual links between information, Cunningham came up with a means for users to organize information and collaborate within a website. Previously, web developers and content managers needed to interact synchronously—often in person—to collaborate on website changes (this was partially due to the complexity of tracking and, when needed, reverting changes). Cunningham's approach made it possible to easily collaborate on creating and editing new website content asynchronously on a scale never before possible. He called his project WikiWikiWeb, which came from a trip Cunningham took to Hawaii, where he'd taken the "Wiki Wiki"—or *quick*—bus from the airport.

Around that same time, Jimmy Wales, CEO of the web portal company Bomis, founded the online encyclopedia known as Nupedia. The idea occurred to him when he was a graduate student and became interested in open-sourcing, or creating and sharing software for free. He wanted Nupedia to become a publicly editable online encyclopedia that would be written by volunteer contributors. Unfortunately, Nupedia's article review process and advisory board were too clunky to allow for the rapid modification of existing pages and creation of new ones. By 2001, fewer than twenty-four articles had been completed. In terms of creating an efficient information-sharing platform, Nupedia wasn't looking good. Enter Larry Sanger, Nupedia's editor in chief, who suggested using Cunningham's wiki approach to make an open-sourced encyclopedia.

The team relaunched Nupedia under a new name, combining an emphasis on quick from *wiki* with *encyclopedia*. Thus, Wikipedia was born.

This innovative approach to information sharing had numerous advantages. Wikipedia leveraged virtual asynchronous interactions in a way that massively increased the productivity of encyclopedia article creation and updating. By allowing experts and contributors to instantly edit articles at their convenience, and for others to be able to track and revise those changes, virtual communication didn't just increase contributors' productivity—it made the whole enterprise possible.

Originally, Wales and Sanger intended for Wikipedia to be used as a space for authors to draft articles, which would later be published on Nupedia. However, when it became clear it could be used as a virtual house for collaborating on both drafts and final products, Wikipedia rapidly overshadowed its predecessor. It provided a forum where brief back-and-forth conversations could be held to quickly resolve issues, which eliminated the need to schedule dozens of formal meetings to accomplish the same task. And given the fact that there was no central organizer, using Wikipedia as a means of communicating with each other made it feasible to get hundreds of experts "in the same room"—a feat that would be impossible in more conventional contexts.

In spite of its various setbacks, Wikipedia began to flourish. Within a year of going live in 2001, there were 20,000 articles that had been translated into eighteen languages. By September 2018, Wikipedia recorded 15.5 billion page views in a single month. What began as a scrappy platform used to share resources among a group of programmers transformed into an information and collaboration powerhouse.

Wikipedia is only one of many success stories about how virtual communication has enabled innovation and productivity at a global scale that never would have been achievable without such technology. To this point, I had the opportunity to speak with David Heinemeier Hansson, creator of the web application framework

Ruby on Rails, which underlies several essential components of the internet as we know it, about how technology tools have improved virtual collaboration and productivity. Hansson told me,

> All of the open-source community is organized through remote work first, and has been since probably at least the late eighties. So, the open-source community for me was the first introduction to collaborative communities where remote is not just an option, but the default. I've worked together with hundreds, if not thousands, of programmers over the years—building Ruby on Rails and other open-source tools—who I've never met. The entire history of the internet is one of remote work.

Like Wikipedia, Ruby on Rails leveraged virtual communication to bring together experts from all over the globe on a scale that would have been inconceivable without communication technologies.

While we're talking about virtual communication rather than remote work in this book, the former is the underpinning that makes the latter possible. Collaboration is no longer limited by organizational boundaries, physical proximity, or even continents. Virtual communication enables us to reach whomever we want, wherever and whenever we want. Instead of spending hours flying cross-country to a meeting, videoconferences have taken their place. Time spent walking to a coworker's office on another floor to ask them a question, which would also likely interrupt their workflow, is now replaced by instant messages that can be responded to at their convenience. The ability to reach out to others with a few taps of a keyboard or smartphone has increased productivity in a host of ways. However, with so many new communication options at your fingertips, it has become more challenging to harness the productivity potential of virtual communication without allowing all the emails, instant messages, and meetings to bury you alive.

Wired for Success

In this chapter, I'll share strategies to help you become even more productive through your virtual communication routines and practices. First, I'll discuss the types of productivity sinkholes that result from virtual communication. You'll see why the pursuit of productivity through communication multitasking can actually be costly, and why communication productivity "hacks" should be approached with caution. (Incidentally, this advice probably holds for any viral social media hack—but given that I'm only an expert on virtual communication, I'll reserve my judgment on the ones outside my purview. I will just say that if you're planning to make cotton candy in your drying machine, maybe first look into how to avoid getting lint in your dessert.) Extreme methods of reducing interruptions from both meetings and text communication aren't always all they're cracked up to be, which will become clear as I introduce research-proven methods of saving time and increasing efficiency. I'll answer the question of whether you should choose to have a meeting or send an email, and how to decide which communication mode will most expediently accomplish your goals. While it may seem risky to let a message go unanswered, you'll learn why your messages require less urgency than you might think, and why it sometimes makes sense to delay your responses. Finally, I'll show you how to build virtual communication habits that facilitate productivity and ensure you don't fall into old patterns.

Virtual communication is not a new phenomenon—what's changed is how many options there are, and the expectation that we're "on" at all times of the day . . . which limits how much we can accomplish otherwise. By the end of this chapter, you'll have the tools necessary to increase your productivity through your communication practices, choose the right digital mode to fit the task, and make the most of your meetings. Rather than being pointless interruptions, you'll find there are ways to make your virtual communication, in a sense, work for you.

Frenzied Focus

A 2023 survey of thirty-one thousand employees across industries found that workers were spending over half their day communicating in meetings, email, and chat. If you dedicate all your time to your messages and meetings, then you're never going to get work done. For most people, however, inefficiency doesn't just come from the absolute number of interactions—it also comes from choosing a suboptimal interaction mode for each task. We can all relate to the feeling of sitting through an hour-long meeting, only to discover that the takeaways could have been summarized in a two-sentence email. Or, conversely, there are times when you spend hours emailing back and forth with a coworker to discuss an issue that could have been resolved in a quick phone call. There are only so many hours in the day, and the more time spent on communicating about work, the less actual work is getting done. It's not surprising, therefore, that *productivity* has become a business buzzword in the context of virtual communication, with all the advice and life hacks that go with it. #Productivityhack has hundreds of millions of social media views, for instance. There are many influencers who make a living out of creating content to help workers communicate more productively. These suggestions range from using AI assistants to transcribe meetings, to digital whiteboards for better brainstorming, to software that tracks the number of hours spent on each work task. And then there are the less obvious and more head-scratching ones, like chugging water to clear your inbox faster, racing paper boats to enhance collaboration, and taking work calls while (literally) surfing.

The sheer number of virtual communication tools at our disposal has hampered many workers' efficiency and downright paralyzed others. Enter the oft-cited (and even more feared) necessity of multitasking. Even some of the most prolific virtual communicators in the world are overwhelmed by the amount of effort it takes to keep pace. Jimmy Donaldson, known to most of the internet as MrBeast, has one of the most subscribed-to YouTube channels of all time. Known for producing content that's authentic (more on this in Chapter 5) and humorous, Donaldson takes his productivity so seriously that he conducts work calls while he's exercising. This need to constantly do work and juggle projects has taken a toll on Donaldson's mental health, to the point where he has admitted, "I have a mental breakdown every other week because I push myself so hard." If you can relate to this sentiment, you're not alone. With multitasking becoming the norm and busyness a status symbol, it's hard to prioritize the tasks that matter the most. The result is less attention and fewer cognitive resources dedicated to your actual job, which leads to worsened job performance and heightened risk of burnout.

Many workers go about their day, multitasking and dealing with the constant inflow of digital communication, without considering the quantifiable cost to productivity caused by all these interruptions. As Jared Spataro, corporate vice president of modern work and business applications at Microsoft, noted, "Over the course of the last [few] years, communication, collaboration and coordination [have] become a bigger part of our jobs." In the process of talking about work, the actual work seems to get lost in the shuffle. And if you don't have time to do work beyond communicating, then you won't be able to be productive. When jumping back and forth between tasks, it's difficult to focus, especially when you're interrupted by a constant series of notifications. Workers find themselves in a paradoxical loop of chasing productivity through multitasking and time-saving hacks, but fragmenting their attention and workflow through these virtual communication-related interruptions. The challenge, then, is to use virtual communication to prioritize—rather than detract from—productivity.

Time Is Money

Shopify, a Canadian e-commerce company with more than eleven thousand employees, decided it was time for a drastic change to the out-of-control meeting culture that was preventing anyone from getting real work done. When employees returned from their holiday break, it was to discover that every recurring meeting on their calendar with three or more people had been canceled. For two weeks, employees were required to carefully consider which meetings were most critical and then, after the two-week period was up, they could add meetings back to their calendars. Kaz Nejatian, the chief operating officer and vice president of product, warned Shopify employees to "be really, really critical about what you're adding back." He reminded his team that "[p]eople join Shopify to build. . . . Meetings are a bug along that journey."

That may sound like a pretty drastic measure, but Shopify didn't stop there.

They also instituted rules like "meeting-free" Wednesdays and specified that large meetings could only be scheduled during a six-hour block of time on Thursdays. The goal was to give employees more time to focus on their core functions, thereby improving efficiency for the entire organization. To make sure no one slipped back into old patterns, managers were held accountable for sticking to the new policies. Shopify even added a bot to employees' calendars that displayed an alert to anyone attempting to schedule a Wednesday meeting.

Because of these changes, an estimated 10,000 calendar events— which equated to roughly 76,500 hours of meetings—dropped away.

To bring even more attention to the cost of meetings, a cost calculator began appearing on Shopify employees' calendars. Every time they scheduled a calendar event, the calculator would estimate the amount of money being lost during the meeting, accounting for "average compensation by discipline and subdiscipline, along with attendee count, and meeting length." The estimated cost for a thirty-minute meeting with three employees was between $700 and $1,600. That meant that if just three meetings were removed from each employee's calendar per week, the company would save 15 percent. To put these numbers on an even broader scale, a survey conducted by Professor

Steven Rogelberg of the University of North Carolina at Charlotte found that large organizations lose an estimated $100 million each year as a result of unneeded meetings.

It's one thing to say that meetings are eating up your work time, but it's another to quantify those losses. Seeing dollar signs in the thousands and millions really puts the time cost of meetings into perspective. As Shopify's president, Harley Finkelstein, succinctly noted, the new company policies would result in "[l]ess meeting time, more time getting sh*t done." As a result of these policy changes, Shopify was able to reduce the amount of time spent on meetings by 33 percent and anticipated a 25 percent increase in completed projects.

When your goal is to have the most efficient use of your time, you're going to want the quick—or "wiki"—option. We've all been in the position of getting out of a long work meeting only to think *that whole meeting could have been an email*. . . . There is no debate that the meeting culture of modern employment has gone beyond the point of useful to excessive. For those of us who feel like our day is a Swiss-cheese series of meeting interruptions that prevent deep work from happening, the more extreme Shopify approach (or as close to it as your organization will permit) might just be the answer.

Shopify isn't the only organization that has taken a stab at making communication more productive.

What do Jeff Bezos, Mark Cuban, and Elon Musk have in common (aside from the fact that they're all billionaires)? They all think meetings are a waste of time. Mark Cuban told *Inc.*, "The only way you're going to get me for a meeting is if you're writing me a check." Ditto for phone calls. Elon Musk said, "Excessive meetings are the blight of big companies and almost always get worse over time." Jeff Bezos "refuses to set up or attend a meeting if two pizzas won't feed the entire group." These men, who have far too many requests on their time to fulfill them all, have seemingly solved their productivity woes with email. When asked about email, Cuban said, "Love it.

Live on it. Saves me hours and hours every day. . . . No meetings. No phone calls. All because of email. I set my schedule."

Similar to the Shopify approach, this sounds great—in theory. Except for the fact that most of us already have email inboxes fit to burst . . . along with an ambitious meeting schedule. Yet, data indicates there are downsides to having a fuller inbox, especially for employees at the highest level. University of Arkansas professor Christopher Rosen and his colleagues discovered that higher numbers of emails result in organization leaders becoming less effective. Because managers function as the "nerve centers" of the organization, interruptions from email overflow have a substantial negative impact on them. When leaders focus on the more incremental tasks of responding to emails and fulfilling short-term email requests, they end up pulling back from work activities that could bring about more consequential changes at the organizational level. The loss of a predictable daily structure and sense of routine due to virtual communication interruptions prevents managers from engaging in "transformational" leadership behaviors (e.g., inspiring workers) because so much of their day is spent managing their inboxes. Further, there can be a trickle-down effect in which the more emails managers send, the more time their subordinates end up spending on email (which means less time for other work tasks). The result is a reduction in everyone's productivity. It's simply a matter of email cutting into time that could be spent on other work tasks, which results in diminished efficiency for the organization as a whole.

The obvious solution would be to minimize the number of meetings and emails we have (and thus create more time for work productivity). Unfortunately, most of us don't have the option of reducing the absolute volume of our workplace interactions (unless your last name is Bezos, Cuban, or Musk), and many of these interactions are vital for obtaining work task-relevant information. However, for a large portion of these interactions, we often do have the option of *how* we interact, such as deciding whether to request a meeting, have a phone call, or send an email or instant message. One of the first questions I'll answer is how to approach these choices strategically to improve your productivity.

Virtual (Communication) Reality

When it comes to the most productive use of your time, there is nuance to deciding whether a meeting or asynchronous communication (e.g., email or instant messaging) is best. The good news is that there is a straightforward answer—it's just one that most people miss by either mindlessly approaching their virtual communication or insisting on extremes that get them into trouble. The solution isn't to eliminate meetings altogether. Rather, it's about knowing when they make the most sense. In order to make that determination, you'll need to put some thought into what your communication is meant to accomplish.

During the first year of my PhD, a senior professor approached me with an amazing opportunity. She offered me a great idea for a research project, a company full of willing volunteer subjects, and a grant that would fund the research. All I had to do was come up with a study design that would work. Easy peasy. I threw myself into the task, designing new experimental scenarios and running test after test. The problem was that none of my study predictions were working. As my failed experiments and costs added up, so did my stress. To make matters worse, I was working with study participants halfway around the world, which meant an ungodly number of 3 a.m. meetings. I knew that if I kept up the same pace, I was going to burn out. So, I made the agonizing decision to drop out of the project, knowing that I would need to admit failure and let down my professor in the process.

I spent days crafting an email to my professor explaining my decision. I agonized over every word, wanting to make the best of what felt like a career-ending decision. I asked my wife to proofread the email . . . multiple times. Finally, after almost week, I was satisfied. Ten minutes after I sent the email, my professor poked her head into my office. She said, and I'll never forget this, "Your email was really long, so I didn't read the whole thing, but I agree we should kill the project." There may have been some conversation about our weekend plans after that—I don't remember. What I do recall is that, after I'd shaken off the sting of spending hours deliberating over an email that went mostly unread, it occurred to me that it would have been better—and unambiguously quicker—to have a conversation with my professor rather than sending an email.

An oft-overlooked downside to text communication is the amount of time we spend drafting and optimizing our messages. When it comes to the most complicated and delicate situations, many of us feel most comfortable having the conversation via email. It seems easier to organize our thoughts, clarify questions, and provide action steps for message recipients. And in my case, it felt "safer" to communicate from behind a computer screen. Unfortunately, this can be the wrong decision. More complex conversations often require a great deal of back-and-forth, which can occur more expediently via a real-time conversation. For instance, if your boss asks when you'll finish the report they requested, you can answer their question in fewer than thirty seconds when you're in a synchronous (real-time) meeting. If you're communicating via email, however, you'll spend significantly more time crafting your message, adding extra details, and proofreading. We all know that feeling when a voice in our head, or perhaps someone looking over our shoulder, shouts, "Enough, just send the darn thing already!" The result of overcrafting your messages is a decrease in productivity and performance. If lots of clarifications are needed, even instant messaging will be slower and more interruptive than having a quick meeting. Not knowing whether the recipient will respond to your most recent message in thirty seconds or thirty minutes can make it difficult for you to decide if you should begin a different task or wait for their response. Although meetings are not the linchpin of efficiency (which I'll be discussing more in this chapter), if everyone in your organization is afraid of meetings due to the time and financial cost (à la Shopify), then you're going to make suboptimal communication choices.

Aiming to discover the extent to which we thoughtfully (or thoughtlessly) approach our interactions, Harvard University psychologist Ellen Langer and her colleagues at the City University of New York came up with an interesting experiment. In the study, a person cut to the front of the line at a public copy machine and asked the person who was about to use it if they could make their copies ahead of them. The person on line was asked this question in one of three ways: 1) "May I use the Xerox machine?" 2) "May I use the Xerox machine, because I have to make copies?" or 3) "May I use the Xerox machine, because I'm in a rush?" Presumably (and logically), the first and second requests should garner the same response, since they convey the same information. After all, the explanation of "because I have to make copies" doesn't provide any additional information (because who would be at the Xerox machine if they didn't need to make copies?). If the individuals hearing these requests were making choices based on relevant information, then they would likely be more willing to acquiesce to the line-cutters for only Reason 3, and take pity on the person who was supposedly in a rush.

Instead, the researchers found that participants were "mindless," and Reasons 2 and 3 garnered the same number of compliances (and more than Reason 1). As a result, just that little bit of effort on the part of the prospective line-cutter in giving a reason, even if that reason was "I need to make copies," was enough to achieve a favorable outcome. The actual reasoning itself didn't matter—whether the line-cutters gave a bogus reason of "I have to make copies" or a more reasonable excuse ("I'm in a rush"). The idea here is that people often don't think too deeply about their choices or process information carefully, such that anything seemingly resembling a reason will suffice.

When it comes to virtual communication mode choices, the simple act of stopping for a moment to consider more deeply why you are making a decision and what your goal for that interaction is—rather than just following normal routines—can substantially improve your communication productivity.

With this mindful-meeting approach in mind, instead of taking the no-meeting extreme, Netflix found an effective method of restructuring their board meetings to avoid a lot of the inefficiencies that come with large meetings. Instead of the board members leading meetings as was the norm, they were asked to observe meetings conducted by senior managers. The initial purpose in listening in on these meetings was to get a broad overview of what everyone in the organization was working on. Then, instead of having their own meeting directly after their observations (which is what happens in many organizations), board members received short summaries in the form of an online memo that contained access to company data, graphs of performance metrics, notes about important industry trends, lists of potential concerns, and links to supporting documents. Managers were also able to write questions and provide comments directly within the memo. Netflix's founder and CEO, Reed Hastings, explained that the changes were "an efficient way for the board to understand the company better." This process created a domino effect: because board members were more informed about what was going on in the company before their meetings, they were much more focused and productive when they did get together.

How did Netflix find its way to such an efficient system? By setting meeting goals and mindfully following them. Because Netflix's focus was on "results rather than processes," the company's leaders decided that transparency was critical to the business's success. The pre-board-meeting memos ensured that everyone had access to the same information, which meant employees didn't need to spend time updating the board members. This approach met Netflix's goal of increasing efficiency and providing all stakeholders with a better understanding of the company.

As a different means of being mindful about communication efficiency, two entrepreneurs came up with a bold way to make sure they never lost sight of a meeting's purpose. The founders of Apostrophe, a New York City startup, decided that they would begin standing throughout entire meetings. They conducted interviews, planning meetings, and catch-up sessions . . . all while standing. Now, I would not suggest you propose initiating "all-stand" meetings at your organization. It might not be feasible due to health or accessibility for some employees, and it's just plain weird to have video call participants standing (especially if everyone isn't attentive to repositioning their cameras to focus on their faces rather than their pants). However, there is a useful takeaway. When meetings take place, they should be goal-focused to avoid getting sidetracked.

These points about being mindful about when to avoid meetings and how to keep them from taking up your whole day are particularly relevant to virtual communication. The number of virtual meetings has increased dramatically in recent years, in part because they're so simple to coordinate and don't necessitate everyone being colocated. Because it's so easy to get distracted or multitask when everyone is looking at a tiny thumbnail on their screen rather than a live person sitting across the conference table, virtual meetings in particular can drag if everyone isn't attentive to the meeting goals (i.e., why the interaction is a meeting instead of an email in the first place).

Thus, making the most of virtual meetings has become a workplace necessity.

When it comes to choosing virtual meetings, there are a variety of methods to ensure participants stay focused on the intended goal. One research-supported strategy is for the coordinator to send the other participants an agenda the day before the meeting. The agenda should include any necessary background information, clearly defined meeting goals, and an estimated time allocation for each conversation topic. This will help keep everyone on track and avoid the slippery slope of getting sidetracked, especially when there are a lot of participants. Furthermore, the agenda will help everyone in the meeting identify when the objectives have been met so they can end the call and move on to other tasks. This will eliminate the feeling that everyone needs to stay in the meeting for the allotted time, regardless of what is (or isn't) accomplished. For bigger work goals that can't be completed in a single meeting, set milestones to reach your group's ultimate objective.

Additionally, it's beneficial to choose meeting attendees with care, and only include participants who can directly contribute to the agenda topics. Everyone else can be updated via a summary email later. Finally, if you are a manager, you can help make sure the meeting runs as smoothly as possible. Emphasize problem-solving rather than counterproductive behaviors, such as complaining and talking badly about others. One study of more than ninety teams across industries found that during hourlong meetings, there were only an average of two statements that could be categorized as action planning compared to over thirty that were categorized as "complaining." Being goal-focused during virtual communication meetings will go beyond just ensuring employees are more productive to helping to keep meeting attendees happier and more engaged.

Virtual meetings in and of themselves aren't necessarily bad— sometimes they really are the most efficient means of communication. Instead, *bad meetings* are the enemy. Effective preparation and diligence during the meeting itself will make all the difference.

Brain Storms and Productivity Sinkholes

One of the trickiest situations to find a balance between productivity and communication is in the context of brainstorming. Because there are so many different ideas and people involved, these meetings often take a lot of time without producing actionable results. Several executives I've spoken with insist that meetings are necessary for brainstorming sessions. After all, it's difficult to imagine how text could be better for the quick back-and-forth that new-idea generation requires. Right?

According to research, real-time meetings are actually the wrong mode to use in order to foster productivity and innovation during early-stage brainstorm sessions. Experimenters from Queens University found that "verbal brainstorming groups of three or more members have consistently produced fewer ideas, and fewer high quality ideas" than when people brainstorm separately and then combine their ideas later. Interestingly, these researchers found that it was the anonymous quality of virtual brainstorm sessions, especially when it comes to controversial subjects, that made for the most productive sessions. Why is this so? Because when you're in a group of your peers, there is a tendency to hold back the more divergent ideas that might make you look bad in front of the group. Unfortunately, it's these divergent (and often seemingly outlandish) ideas that result in the most productive innovations. Additionally, a study conducted on participants from Portugal, Finland, Israel, Hungary, and India found that when initial brainstorming and idea-generation sessions are held via video, participants are often more focused on nonverbal physical cues (e.g., facial expressions), to the point where attention is taken away from the task at hand.

There's another reason why real-time conversations can undermine productivity during a brainstorming session. Counterintuitively, the *almost* in-person-like back-and-forth that occurs during a synchronous meeting can be derailed by the slight delays that often disrupt the completely natural flow of a virtual conversation, which can be frustrating and result in the loop of "Oh sorry, no, go ahead" I mentioned in Chapter 1. This slightly longer pause that often occurs between speakers during video and audio calls can cause confusion about when it's okay to speak (e.g., Is the other person just thinking about what they're going to say, or is there a sound delay in the video?). The last thing you want during a brainstorming session is for people to interrupt each other *more*. Researchers timed the delay between speakers with in-person versus video meetings, and the difference was stark. Time between speakers during video calls in the study averaged 577 milliseconds, while in-person conversation lags between speakers was only 279 milliseconds. Here's the thing: the extra pause between speakers in video meetings wasn't solely because of the time lags we've all come to associate with this medium. In fact, there were only audio lags of 30 to 70 milliseconds, which is nowhere near large enough to account for the additional silent time between speakers on video calls.

What accounts for this difference? When you're in person, there are more cues (both verbal and nonverbal) that provide necessary information about when we should speak. These clues are more minimal or lost altogether in video, however, which makes it more difficult to appropriately time your responses. The result is a lot of extra interruptions and awkward periods of silence that could hurt rather than help your collaboration efforts.

If you want to have the most productive brainstorm session that results in the best ideas, each person should conduct the exercise individually, and then anonymously submit their ideas to the entire group for evaluation. You'll get much higher idea-generation productivity (and quality) than if the conversation was had synchronously and non-anonymously. Once you've reached the stage where your group needs to evaluate the brainstorm list and decide on the best idea, text is no longer the most productive mode. Because there is a lot of back-and-forth at this stage when agreement needs to be reached, synchronous voice or video avoids the time lapse of text and is thus more efficient.

By now, you should be seeing a theme: choosing the right communication mode isn't as simple as *meetings/emails are good/bad*. Instead, it's about being cognizant of the context and your intended productivity outcomes (the "goals" element of the PING framework). Sometimes a hybrid of text communication and synchronous meetings is needed to reach your intended outcome. And the process of enhancing your productivity via virtual communication begins with being clear on the purpose of your communication. When considering whether to choose a real-time or asynchronous mode, consider the complexity of the situation. In general, more complex situations necessitate richer communication modes.

To increase productivity, choose *less rich* modes of communication—such as email or instant messaging—when one or more of the following is true:

+ There is straightforward information that won't require much back-and-forth.
+ You want unambiguous certainty in communication (i.e., it's particularly useful to have a written record of the conversation that you can easily find at a later date).
+ You want more concurrent/simultaneous communication (such as with early-stage brainstorming, when text communication will allow you to avoid the limitations of only one person communicating at a time).

Alternatively, to maximize productivity, choose *richer* modes of communication—including video meetings, audio meetings/phone, or in-person—when one or more of the following is true:

+ There is complicated information.
+ It is a situation where you are likely to "overcraft" because you are overly concerned about how your message will be interpreted.
+ There will likely be a lot of back-and-forth that would be faster to resolve synchronously.

There is, of course, a multitude of other conditions that can influence how productive a given communication mode is—for example, maybe someone is unfamiliar with how to use your videoconferencing platform—but the listed criteria tend to have the broadest impact across situations.

Up to this point, I've been discussing each element of the PING framework in isolation, such as using perspective taking to understand the type of message your recipient is expecting, and taking the initiative to choose a more productive technology tool than the one your collaborators defaulted to. Now, I want to bring the framework together as a whole. For argument's sake, let's say that you get to the end of this book, and the only detail you remember is the framework itself. When faced with your next virtual communication challenge, what should you do in a situation where improving productivity is key?

First, engage in *perspective taking*. Often without realizing it, our communication doesn't always relay the information and tone we intended. Rather than jumping right into your communication, take a few seconds to consider how your message will come off to the other party so that you can avoid lost time due to miscommunication. Second, take *initiative* and decide whether the mode you're using is the most productive or the best choice in the situation, even if it seems like more effort in the short term to switch to a different mode. For instance, instead of just defaulting to hitting reply to an email that contains a complex question and necessitates a long response, consider suggesting a short meeting to avoid needing to type up an eight-paragraph-long email and having to answer multiple more emails' worth of clarification questions. Third, consider which types of *nonverbal* behavior might make your interaction either more or less productive. Recall the email I mentioned earlier, in which I described my decision to discontinue a research project in such painstaking detail that I caused my professor (the message recipient) to lose interest after the first few sentences. If I'd been more thoughtful about my communication mode and met with my professor in person, I would have noticed when my professor's eyes started glazing over and adjusted my five-paragraph-long explanation to save us both time. Fourth, and finally, consider your *goals* for the specific situation. Sometimes you'll value clarity over productivity. Other times, getting your message across succinctly is most important. Defining your goals will enable you to optimize your approach.

By being more deliberate about which mode you choose for each situation, and how you handle the communication itself, you'll prevent your virtual communication from becoming a productivity sink. You'll also avoid the time cost that has preceded so many of these extreme "no meeting" cultures in the first place.

Alas, identifying how to choose the right communication mode to optimize productivity is only half the battle. There are still only so many hours in the day, and with frequent communication being an inescapable reality of most jobs, it's necessary to optimize your virtual communication time management so your workday isn't just one long set of interruptions.

Holes Are Good in Cheese, Not Workflows

You sit down at your desk to begin working for the day. After checking your email, you pull up the project you've been working on in fits and starts all week. You're just getting down to business when your phone rings. After wrapping up your call, you're about to return to your project when a colleague sends you an instant message asking how your weekend went. After responding, it takes several minutes for you to remember where you left off. You're just getting into the flow of work when your inbox pings with three new emails. By the time you finish getting back to everyone, it's lunch . . . followed by a phone call from your manager that necessitates more time spent away from your project. Before you know it, the workday is over. You're about to log off for the day when you discover that you've written exactly one paragraph for a project you'd hoped to complete.

Does this situation sound familiar?

Beyond the time employees spend on emails themselves, in one study, researchers found that it takes over a minute to get back to work after checking email. If your inbox looks like mine with well over sixty emails per day, you can easily spend more than an hour each day just *recovering* from email interruptions. Forget about the amount of time spent actually reading and responding to those emails (and dealing with all your other digital communication). The result is a chaotic workday where productivity is as elusive as an empty inbox. The simple truth is that time spent on emails reduces productivity in other areas of your job.

I've heard many business leaders suggest knocking out emails all at once, often either at the beginning or end of the day; however, research on the topic offers a different recommendation. These leaders are right in that it's better to set bounded times for email, instant messaging, and meetings to avoid interrupting concentration throughout the day, but the once-a-day approach is an oversimplification of the optimal strategy. Contrary to what is so often suggested, you shouldn't aim to have a single portion of your day allotted to virtual communication. Instead it's better to allocate several confined periods throughout the day. For me personally, I like to check (and respond to) my messages during three confined periods: one hour into my workday, one hour after lunch, and one hour before signing off for the day. I've found that this schedule provides me with an effective balance between allotting time to engage in deep work while ensuring important messages are promptly addressed. You may need to play around with this exact formula to suit your needs, but the point is that some strategic restructuring of your day will help you manage interruptions and also reduce mistakes.

There are three key benefits to chunking your virtual communication into a few time blocks each day. First, by confining communication to certain times, you'll have fewer interruptions and thus be better able to focus on your primary work tasks. Not only is it time-consuming to go back and forth between activities, but research also shows that people are more likely to make errors after switching between tasks. Thus, the less task-switching that occurs throughout the day, the fewer errors are likely to occur. You can think of it as a mental gearshift, where each change requires a certain amount of energy and attention. Second, it's better to check your messages in batches rather than save them all for a single time, because your communication can often include time-sensitive, task-related details that will save you time on more complex assignments. This will reduce the likelihood of you missing out on key information that could speed up your work task and maybe even prevent you from having to redo parts altogether. And third, using social tasks that require minimal cognitive resources (i.e., replying to email is often a relatively time-consuming but easy activity) can act as breaks during your day, thereby increasing both creativity and motivation.

Researchers found that interspersing periods of working on more challenging tasks with occasional "mindless work" (i.e., tasks that don't take a lot of concentration to complete) doesn't just make you more productive; it actually makes you more creative. Why? Because these mental (and time-bounded) breaks provide the chance to reset and rejuvenate, which allows creative opportunities to emerge. The reason is that if you focus on a single complex task for too long without a break, your mind gets overloaded and can become dulled. Taking a break from your primary task every so often to do something mindless will allow your brain to refocus. So, in addition to avoiding the irritating stream of constant interruptions, using your virtual communication as a break (rather than an interruption) can help enhance the productivity of your day without changing the number of messages you're responding to.

There's another benefit to this approach, as well. In the next chapter, we'll explore why sending messages at different times of the day is an effective means of showing engagement, especially if you aren't sitting within viewing range of your manager. The chunking strategy applies to your meetings, too. Especially when it comes to video and phone meetings, it's even easier to batch them close together than in-person meetings, since you don't need to pad in time to drive between buildings or walk between rooms. This way, you'll also avoid being left with that awkward thirty-minute chunk of time between meetings, when it doesn't make sense to dive deep into your work. By the time you reorient yourself with where you left off and get in the zone, it will be time for your next meeting. Chunking your meetings can also help keep you honest about cutting off meetings at their planned end times, since you can cite your next meeting as an excuse to wrap up the conversation. The bottom line is that chunking your virtual communication into two or three confined blocks within each day will give you more uninterrupted focus time, so productivity isn't lost due to task-switching and interruptions, and will also give your mind much-needed resets throughout the day.

Now, I know it's one thing to plan blocks of communication-free work time; it's another to stick to your schedule when you get a notification during one of your non-email work periods. How are you supposed to stay on the productivity wagon, as it were, when your phone is alerting you to a near-constant stream of notifications?

Psychologists have found that the mere presence of your smartphone, even if you aren't using it, results in "brain drain," because we allocate too much of our limited cognitive resources to our phones, which results in lower focus on everything else. It's that feeling when you're trying to get into a task but your mind (or thumbs) keep wandering back to your phone. By being constantly connected and using our devices to multitask, we're actually becoming less productive.

When people are on a diet, they hide their junk food to reduce temptation—out of sight, out of mind. The same philosophy can be applied to your virtual communication.

There are a variety of methods for making incoming messages less obvious, and therefore less of a disruptive temptation. If you get a sound notification every time you receive an email or instant message, choose a softer sound or mute the alert altogether. The same goes for removing the pop-up on your computer screen. If you're not jolted to attention every time you receive a message, it will be easier to resist the temptation to respond right away. You can also apply rules to your email inbox so your system only checks for new messages at certain intervals (rather than continuously syncing). Out of sight, out of mind.

A more extreme version of this strategy would be to log out of your email (or chat) altogether, and then log back in at the times you've designated specifically for this purpose. For instant messaging, utilize the "do not disturb" status on your work communication platform when you're outside of message-responding times. If you're worried about how it will appear to others when you don't immediately respond to their queries, Tim Ferriss (entrepreneur and *New York Times* bestselling author) suggests setting up a short automatic response. Your message might say something along the lines of "I'm deep into X project and will respond to any non-urgent messages by 4:30 p.m." And if you are in a work environment where "urgent" issues occur, you can let coworkers know how to reach you (e.g., text your cell phone). Think back to the copy machine study I discussed earlier, and remember that simply providing any reason for a behavior (in this case, delayed responses) can make others more understanding.

You'll likely find that people are more receptive to this strategy than you expect, and you may end up being a trendsetter for your entire team. After all, who is going to argue when your reason for a slightly delayed response is that you're focusing on higher-impact initiatives?

If you're a leader, set standards for when (and how promptly) you expect messages to receive a response. You should also be cognizant of how many people you're adding to an email chain, and only include those who are directly relevant to the subject. Also, as we'll discuss later, be wary of replying-all. Beyond harming the trust you've established with your colleagues, this practice will also increase the number of emails in your inbox—and therefore decrease your productivity.

I don't expect you to implement all these changes overnight. Changing your workflow cadence will take practice, along with a hearty dose of self-control. Every time you hear your messages ping (no pun intended), you're going to have the urge to check them immediately.

But if your objective is productivity, try to take steps that will help you resist the urge. It will get easier over time.

I want to be clear that I understand how strange these suggestions will seem to many of you, especially if you're used to responding immediately to any message that appears on your screen. And I get it—it's much harder to delay your responses when the message is important or coming from someone above you in the organization. Most of us don't have the authority of Bezos, Cuban, and Musk, and therefore we need to be more receptive to responding to messages even if it's inconvenient for us. Fortunately for all of us nonbillionaires, we have more flexibility in timing our emails than we think.

Fast & Furious Is a Movie, Not a Communication Strategy

Because of blurred lines between work and nonwork hours, as well as the "always-on" culture that has become the norm, we've grown accustomed to responding to messages *right away*. If you've ever come back from a quick lunch to find several important emails—and incidentally felt your heart rate increase—you're not alone. Researchers have labeled this tendency *email urgency bias*. London Business School's Laura Giurge and Cornell University's Vanessa Bohns discovered that email recipients overestimate how quickly the sender expected them to respond to nonurgent messages. They also found the email urgency bias to be especially true for messages sent after normal work hours.

This mismatch in expectations is frustrating for both parties. It's also unproductive.

You can help prevent this need to be "always on" by taking your message recipients' perspective. If you recall, the first letter in the PING framework stands for *Perspective taking*. Since there's a tendency on both sides to make assumptions about when a response is expected (the sender might assume a response will be forthcoming in the next week, while the recipient believes the response is needed within the hour), perspective taking is useful for avoiding unnecessary urgency. Relatedly, if you find yourself apologizing for the lateness of an email response, don't. Unless you promised to send something by a certain deadline or you took an unusually long amount of time to respond, you have nothing to be sorry for. This is especially true for women, who are quicker to apologize than men. There are even times when strategically delaying a response can make you look better rather than worse.

In 2016, Beyoncé released a trailer for her new album, *Lemonade*, but with a twist (not the Arnold Palmer kind): there wasn't a release date. Fans went wild speculating when the album would drop, and what it would be about. When it finally aired, *Lemonade* was an HBO exclusive being shown at 9 p.m. on a Saturday. In that one decision about timing, Beyoncé communicated her power. Those who wanted to see her new creation needed to cancel their Saturday night plans. Media members who would be covering it had to work on the weekend. This is an example of a reigning "queen" exerting her dominance and authority over an entire industry.

You too can be royalty (sort of) with your message timing. A research study of four thousand email recipients showed that delaying email responses can actually be better under certain circumstances than a near-immediate response. Not only do people overestimate how much recipients care about getting a fast reply, but slower responses (within reason) can make you seem more important and powerful. This study found that sending a task-oriented work request after normal work hours is seen as a more dominant *nonverbal behavior* (**N** in the PING framework) than one sent during the day. In other words, higher-power people are more likely to send an email for work tasks at a counternormative time. Likewise, longer response delays signal higher authority than prompt responses. Why is this the case? Because more powerful (dominant) workers are seen as busier/more in demand, less concerned with their communication timing, and having more control over their work timing; therefore, they'll be more likely to violate communication timing norms. Conversely, if you respond to every message the moment you receive it, others may assume you aren't working hard since you are always available to respond immediately.

A word of caution here: use this strategy with extreme care. You don't want to signal power at the risk of harming trust (something we'll explore more in Chapter 6). Being selective about when to use this tip goes back to defining your goal for the interaction. If you're trying to demonstrate authority and power, then sending delayed responses (or sending work-related tasks outside of normal working hours) will make more sense. But be wary of the interpersonal ramifications of leaning too heavily on any show of dominance, as it can result in backlash if that power is unearned.

A general rule of thumb is that so long as you respond to a message within a day (e.g., if it's the beginning of the day, respond by end of day; if it's later, by the next day), there won't be any negative repercussions on your reputation. This is just a general rule, though, and there will always be exceptions depending on the norms of your organization or your communication mode. If you're interacting via instant messaging, for instance, there will generally be an expectation of a faster response time than there would be with email. In some specific cases, there will be an expectation of quicker response times regardless of mode (e.g., your manager needs information for a slideshow they're presenting to an important client in an hour).

To ensure you receive urgent messages when they arrive, consider setting up appropriate expectations with your regular interaction partners. For instance, you could tell your team to expect a response on any nonurgent communication within twenty-four hours. This way, they'll know not to start knocking down your door (virtually or otherwise) until that amount of time has elapsed. If you need contingencies for urgent communication, consider asking your colleagues to text your personal cell, or include the word *urgent* in their email subject heading. That way, you'll know when it's worth interrupting your other tasks.

This strategy of having multiple interaction processes depending on the situation's urgency would have benefited the United States' Strategic Air Command Headquarters (SAC HQ) and North American Aerospace Defense Command (NORAD), when a lapse in communication almost resulted in the decision to launch nuclear missiles. In 1961, the SAC HQ lost contact with an early-warning radar in Greenland. When they tried to confirm what the issue was, the NORAD phone line was dead. For these reasons, it was assumed to be an attack. Thankfully, a US bomber flying over Greenland was able to make contact with the early-radar facility and the SAC pulled back its planes. Crisis averted. It was later discovered that AT&T, the company responsible for the telecommunication system, hadn't established redundancies, such as setting up radio transmitters in the missiles themselves that could have been used to communicate with crews on the ground. Taking those additional few steps might have saved everyone a lot of anxiety and more quickly prevented this almost-disaster.

Urgent matters aside, rest assured that we tend to overestimate the speediness with which we need to reply. As Adam Grant, bestselling author and Wharton professor (and my mentor), so succinctly explains, "How quickly people answer you is rarely a sign of how much they care about you. It's usually a reflection of how much they have on their plate. Delayed replies to emails, texts, and calls are often symptoms of being overextended and overwhelmed. If the message isn't time-sensitive, we should count delays in weeks or months, not days or hours."

Earlier, I discussed ways to reduce the chances that your coworkers will be put off by your delayed responses. On the other side of the communication equation, there are steps you can take to alleviate your colleagues' concern about needing to respond faster than necessary. When you're the one sending an email request, you can include something along the lines of "I don't need a response until next week, so take your time on this." This relatively small effort on the part of the email-sender can have a significant impact on the email-receiver and help manage expectations on both sides. Taking these steps will ideally inspire others to add similar qualifiers to nonurgent messages. Eventually you can all dispense with the need for timing clarifications, because you'll have helped reverse your team's "always-on" mentality. In its place, you'll establish a culture where individuals are empowered with the ability to arrange virtual communication in the most productive way possible.

Two *Pees* in a Productivity Pod

Imagine you're a research assistant—motivated, eager, and ready to conduct experiments that will inform the next generation of business leaders. The professors you're working with let you know that you're going to have an important role in their new study on personal space. *Great news!* you think. This experience will teach you so much about the research process and give you lots to talk about during your future job interviews. The only question that remains is how soon you can get started.

Fast-forward to a few weeks later. You find yourself huddled in a bathroom stall with two stopwatches clutched in your hand while you methodically record how long it takes men to—er—start and finish up their business at the urinals.

Not quite the transformative research experience you'd envisioned. . . .

This scenario was the foundation of an actual research study conducted by three university professors who wanted to develop a better understanding of personal space. And I thought I had it bad when I was a junior research assistant, and I had to get my professors' oddly specific salad orders exactly right. (Precisely fifteen—never fourteen or sixteen—dried cranberries, thank you very much.

That summer also taught me more about microgreens than I ever needed to know, but that's a story for a different time.)

Back to the urinal experiment, and the poor research assistant hiding in a bathroom stall. The team leading this study wanted to gain a better understanding of personal space, which they investigated by examining whether men finished urinating more quickly when someone else was standing at a urinal near them. Just a little added weirdness in a public bathroom experience . . . no biggie. To test their hypothesis, one research assistant hid in the stall with two timers (to record when urination began and ended) and another research assistant (who was pretending to be another person going to the bathroom rather than ~~creepily~~ strategically being placed there) randomly stood either right next to or one urinal separated from a man who had just entered the restroom. They discovered that, in fact, business got wrapped up faster when there was a second man standing directly next to them at the urinals.

What does any of this have to do with virtual communication productivity, you ask? Fair question. These researchers found that when someone is near you, you tend to alter your behavior. In a way, you can think about your virtual communication practices like using the bathroom: sometimes we just end up sitting there and forgetting what we were supposed to be doing, but when someone else is knocking on the door, we're more likely to finish up our business and get back to business (sorry . . . I'll see myself out now). In all seriousness, though, the same logic discovered in the urinal study applies to your virtual communication productivity. Obviously, I'm not suggesting you ask a coworker to hover over you (or hide in a utility closet) with stopwatches as you engage in your emails and meetings. But if you find yourself struggling to stay on target with your productivity goals, you can realize the same benefits by having an accountability buddy—a partner, friend, or coworker—with whom you regularly discuss whether you are meeting your communication productivity goals.

Every day, my wife and I check in with each other about how we felt productivity-wise about our virtual communication for each of our jobs, and whether the time we spent communicating impeded our actual work output. By taking the *initiative* (**I** in the PING framework) to be mindful of our interactions and routinely have this conversation, we ensure we aren't wasting time that could be allocated to either improving our work or just enjoying life outside of our jobs. Some days we get the balance right and some days we don't, but the point is that it's top of mind and we're holding ourselves accountable.

Accountability helps direct our efforts, both on an individual and wider scale. When we use the virtual tools at our disposal to communicate deliberately and thoughtfully, the result can establish strong habits that will improve productivity over the long term.

Sync or Swim

In 2010, Mohammed Bouazizi, a young merchant living in a small town in Tunisia, was told by authorities that he wouldn't be able to sell his goods unless he paid a bribe. Bouazizi couldn't afford to pay, so he appealed to the governor. When the governor did nothing to help, Bouazizi took drastic action to protest the corruption. He lit himself on fire.

After this horrifying incident, social media users across the Middle East and North Africa began to see posts pop up on their social media that showed, in real time, what was happening in this small Tunisian town. Watching this horrific event began a wave of passion for democracy over authoritarianism. Bouazizi's face became a symbol against the oppressive regimes. Citizens across a host of Arab countries rallied together, using blog posts, tweets, and Facebook posts to share news and organize protests. Millions of messages were exchanged via social media. In this way, a revolution was born.

Virtual communication provided a means of ensuring that everyone was on the same page, virtually speaking, and working toward a common goal. The movement snowballed and captured worldwide attention.

If the same message had been spread via individual in-person meetings or phone calls, only a handful of people would have been made aware of the incident. Between time lags and limits on how one person could conceivably repeat the story, more traditional means of sharing information would have been wholly inefficient. This same incident would have garnered a fraction of the attention—and at a much slower pace—without virtual communication. Due to media suppression and government restrictions, these social media posts were, for many, the only means of sharing and obtaining information.

Because there were so many voices speaking as one, leaders in the region were forced to listen. Bouazizi's death, and the subsequent social media movement around it, was the catalyst for what became known as the Arab Spring—a series of protests that led to the eventual flight of Tunisia's president from the country and an established democratic election process. It was the start of a future where citizens would be able to choose their leaders in a way that wasn't dictated by violence.

A lot of this chapter has focused on the negatives that inevitably come with so many virtual communication options, and ways to manage the clutter. I'd be remiss, however, if I didn't address the fundamental and largely positive ways in which technology shapes the productivity of individuals, organizations, and nations. The Arab Spring protests represent a degree of communication productivity that never would have been achievable without technology.

As you saw earlier in the chapter, an idea for an online encyclopedia transformed into the information and collaboration powerhouse Wikipedia. By allowing experts from around the globe to easily interact (virtually, of course) and share resources, Wikipedia was able to accomplish feats that never would have been possible without virtual communication. The same can be said for giants like Apple and Google. These organizations wouldn't have been able to scale as quickly, or have such a massive worldwide impact, if they had been limited solely to in-person meetings, letters, and phone calls. As our inboxes continue to fill up and our meeting calendars look like a scary version of *Tetris*, it's good to remind ourselves of the bright side of virtual communication.

KEY LESSONS
Perspective Taking
+ Your message recipients generally don't expect message responses as quickly as you think they do. By taking your message recipient's perspective, you'll be less likely to make assumptions that could lead to a false sense of urgency.
+ When you're the email sender, you want to know: 1) that your recipient isn't just ignoring you, and 2) when they'll get back to you. Communicate your virtual communication expectations via conversations or away messages to others, so it gives you flexibility and doesn't leave others wondering.

Initiative
+ Virtual communication multitasking isn't the answer, as it can split your attention and cognitively exhaust you. Instead, take the initiative to chunk your virtual communication into two or three time blocks each day. This will limit interruptions, provide you with needed information to complete your work tasks, and give you a respite from more mentally taxing tasks. Strategically restructuring your day in this manner will make you more cognitively present in your work, which will allow for more creative ideas to emerge.
+ To avoid the temptation to check your messages during your nonvirtual communication work times, use your "do not disturb" status for instant messages and set up an automated email response

that notifies colleagues when you will be checking your messages. Provide a way for them to reach you in a truly urgent situation (e.g., calling or texting your personal cell).

✦ Choose an accountability partner to make sure you aren't getting so sucked into—or distracted by—all your communication that you lose focus on your work (or life) tasks.

Nonverbal

✦ By not always responding instantaneously, or sending work requests during nonwork hours, you can communicate power. Just be careful to use this strategy sparingly, and don't use it to the detriment of your relationships.

Goals

✦ If a situation likely involves complex information and/or requires a great deal of clarification and back-and-forth, then synchronous modes (e.g., audio or video calls) will be most efficient. If you want unambiguous certainty in communication, then text-based communication will likely be most productive.

✦ When it comes to productive brainstorming, the most creative outcomes arise when everyone generates initial ideas separately. Once everyone has reviewed the submissions separately, have a meeting to discuss them.

✦ To make the best use of meeting time, do the following: Create an agenda and send it out to participants in advance of the meeting. Define the meeting objective(s), and assign an expected time limit for each topic to avoid conversations getting off track. Ensure that only people who can contribute to the agenda topics are present in the meeting, with others simply receiving a summary email afterward. Avoid negative meeting behaviors, like complaining and talking badly about other people.

3

Seeing Is Believing. Or Is It?

How Your Communication Can Make You Seem More Effective

To err is human; to really foul things up requires a computer.
—BILL VAUGHAN, COLUMNIST

In 2017, the internet was abuzz about what was promised to be—conservatively—*the* festival of the year. After all, who wouldn't want to travel to a private Bahamian island where you could spend days enjoying live music, gourmet food, and performances by the hottest names in the industry? Advertisements displayed crystalline Caribbean water dotted with models atop Jet Skis and white-coated servers bearing trays of fruity cocktails. There were promises of packed nightclubs with bottle service and the world's top performers, as well as the chance to mingle with celebrities the likes of Jamie Foxx, Queen Latifah, Lil Wayne, and Iggy Azalea. As if that weren't enough, activities included yoga on the beach, water trampolines, and "$1 million of real treasure and jewels hidden around the island."

Forty-eight hours after the first ads appeared, the festival was the talk of the internet. It had 300 million social media views, as well as mentions from big-name influencer "ambassadors" with millions of followers such as Kendall Jenner, Bella Hadid, Emily Ratajkowski, and Chiara Ferragni. Media venues like *Vogue*, *Bazaar*, *Sports Illustrated*,

TMZ, and Fox News couldn't stop sharing enticing sound bites about the festival. They noted that it was going to be "a life changing experience," "the next BIG destination event," "The New Coachella," and "the biggest FOMO-inducing event of 2017." It was all anyone could talk about, and it hadn't even happened yet.

Sure, the best tickets cost upward of $100,000, but you can't put a price on experience . . . especially when it comes with "the best in food, art, music, and adventure." Right?

When you were younger, your parents might have warned you about things that seem too good to be true. Or all that glitters isn't gold. Pick your cliché—suffice it to say the reality didn't live up to all the hype. When the weekend of Fyre Festival finally arrived, eager ticketholders arrived in paradise . . . only to discover they'd walked into a nightmare.

Instead of the lux experience promised, festivalgoers arrived to find shark-infested waters, mattresses lying on the wet ground, luggage tossed in a random parking lot, and undrinkable water. An image of the attendees' "gourmet" meal—a limp cheese sandwich and soggy salad served in a Styrofoam container—went viral on social media. Talent producer Chloe Gordon described the whole fiasco: "This was a development lot covered in gravel with a few tractors scattered around. There was not enough space to build all the tents and green rooms they would need. There was not a long, beautiful beach populated by swimming pigs. There were, however, a lot of sand flies that left me looking like I had smallpox."

Talk about expectation versus reality.

After the fact, images surfaced of water trucks on their way to the festival that had been seized by Bahamian customs because the $175,000 import fee wasn't paid. It was also discovered that concerns about the lack of adequate plumbing on the island were alleviated in one internal email, which noted that "[n]o one is eating, so therefore no one's pooping."

Um, sure. . . .

Being a glass-half-full kind of guy, Fyre Festival's chief management officer, Grant Margolin, tried to assuage people's reactions to the disaster by pointing out that "nobody got murdered."

I feel better now, how about you?

One year later, the festival's founder, Billy McFarland, was convicted of fraud. He was sentenced to six years in jail and ordered to repay $26 million in settlements. In 2019, two documentaries about the event were released: Netflix's *Fyre: The Greatest Party That Never Happened* and Hulu's *Fyre Fraud*.

It would seem that even the hottest *fyre* can flame out.

Countless articles and internet personalities gleefully theorized about how McFarland and the Fyre Festival organizers (who dubbed themselves "The Fyre Squad") managed to hoodwink so many A-listers into attending such a poorly planned and executed festival. While there is undoubtedly myriad factors that led to a perfect storm of high expectations meeting a dismal reality, McFarland and his team did one thing with a shocking amount of success (and which resulted in the fraud charges). They managed to make it seem like they'd created an event that would be reminisced about for years to come, when in fact, very little work had actually taken place. The Fyre Squad were masters at managing other people's perceptions of their performance.

In McFarland's case, this perception management was clearly immoral and landed him in jail. However, consider this hypothetical situation. Let's say you organized the best festival in the world—one that actually made good on all of Fyre Festival's promises. All that hard work would be for nothing unless you were able to get the word out and communicate the festival's awesomeness to others. And there would be nothing unethical about that. After all, what's the point of creating an incredible experience if there's no one there to enjoy it? In virtual interactions, there is often a disconnect between impressions and reality. When it comes to virtual achievements, optics matter. It's often not possible for those interacting with us—whether it be managers, coworkers, or customers—to physically see how hard we're working. Thus, the need for impression management arises. Because seeing is believing.

If a [Digital] Tree Falls in the Forest . . .

If a digital tree falls in a forest and no one is around to hear it, does it still make a sound?

Or, more to the point, if an employee spends ten hours working but there is no one to see it, was their work really accomplished?

You might think your manager only cares about output—after all, why should it matter if you spend twenty minutes or twenty hours on a task, so long as you do it well and before the deadline? As you'll find out, this assumption makes even the hardest-working employees seem less diligent.

In the last chapter, we focused on how to use virtual communication to be more productive at work. However, just because you're being productive, that doesn't necessarily mean your supervisors, colleagues, and customers will be aware of how amazing you are. It turns out that just because we're being productive, that doesn't necessarily translate into others seeing us as such.

If someone isn't physically next to you and watching your screen, there is no way for them to know how hard you're working beyond what you directly communicate. While it is still a reality in some fields that managers hover behind their employees' desks, in most cases (even for those who are located in the same building), managers have less direct observation of their employees due to most of their interactions occurring virtually. The same concept applies to customer interactions. Whereas the old way of working for customers—as a consultant, accountant, or other vendor—used to entail taking residence in the customer's offices, now it is often done at a distance.

This chapter deals with two essential questions: How do we demonstrate that we're highly engaged in our work and interactions when no one can observe us working? And, just as important, how do we manage virtual impressions across various modes?

We'll explore biases that can create a roadblock to signaling competence in virtual interactions. We'll also look at the communication choices that many of us default to, and how they actually make us appear less productive. Finally, I'll share strategies for avoiding these pitfalls and making virtual communication decisions that will demonstrate you're a superstar performer . . . even when others can't see you.

You may be the highest-performing employee at your company, but that doesn't mean others will even be aware of your accomplishments—especially in the context of interactions that occur via communication technologies. So, although it may feel inauthentic at times, it is vital to be thoughtful about the impressions you're creating. This chapter delves into the challenge of demonstrating your work performance and interaction engagement in today's virtual world.

Typo'ing Your Way to Success

In 1962, NASA's unmanned rocket, the *Mariner 1*, exploded five minutes after liftoff. During the investigation into what went wrong, it turned out that someone had missed a single hyphen* in the code that controlled the rocket (give them a little slack—the code was all hand-transcribed). One hyphen . . . and the cost to NASA was $707 million.

In a different instance, the Australian mint misspelled *responsibility* on their fifty-dollar bank note. The error was printed 46 million times, resulting in $2.3 billion worth of misspelled currency that was circulated for years.

---

* *Fun trivia fact: even though this is often reported as the "most expensive hyphen in history" (and I also refer to it as a hyphen for simplicity), it technically was a missing overbar over the symbol R in an equation (R instead of $\bar{R}$).*

And you thought the typo in that email you sent your boss was bad.

There are numerous highly public corporate typo blunders that have cost companies, both in dollars and reputation. And many of them are minor mistakes that could easily be missed, even with multiple checks. The problem with errors made in the context of virtual communication is that they're both more visible and more permanent. If you're having an in-person conversation with your boss and you mispronounce the name of your competitor's product, it will quickly be forgotten. If you misspell the name of that product in an email, the mistake will be much more glaring. Errors that are relevant to your work task (like leaving out a hyphen in mathematical code for a rocket) can make you appear far less competent.

Now that you're appropriately quaking in your virtual boots, let me share the good news: virtual communication mistakes don't necessarily need to be perceived as mistakes. And there are ways to limit the fallout when they do occur.

In my own research alongside Hayley Blunden from American University, we examined how more than 3,700 people evaluated email typos. And we found that typos massively decrease perceptions of sender intelligence, with one big exception. When typos are made in an emotional context, recipients are more forgiving of the typo-makers because, in this type of situation, recipients believe the typos were the result of the sender's emotions rather than intelligence (or lack thereof). The reason is that we're all prone to searching for reasons—or attributions of—why something occurred. When it comes to virtual communication mistakes, the obvious "reason" is that the mistake-maker is careless or unintelligent. However, if there is another more visible reason for the error, then your message receiver will attribute that reason to your mistake instead.

So, if you notice that the message you sent your colleague was riddled with typos because you happened to be in the middle of a crisis with your child refusing to get ready for school, you can send a quick follow-up (ideally error-free) to quickly explain the situation.

Something as brief as "I just looked back at my message and saw all the typos—sorry about that! I was trying to get my toddler dressed for school and she was screaming her head off" will do the trick (and maybe even give you and your email partner something to bond over).

Even including "Sent from my iPhone" in your signature can reduce the negative impact of typos. As University of California psychologists Harold Kelley and John Michela discovered, when this line was included in email signatures, message recipients were more likely to attribute the sender's errors to the technology rather than the individual. Two North Carolina State University professors also found that email errors and etiquette breaches (like messages that are too formal or terse) are viewed less negatively when there's available information that an email was sent by someone from a different culture. So, by providing an alternative "reason" for your virtual communication error, you'll be able to reduce the impact of negative perceptions.

If there's no good reason, then using humor to acknowledge your mistake can lighten the impact and mitigate assumptions that you're careless. The Ace Hotel in New York employed this strategy when they accidentally sent out a broken link to their subscriber list. When they realized the error, they sent this follow-up message:

ACE HOTEL
NEW YORK

View in Browser

Surprises are great, but not without risk.

The other day we sent a deal into the universe. The hope was to stir your soul and hand you the keys to your own New York adventure. Instead, it was all hype with a broken link.

Today, we fix that with a code that works. Book now through May 30 and get 20% off any room you want, with late checkout and $20 at the bar to get your wheels turning.

ESCAPE TO NEW YORK

Similarly, Fab, an e-commerce home and life accessories company that was later acquired, also found a tactful way to address a virtual communication blunder. After accidentally sending a test email with just an image of a cat to all their subscribers, they sent this apology message:

I'm a sucker for good puns, so I especially appreciate the clever way Fab navigated the error. At the end of the email, they added, "On a serious note, please know that we sent this cat email unintentionally and are taking steps to ensure that this doesn't happen again. Ok, enough from us." In this email, Fab found an effective balance between humorous self-deprecation and an assurance to do better.

With so many virtual communication options at our fingertips, there's more room for catastrophe that becomes impossible to recall once it's out there. No pressure or anything, right? The truth is that errors are bound to crop up from time to time no matter how diligent you are. To minimize the harmful reputational (and possibly fiscal) effects of your typos, acknowledge the error, provide a reason, and then move on. It's not the last error you'll ever make.

Counter Clock-Wise

Let's say you were given two presentations to watch that were nearly identical. Afterward, you were asked to decide which was better. Your answer? They're identical insofar as quality . . . so they're equally good.

What if I told you that one presenter took thirty-seven minutes to create the presentation, while the other took eight hours and thirty-four minutes? Remember, the presentations are identical in terms of quality, so neither is better than the other, regardless of how much time they took to prepare. Seems like common sense that, if the two presentations are exactly the same, they'd be rated as such. Right?

Wrong.

Evaluators who were told the presenter spent more than eight hours preparing rated the presentation as 24 percent better than evaluators who were told the presenter spent only thirty-seven minutes preparing, even though both presentations were identical. The culprit of these nonsensical evaluation differences is referred to as *input bias*, which addresses how our judgments are shaped by details that are irrelevant to the outcome.

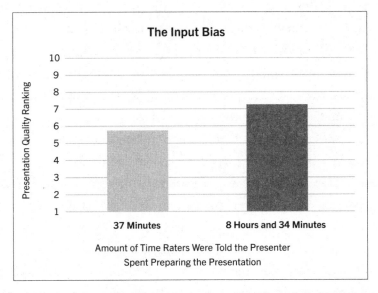

Despite both presentations being identical, raters evaluated a presentation as 24 percent better when they knew the presenter took a lot more time to create it.

When we hear that someone spent eight hours working on a presentation, we assume the output is good, because eight hours represents a lot of effort. Similarly, a task that only took thirty-seven minutes couldn't be nearly as good, because that doesn't seem like enough time to create something high-quality.

Let's consider another example. Suppose I gave you two samples of fudge to taste (yum): Fudge A and Fudge B. Right before you gobble up the tasty morsels, I inform you that both samples were made with the same ingredients, but Fudge A was made with an expensive machine. How much the machine costs should be mostly irrelevant if the two fudge samples are made with the same ingredients, so that detail shouldn't make a difference in your evaluation. However, when this scenario was presented to study participants, they rated the fudge sample that was supposedly made with more expensive machinery as tastier.

By this point, you should be starting to see why the input bias is so problematic when much of our communication about our work occurs virtually. Here's the other problem: most jobs lack clear performance metrics (with the exception of careers like sales, which are judged on more easily quantifiable criteria like sales numbers). Can we really measure precisely how well a manager manages, for instance? Or how good a consultant or investment banker really is? Even for a software developer, there is messiness, since assessing the number of lines of code generated is a problematic metric of productivity. More concise code that accomplishes the same goal tends to be better than lengthier code, for example. Just because a program was developed, that doesn't mean it was completed in the most optimal way (and there is no true "optimal" product to compare against anyway). As a result of a lack of objective criteria on which to judge employees' performance, employers fall back on the input bias—using more easily observable but irrelevant details to assess work quality. And one of the most misused measures of work quality is perceived time or effort spent working. This is why an employee who is in the office from nine to five will often be rated more favorably than another employee who accomplishes more work but leaves at three. It feels fairer to rely on something salient, like time spent working, even though it isn't a good indicator of someone's job performance.[*]

Using time and effort spent working isn't just an ineffective metric—it's detrimental. As a manager, would you rather hire the person who takes eight hours to complete a task, or someone who can finish the same task in thirty minutes? The latter candidate is the obvious right choice, since they will have the rest of the day free to achieve other goals. And yet research shows that without other easy, objective ways to evaluate a task, evaluators rely on time spent working as a proxy for how much effort was put into a task. Even when people acknowledge that inputs shouldn't matter in a situation (and believe the input information didn't matter), they are still a factor in their judgments.

The input bias plays a particularly noteworthy role in the context of how much face time—or time spent within view of supervisors and colleagues—employees are exhibiting. University of California and University of North Carolina professors set out to understand how "passive face time"—the amount of time others spend observing you without actually engaging—affects perceived work performance. Through conducting dozens of interviews, a trend emerged. The general perception was explained by one manager, who said, "I've been a supervisor for I don't know, seven, eight years, and without a doubt, if I see the person at their desk I know they're working. Or if my boss sees me in the office, he, she, knows I'm working. If I am not physically in the office, they have to assume I'm working. So it's an easy way for them to check if I'm doing what I'm supposed to be doing."

---

[*] *For managers who are looking to ameliorate the effects of the input bias in employee performance reviews, it is helpful to focus more on evaluating worker output, decision quality, and how employees are contributing to the organization as a whole, rather than how much time they spent working.*

These professors found that workers who put in more observed face time at the office are characterized as more responsible, dependable, committed, and dedicated. Even more troubling, these snap judgments about an employee's performance based solely on how much a manager sees them working can occur subconsciously.

Another area where biased evaluations crop up is in patient satisfaction, which is a criterion often used to judge a doctor's performance. In theory, more satisfied patients should be healthier, as their perception of physician effort should drive outcomes. Yet, in a nationally representative study of tens of thousands of patients from the United States, patient satisfaction didn't just fail to yield better outcomes; in fact, more satisfied patients were also more likely to die. These results point to the possibility that patients are more satisfied when doctors order more tests or treatments than strictly necessary and are more willing to "fulfill patients' requests" (even when those requests are not the best medical treatment). It is possible that other factors impacted these results as well (e.g., patient degree of illness, which was controlled for but not fully eliminated). However, the fact that higher patient satisfaction had a big impact on mortality in this study means that even if it were possible to design a flawless experiment, it would still be unlikely to find the opposite—where more satisfied patients boost survival rates.

The input bias occurs across industries and is further complicated by the increasing use of virtual communication. Before mobile devices were a widely available communication mode, for instance, construction foremen needed to stay at work sites all day to manage tradespeople. Whenever the homeowner (or whoever was paying for the construction) stopped by, the foreman would be seen working. Now, foremen can be even more productive by managing these tradespeople via text messaging and video calls while simultaneously engaging in related work off-site, such as purchasing materials or hiring employees who will be needed later in the project. They might visit their sites once a day rather than being at a single location for the entire day, thereby potentially doubling their productivity. If a customer stopped by their in-progress home and didn't see the foreman there, however, they might assume the person wasn't doing any work because they weren't visibly present.

When auditors and accountants used to spend all day (and sometimes weeks at a time) in a customer's office going through their paper files, the customer saw them working. Now, these employees work at their headquarters instead of being flown all over the country. As a result, the only information the customers receive is what the accountant communicates.

In bygone days, it was necessary to walk to your colleagues' and manager's office every time you wanted to give them an update. Now, regardless of whether you work in the same office as your team, most of this communication is handled through instant messaging and email. Thus, there is far less reason to visibly see coworkers' spaces (and whether they're in them ostensibly doing work).

To consider the real-world value of demonstrating effort virtually, let's return to the Fyre Festival debacle I discussed earlier in the chapter. The Fyre Squad likely recognized that the perception of how hard you're working is often as important as the work output (at least, until the stakeholders show up at the event and find only a barren parking lot and sad cheese sandwiches awaiting their arrival). While their actions were unquestionably fraudulent, there are many times when showing how hard you're working is an essential element of job performance. When it comes to our virtual communication practices, it's not enough to provide others with the result of our work. To manage optics and demonstrate your work efforts, virtual communication requires explicitly communicating about your work process in ways that were never before necessary. After all, if your manager, customers, or colleagues can't physically see you working, then who's to say you're putting in the effort rather than spending 90 percent of the day napping?

Making Your Virtual Presence Felt

In 2017, Uber was getting some seriously bad press. Workers described being pitted against one another while executives got away with all manner of poor behavior. There were reports of sexual assault on company retreats, homophobic slurs being shouted during meetings, and even a manager who threatened to beat an employee's head with a baseball bat.

Something obviously needed to be done. Arianna Huffington, a board member at Uber, helped lead the effort to address the company's toxic culture in an email.

> Hi everybody, I'm writing this from the plane back to New York after two days in the office listening to your concerns, your experiences, your expectations for Uber—and to all the things you want to get done to improve it. I have talked with Eric Holder and Tammy Albarran who are both planning to be at 1455 Market tomorrow to continue their work. And while the investigation is continuing, I wanted to share a few impressions before I head back. First, know that in all my conversations with Travis and members of the leadership team, everyone is absolutely committed to making any and all changes that need to happen. I also want to let you know how many people wanted to talk to me about how much they love Uber and its mission, and how much they want to be part of the team that fixes everything that's not working to create a workplace where everyone feels respected and valued.
>
> I have set up calls with those of you I was not able to meet, and also next week will be in the New York and Vancouver offices and we will set up time with anyone who wants to meet with me.
>
> More soon,
>
> Arianna

It would have been easy enough for Huffington to assume that Uber employees would realize she was working hard on the situation. She could have simply said she and the rest of the board were going to come up with a resolution and left it at that. But that would have been a mistake. Many employees would likely assume that a media mogul worth over $100 million, like Huffington, would not devote much time and just swoop in to make whatever decision she felt was best. She also didn't take the approach of simply listing the number of hours she would spend working to resolve the issue, which would have come across as forced. Instead, she made a point of actually demonstrating her effort via her communication (e.g., "two days in the office listening," "I'm writing this from the plane," "I have set up calls with those of you I was not able to meet," and "next week will be in the New York and Vancouver offices and we will set up time with anyone who wants to meet with me").

It's like that digital tree-falling-in-the-woods analogy I made earlier. We often incorrectly assume that just because we're working hard, others will recognize our effort. Instead, we need to find ways to show this effort through our virtual communication. Rather than jumping to tell your client or boss how quickly you were able to complete a task (e.g., "I was able to finish it in half the time expected"), the best virtual bang for your buck comes from focusing on the effort you put in (e.g., "Given how important I know this task was, I made sure to block out a large chunk of time with no meetings or emails, so that it had my full and uninterrupted attention"). And beyond the actual messages themselves, there are ways to highlight productivity through nonverbal virtual communication behavior.

Email Is Like Naptime: Sometimes It Needs to Be Scheduled

What would you think about a coworker who only sent you emails between 4:00 and 4:30 p.m.? Based on what research has shown, you would most likely assume they aren't working most of the day, even if that is completely false. Researchers from the University of California conducted their own series of interviews to examine the relationship between message timing and employee performance evaluations. George, an engineer working from a subsidiary office halfway around the world from his company headquarters, told the research team, "I used to send an update to [headquarters] at the end of the day of the things I did. It was one big email." The problem was that, because of a lack of face time, there was no way for his managers to know he was actually working all day long (instead of just the few hours leading up to his end-of-day email). There was also the *out of sight, out of mind* concern, where his name only appeared in his bosses' inboxes once a day. George tried out a new strategy, where he sent multiple, smaller updates throughout the day. He explained, "[Now] I just send lots of emails during the day so when they open their mail they see in their inbox lots of messages from me from all times of day, and they know I am working. What is good about that is that if they ask me to do something else, they already know I am very busy and working hard, so when I say yes, it looks extra good like I am doing it just for them."

In a sense, George discovered how to use email to show "face time," without ever actually showing his face. The best part about this strategy is that it doesn't require any extra work. Although others may not "see" you working all day long—whether you are remote, working in a satellite office, or located on a different floor in the same building—you can engage in virtual communication sporadically throughout the day to "show" you are working. Rather than going through your inbox and instant messages at the beginning of the day and replying to all the messages at once, spread out your responses in a few dedicated blocks throughout the day to counteract the face-time effect (as we discussed in Chapter 2, this practice has the secondary benefit of providing short breaks between more difficult tasks to help replenish your cognitive resources). If you want to take it a step further, there are many technologies that allow you to delay or schedule the sending of text-based virtual communication messages that you already wrote, so you can make it seem like you are communicating outside of normal work hours (i.e., going above and beyond), even when you aren't.

A similar logic, with a twist, is related to scheduling meetings. On one hand, you may want to show how excited you are to meet with a given party (e.g., a manager, coworker, or client), and that you are "at work" all day by having broad availability to meet at nearly any time. The problem with this approach is that it will make it seem like you aren't busy working because your schedule is too wide-open. Rather, if your goal is to provide evidence of your productivity, the best approach is to offer a limited set of potential times at differing parts of the day and week. As an example, you might say:

> Given my current meeting and work schedule, my remaining open times for the next couple of days when I could meet are Tuesday: 8:30am–9am or 2:00pm–3:00pm; Wednesday: 10:00am–11:30am or 4:30pm–5:00pm. I'm also happy to provide times further out in the week if there isn't overlap.

Just be careful not to be too stingy with times so that it becomes a headache to schedule with you. Instead, being diverse and limited with your open times can create the perception both that you are busy with work and that you are working throughout the day.

This advice matches that of negotiation experts Deepak Malhotra and Max Bazerman from Harvard Business School. They suggest that when house sellers limit house viewings to one hour, or that when entrepreneurs offer schedules for only a few available dates, it signals they're high in demand and busy with other potential buyers. Even if that's not the reality, this limited schedule signals information to others—both scarcity and "social proof"*—which can create a sense of urgency for potential buyers.

---

* Incidentally, social proof is the reason why, when you see the line out the door for a bakery, you might be tempted to join the crowd. Even if there are five other lineless bakeries on the same block, the line provides information, valid or not, that this is the bakery to visit.

At this point, I'm sure some of you are thinking it seems like a poor use of time (and limited mental energy) to need to be thoughtful about scheduling your virtual communication. In fact, the term *productivity theater* has been coined to describe these kinds of approaches. There are a myriad of articles noting that productivity theater doesn't help organizations and is a waste of employees' effort.

Here's the thing—I fully agree. This process is pointless for organizations and should be unnecessary for you to do, as your work decisions and outcomes should speak for themselves. If this was a book solely for CEOs, I would be describing ways to design organizations and performance evaluation processes to avoid the need for this showmanship. But this is a book for you as an individual about how to improve your outcomes within your work environment. Unless you are lucky enough to be in an organization that doesn't care how much time you spend working so long as you meet performance metrics, most employees will need to engage in productivity theater. After all, managers are only human, and we all enjoy theater. Given that true work performance is nearly impossible to judge objectively in most jobs, managers are left falling back on more easily observable information, such as perceived effort and time spent working. As a result, it often isn't enough just to work hard—you need to be strategic in showing how hard you are working.

Scintillating Pixels

Demonstrating productivity in your job is about more than proving you've spent your contracted hours toiling away at your computer. It's also about showing you're engaged in one-off interactions.

A technology executive acquaintance of mine—let's call him Amari—told me a story about a memorable experience he'd had during his last job hunt. He was fortunate enough to receive two competing job offers from midsize technology companies. Before deciding which offer to accept, Amari scheduled meetings with both of his prospective teams to get a feeling of the culture at each organization and where he might be able to contribute the most value. Both conversations occurred via video calls, but his experiences during the two meetings were drastically different. When Amari spoke with the team at Organization A, everyone had their webcams on. They asked lots of questions, laughed at his (self-professed) corny jokes, and nodded along as he discussed suggestions for new initiatives. They had a great conversation, and Amari received several follow-up emails asking for resources he'd mentioned.

At Organization A, Amari knew that everyone was paying attention and engaging in the conversation. His experience at Organization B was a *little* different.

Only two people in the virtual room (Amari included) had their webcam on. And everyone aside from three people kept themselves muted for the entire meeting, except for a few excruciating seconds when someone accidentally unmuted themselves, and everyone was privy to the fact that they were talking to someone else in a separate conference call. Needless to say, there was no stimulating Q&A, no follow-up messages, and no discussion of future projects. The whole experience left a bad taste in Amari's mouth, because it was clear no one had been paying attention. He felt like the conversation had been a waste of everyone's time. To no one's surprise, Amari took the job at Organization A and never looked back.

There is one slight aside that I'd be remiss if I didn't highlight here. A good strategy that the members of Organization A employed after Amari's call—and one I recommend that you use whenever it's relevant—is to send thank-you notes. It can be a simple, personalized two-sentence email after a job interview or meeting with a client, but it's a surprisingly underutilized—and relatively low-effort—means of both warmly acknowledging the other person's time/contribution as well as highlighting your own engagement/effort in the relationship (i.e., you can both be a kind person and positively manage optics using the same behavior). A quick "Thanks so much for taking the time to meet with me yesterday about X. It was really interesting to hear more about Y, and I look forward to learning more" will show you were really present during the conversation.

For my MBA courses that I teach online, one of the first things I tell my students is that their cameras need to remain on for every class (unless they've messaged me beforehand with any valid reason, from having technology issues to just needing a mental health day; I'm not a total monster). When I make this announcement, I can practically hear the groans. In my beginning-of-course survey, one student actually noted that cameras-on "isn't why I signed up for an online class!!!" The three exclamation points were a nice touch. And I can see their perspective; especially since my first class begins at 8 a.m., I can imagine how tempting it would be for students to not even get out of bed to join the class. Aside from the obvious pleasure all professors take in torturing their students (just kidding), there is a legitimate reason why I have this requirement.

When your goal is to demonstrate engagement and productivity, a richer communication mode, like video, is generally going to be your best choice.

Sometimes you won't even need to say anything. For instance, if you are in a meeting with twenty people and your manager is presenting quarterly results, and most (but not all) attendees have their webcam off, it would be strategic to turn your webcam on. In this situation, being visible will make you seem more engaged, regardless of whether you actually are (e.g., you could have unrelated emails up on your computer screen, but no one would know. Not that I'm condoning multitasking, of course).

Many managers assume—albeit often incorrectly—that employees whose webcams are off during meetings are not fully engaged in the conversation or their work. Thus, while it can be a pain to make yourself camera-ready and monitor your facial expressions throughout the entirety of a video call, that effort can actually make you seem more "present."

This strategy allows students to show their engagement not only with me, but also with each other. In my MBA negotiation courses, students would likely feel uncomfortable telling an embarrassing story about a time they did poorly in a negotiation if they were talking to a bunch of static head shots on their computer screen. When they share their story with everyone's cameras on, however, they can see their class-mates reacting and putting in the effort to listen to them. I leave my own camera on (not least because it's weird to require attendees to have their cameras on when the leader has theirs off) to show my own en-thusiasm for the course. And it works. By the end of the semester, my students' initial grumblings about the cameras-on rule have shifted to an overwhelmingly positive postgame analysis. In the anonymous end-of-class survey I give out, my recent cohort of students made comments like "At the beginning I didn't see the point [of cameras on], but if we hadn't done that, I wouldn't have gotten to know anyone in the class. Seeing and hearing them made it feel like we were in person . . . with-out having to actually be in person." Another student wrote, "Seeing how excited Prof Brodsky gets when he talks about his research made the class more interesting and kept me from zoning out a lot of times."

In case you were wondering, I take all parts of that last comment as a compliment, thank you very much.

Video can be even more useful when working in a group that you have no prior history with. In these cases, using video will make you seem more present. The need for cameras on becomes less necessary, however, for a group that has a history of working together. A study that looked at audio-only versus video found there wasn't much differ-ence in terms of participation and cohesion when the group was already established. When the people you're meeting with know you well, their assumptions about your work ethic will be more accurate, which means there will be less benefit to you "showing" how hard you're working with your camera on. As we'll discuss later in the book, different goals, such as conserving your ability to engage in other tasks, might necessitate turning your camera off. But if you don't know the other people well and your goal is to demonstrate you're working hard and engaged, video will help show it.

Beauty Is in the [Virtual] Eye of the Beholder

When you're having an in-person conversation with someone, with a few exceptions, it's standard practice in many countries to maintain at least some level of eye contact. If your gaze stays fixed on a spot to the left of the other person's face, they're going to be confused. At best, they'll think they have something stuck in their teeth and you're being too polite to stare. At worst, they'll think you aren't paying attention to what they're saying. When you're communicating virtually in video interactions, there's the same expectation of maintaining eye contact, but with some additional challenges.

If you're talking to someone standing right in front of you, the other person will naturally draw your attention. You generally won't have to think about maintaining eye contact—it will just happen naturally. When their face is just a little square on your computer screen, however, it feels less natural (and even slightly disconcerting) to stare at them.

Have you ever been on a video call, dutifully trying to maintain eye contact with the speaker, only to find that the other person is staring off in a direction that's nowhere near your eyes? Maybe they're looking at notes on their screen, focused on the video display of themselves, or staring off into space as they carefully consider your brilliant commentary . . . or playing a game on their phone. When it comes to video communication, there is a lot more that you can look at and do (and that people feel comfortable doing) besides keeping eye contact. To complicate matters further, activities that would be normal in an in-person situation, like breaking eye contact to consult your notes, will make you seem inattentive during a video call, because all the other person can see is that you're looking away from your camera.

A third issue during video calls is that people aren't attentive to where their webcam is located—and the fact that it often doesn't sync with where other people's faces are appearing on their screens. For most computer setups, there will be a mismatch between where the other person's face appears on your screen and where your webcam is located. While you might be looking at the person's video feed, to them it seems like you're staring somewhere off to the side or above them. Not ideal, especially when you consider that numerous research studies have shown that eye contact in the context of video conversations positively affects impressions of warmth and competence. For instance, research has shown that interviewees are assessed more negatively when they don't maintain eye contact in video interviews. We're also evaluated as less likable and less socially present when our gaze strays from the camera. Nonverbal behavior in video calls is especially significant in forming initial impressions of competence. Even if you're less articulate in your wording, maintaining eye contact will do some of that heavy lifting, without you needing to say a word.

The answer to these video-camera-related challenges is simple (although it's not always easy). Make a concerted effort to maintain eye contact with your camera, rather than the person's on-screen image. Or even better, make sure to move their video display near your webcam (e.g., if your webcam is at the top center of your laptop, drag the video display directly beneath the webcam). By being more attentive to where you're looking, you can avoid seeming uninterested because the other person thinks you're staring at your other screen (or your phone, or your kid, or your dog jumping up and down begging for lunch) while they're talking. When I give keynote speeches for virtual conferences held via video, for instance, I make sure to position my notes and the chat Q&A close to my webcam at the top of my screen. That way, when I glance back and forth between those main components I'm paying attention to, it doesn't seem like I'm looking away from the camera.

If you feel like you're going cross-eyed with the effort of staring at the "wrong" spot, never fear. You can also leverage more mechanical tools, such as hanging or stick-on webcams, webcam stands/mounts, or even tablet teleprompters, to enable your camera to be located center-screen rather than above (although they may cover part of your screen). There are also software tools that will actually "center" your eye contact for you in real time, even when you are looking elsewhere (although this can occasionally end up looking unnatural). So, there's hope for even the most hopeless of us.

Lights, Camera, Action

Most people are inclined to assume that business leaders are too experienced to make silly communication faux pas. This would certainly be the case for the leaders of AMC Entertainment, which was the largest movie theater chain in the world and boasted revenue in the billions. It should follow, then, that the company's CEO would be the crème de la crème of communicators, virtual or otherwise. It was therefore a surprise to everyone when Adam Aron, AMC's CEO, was literally caught with his pants down during a live YouTube video interview.

While discussing stock trading within the company, his camera slipped, showing a brief flash of Aron's, well, briefs. He quickly returned his camera to its rightful place, but the damage had been done. He even got his own hashtag, which was also a play on some of the AMC stock-trading activity at the time: #NakedShorts.

Talk about the opposite of #Lifegoals.

I mentioned earlier in the chapter that my students balk at the idea of cameras on at the beginning of the class but soon come to appreciate the method of my madness. However, while they virtually "show up" to class, many of my students choose to give the class an up-close-and-personal view of them in their pajamas, lounging in bed, as they engage in tense negotiation simulations. Mind you, my students are MBAs, many of whom have had years (and in some cases, decades) of experience in the workforce. When I join virtual meetings with Fortune 100 companies that I'm either leading training for or consulting with, the exact same thing happens. You'd think they would know better. And you'd be wrong.

Too often, I find in both professional and classroom virtual settings that people don't uphold the same standards they would if they were in person. This is a mistake. I'm not suggesting you get into a suit just to sit behind your webcam, as that would often be counternormative, but research has shown that appearance matters, whether you are interacting in person or virtually.

Some employees have tried to find a balance between comfort and traditional work attire—a fusion of outfits that has been termed the "Zoom mullet" and recommended on many a social media post. The idea here is you can get the comfiness of working from home on the non-camera-facing lower half of your body with your favorite pair of sweatpants, while your upper half is all business. And if, by chance, there is camera slippage, at least you won't be caught #NakedShorts. Business on the top, party on the bottom, as it were.

The best approach is to ensure your visible attire is appropriate but won't stick out in a way that detracts from what you're saying. A good general rule is that if you know how the other person (or people) in your meeting will be dressed, choose an outfit that is a similar level of formalness. If you don't know what the other person might be wearing, or it's a higher-stakes meeting (like an interview), then err on the side of dressing more formally.*

The bottom line is that appearance matters, even in the virtual world. Beyond the way we dress, elements of our video call environment can

---

* If this were a book just for executives, I'd discuss the research showing how allowing employees to wear "home attire" can increase feelings of authenticity and engagement. But given that most readers won't be able to set dress codes for their organization, I'll save the topic for a future book of mine that will be addressed specifically to leaders.

also affect how our competence and productivity is judged. In two different studies, interview candidates received lower ratings simply due to having awkward camera angles or poor lighting. It turns out that something as simple as investing in a cheap twenty-dollar ring light to improve your videoconferencing lighting or buying a better webcam can help you get a job.

A study that looked at different virtual video call backgrounds, which could be used to hide communicators' actual backgrounds, found that backgrounds with plants and bookshelves resulted in better impressions of communicator competence, since they're associated with an "established human preference for natural environments" and intelligence, respectively. In contrast, virtual backgrounds with household items (like a couch) and "novelty" backgrounds (like a walrus posing on ice) worsened impressions. The idea here is that out-of-place fake backgrounds or home-oriented backgrounds seem less professional and thus contribute to impressions of the speaker being less competent.

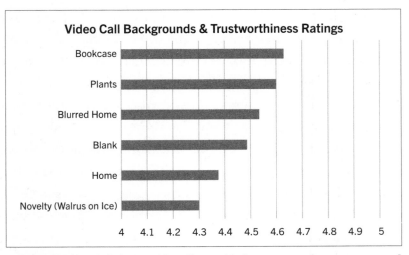

Your choice of backgrounds during video calls can alter how trustworthy you appear to others.

The main takeaway here is that, when it comes to your video calls, people are making assessments about your competence based on what they see—both you and what is behind you.

Don't Talk the Talk If You Can't Walk the Walk

Throughout this chapter, we've examined virtual communication strategies to manage impressions of both your ability and performance. This should go without saying, but you should only engage in these impression management techniques if you have the goods to back up your signaling. In other words, your goal is to emulate the Fyre Festival *lead-up*, where you use your virtual communication to show just how great you are. But—and I want to emphasize this *but*—you need to ensure that when the other person takes a closer look at your work, they aren't finding a soggy cheese sandwich. What I mean is if you are signaling high productivity and ability through your virtual communication, it's essential to actually make good on your promises (even if they're implicit rather than explicit). Violating expectations can result in worse outcomes than someone having a lower impression of you to begin with, so it's not enough to talk the talk. Combining the strategies you learned both here and in Chapter 2 will help you strike the right balance of not only being productive, but using virtual tools to manage your optics . . . even when there's no one else around to witness you working.

KEY LESSONS

Perspective Taking

+ Although you know you're working hard, others lack the
  same frame of reference, especially when you are interacting
  virtually. This is where perspective taking becomes crucial. By
  managing impressions strategically, you can ensure your efforts
  are recognized.

Initiative

+ To create positive impressions at work via virtual communication,
  it's useful to take the initiative to both show (e.g., send emails/
  instant messages at regular intervals rather than sending one long

message daily) and tell (e.g., highlight the effort you put into a task without making it seem forced).

✦ It's not enough to use your virtual communication to show you're a high performer—you need to have the skill and output to back it up and "walk the walk," lest you end up in a Fyre Festival flameout situation.

✦ You can reduce the negative perceptions of virtual communication errors by providing a reason (e.g., mention in the passing that you're emailing from your phone since you wanted to get them an answer ASAP).

Nonverbal

✦ Turning your camera on helps to show you're actively listening and engaged in a meeting. It'll also make you seem like a better performer, especially when meeting with people you don't know well.

✦ In an office, you don't have to worry about your lighting and surroundings; on video calls, these details matter.

✦ Be aware of where your webcam is located and make sure you're maintaining eye contact with the camera rather than the person's image on-screen, as the two are often misaligned. It will make you seem more attentive and competent.

✦ For attire during video calls, try to match the level of formalness of the other people in your meeting. If you don't know how others will be dressed, err on the side of being more formal.

✦ Choose a professional-looking background for your video calls. Plants and bookshelves can make you seem more competent and intelligent.

Goals

✦ If your goal is to avoid having your performance be unfairly judged (e.g., due to the input bias), make sure to use your virtual communication to emphasize your work effort and productivity.

✦ Counterintuitively, if your goal is to show how productive you are, limit your virtual communication meeting availability. Beyond helping you to avoid meeting times that will interrupt your workflow, this approach will make you seem busier, and thus more productive. Just don't take this strategy to the point where it becomes a pain to schedule with you or can't be justified.

✦ When your goal is to demonstrate engagement and productivity, choose a richer communication mode (e.g., video).

4

Ice Ice Baby

How to Start Relationships Virtually

The whole problem of life, then, is this: how to break out of one's own loneliness, how to communicate with others.

—CESARE PAVESE, *THIS BUSINESS OF LIVING: DIARIES 1935–1950*

Most everyone has a memory of a particular virtual interaction that gives them the heebie-jeebies whenever they are forced to recount it. Here's (one of) mine.

My department had hired several new faculty members; however, because most of us were working from home at the time due to the COVID-19 pandemic, there hadn't been an opportunity for everyone to connect as a group. So, in a well-meaning effort to bring the department together to introduce our new hires, one of our colleagues arranged for a comedian to perform during a virtual happy hour.

Seems reasonable enough, at first.

The event began with nineteen management professors arriving in the videoconference. There were some stilted attempts at introductions and small talk before we all realized that one-on-one conversations don't really work with so many people in the room.

There was an announcement that the comedian had arrived, so we all settled ourselves in our home offices and prepared to get some good laughs.

"How many elementary school teachers does it take to screw in a light bulb?"

Crickets.

After an uncomfortably long pause, the comedian answered his own joke: "None; they assign it to their students for homework."

Some forced chuckles ensued.

Not to be deterred, the comedian pressed on: "What's the best way to get a teacher's attention during recess?"

Static crackled over someone's mic.

"You *slide* into their conversation, of course!" the comedian enthused. "Okay, how about this one. Why did the arithmetic book look sad?"

This time the comedian didn't even wait before supplying the answer: "Because it had too many problems!"

Someone's dog let out a plaintive howl.

It had become obvious to everyone in the video call—aside from the comedian—that he had either been misinformed about or misunderstood the nature of his audience. He was under the impression we were all elementary school teachers. There is of course nothing wrong with being an elementary school teacher (my mother was one for over forty years), but the nuances of the experience of monitoring activities like recess were somewhat lost on us as college professors.

As the jokes continued in rapid-fire succession, it was clear from my colleagues' facial expressions that all the people in the video call were asking themselves the same question: Do we interrupt the comedian to let him know about his audience, which would be embarrassing for everyone involved, or just let the show go on pretending we taught six-year-olds rather than twenty-year-olds? To be fair, though, sometimes the latter need their hands held just as much.

With our realization that interrupting the comedian would likely only make everything more awkward, the show forged ahead.

The whole hour felt like a really bad first date: everyone involved knew it was going badly and both parties never should have come out in the first place, but there was nowhere else to go but forward.

The unintentional positive benefit was that our group was texting each other during the hour, bonding over how hilariously terrible the whole experience was. Not that I'm condoning bonding at someone else's expense, but the activity did have its intended effect in a round-about way. We all got a chance to interact with the new members of our department in a setting outside of a work meeting. It also gave us a few humorous ideas about ways to motivate our undergraduate and MBA students (detention, anyone?).

The American inventor and internet pioneer Douglas Engelbart said, "The rate at which a person can mature is directly proportional to the embarrassment he can tolerate." If he was right, then that hour was one of substantial personal growth for us all. Probably even more so for the comedian himself.

Needless to say, that was our department's first and last encounter with a virtual comedian.

The spirit of the whole concept was a good one—it was just the technology that made it a failure. If it had been in person, the comedian would have quickly realized he was at a university rather than staring at our living rooms. Beyond that, there's a reason why sitcoms have laugh tracks in the background. Even though they were not exactly relevant to the audience, the comedian had some great jokes. But it was just bizarre having complete silence with people laughing to themselves on mute after each punch line (I got a few weird looks from my wife, who was sitting at her desk next to me at the time).

The takeaway of this story is not that fun or beginning new relationships can never occur via technology. Rather, you just need to be more thoughtful and strategic in how you approach communication technologies than you would be for a similar interaction in person.

Lost in Transmission

This chapter considers the essential components of initiating new relationships virtually. When you're meeting someone for the first time via a digital mode, there are ways to make up for the lack of physical proximity. I'll discuss how to leverage virtual communication to reach out to completely cold contacts, start up conversations with acquaintances you've had little contact with, and reignite relationships that have fallen by the wayside.

For most workers, communication technologies have become one of the main—if not only—tools for building relationships with work colleagues who may be spread around the world. I've seen dozens of articles and listened to countless executives bemoan the seeming universal truth that, in order to initiate new and lasting relationships, physical proximity is an essential ingredient. In this chapter, I'll overturn the assumption that relationships formed virtually are weaker than ones established in person. It is possible to start and maintain relationships mostly—or purely—through virtual means. It just takes a little more initiative and planning. This chapter will show you how to get your foot in the door, relationally speaking, via technology.

Find Your Uncomfortable Zone

Imagine you're walking through a college campus at lunchtime when everyone is out and about. You're incredibly self-conscious because you're wearing a ridiculous T-shirt with the 1990s hip-hop star Vanilla Ice's face plastered on the front with the words "Ice Ice Baby." That might be an acceptable wardrobe selection for your quirky uncle, but it's not a choice anyone in this decade would make. Everyone you pass is staring at your shirt and, by association, you. At least, that's how it feels.

Psychologists Gilovich, Medvec, and Savitsky tried out a similar scenario, in which they directed students to wear embarrassing shirts (e.g., with Vanilla Ice or Barry Manilow on them) or a shirt with an individual's picture who they felt favorably toward (e.g., Martin Luther King Jr.). Repeatedly, students assumed that a large number of people they encountered would remember the shirt they were wearing. The student participants certainly couldn't stop thinking about it themselves. Yet the researchers found that less than half as many people noticed the T-shirts compared to what the students predicted. This study uncovered a bias known as the "spotlight effect," in which we believe people think about us a lot more than they really do.

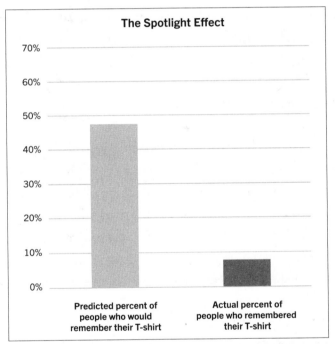

We tend to overestimate the degree to which others will remember what we wear or do.

Earlier in my career, I always felt strange at the thought of introducing myself to someone via email. It seemed like such a disingenuous way to make a new connection, and I figured my awkward introduction email would end up being a shared joke among their friends. But as I learned, my concerns were unfounded. Other people just aren't thinking about me—or you—as much as we think they are.

I've seen a lot of people making communication decisions purely based on how uncomfortable they feel reaching out, especially when it comes to a cold or lukewarm contact. As you can see from the Vanilla Ice experiment, however, these fears are mostly in our own heads. We're not being judged as harshly as we believe. While you may be tempted to bite your nails and stress over how a new acquaintance will judge you for the email you just sent them or what you said during a video call, try not to worry. Beyond other people thinking about you less than you expect, research shows that we tend to believe we come off more negatively than we actually do, and underestimate how positively new acquaintances will react to our message. If your parents ever told you, "It's the thought that counts," they were right. These studies show that message recipients care more about you making the effort to reach out than the actual message content.

Still not convinced? Give it a try: send a warmly worded email (or any other communication medium of your choice) to someone you may not have a preexisting relationship with. Don't worry too much about the message's perceived value. Not every single message will be a success, but remember: others are generally less critical of your messages than you'll be. When in doubt, reach out (sorry, I had to). You might be surprised at the lasting effects of a simple email or phone call.

Words of the Wise

A financial executive told me a harrowing story about the job he'd had—and lost—before deciding to go back to school for his MBA. At the time, he'd just started as a financial analyst and was working on a presentation for his company's most important client. That one client brought in more than $500,000 in revenue each quarter. Keeping them happy was paramount. My student made a few assumptions about how the data should be presented, since he didn't want to bother his new supervisor or the client. After all, he wanted to demonstrate his competence so he'd get put on other high-value accounts.

As it turned out, his assumptions were the opposite of what the client had been looking for—which became abundantly clear during a meeting that included both the client and the analyst's executives. His company ended up losing the account (there were other reasons beyond his presentation, but it was a contributing factor), and he lost his job. His exit interview with his boss stuck with him. His boss asked, "If you weren't sure about something, why didn't you just ask one of us?"

My student had worried that asking for advice would make it seem like he didn't know what he was doing. Paradoxically, it was this concern that led to an actual decrease in his performance and work reputation.

Although my student learned this lesson in an especially harsh way, it's something I think we can all relate to. Sending that first message (or making that first call) is hard. But this fear of reaching out isn't just a disservice to us—it's worse for the person on the receiving end as well. When it comes to a new relationship, one of the most useful conversation starters you can engage in is asking for the other person's advice. The foundation of many new working relationships begins with the other person having access to knowledge, resources, or success that you don't have (and are striving to attain). It may feel like you're being a bother by asking for their advice or perspective, but this intuition is unfounded. It turns out that people generally value being given opportunities to meaningfully help others.

As someone who gets dozens of emails asking for help from a professor (often for topics not even related to my personal expertise) on a weekly basis, I can offer a few research-based strategies for increasing the chances that your query will receive a response. The first strategy is to focus your advice request in a way that makes it clear the advice will meaningfully help you improve—not that you're simply trying to build the connection for your benefit. In a study of 499 supervisor-subordinate pairs in China, Professor Wing Lam's team from The Hong Kong Polytechnic University found that employees who sought advice from their supervisors were viewed more positively when their advice request was perceived as performance-driven rather than for the sake of impression management. If you consider the first element of our framework (perspective taking), this makes sense. After all, would you be more inclined to help someone who is truly looking to improve themselves or someone who just wants to "collect" you as a connection? I'm sure we can all agree on the answer, and it's why you should craft messages in a way that clarifies how the advice will help you improve yourself or your work performance in a meaningful way.

Let's take this strategy a step further. You know the old adage *Give a person a fish and they'll eat for a day, but teach them to fish and they'll eat for a lifetime*? Professor Yihao Liu from the University of Illinois at Urbana-Champaign and his collaborators found that autonomous feedback seekers—people who asked for help with the goal of being able to master a task and any related problems—were seen as more competent and better performers than those who asked for advice with the intention of solving an immediate problem. The autonomous help seekers also received more positive work evaluations because they were viewed as having a higher potential to learn independently, which likely resulted in the advice giver perceiving their advice to be more impactful. As an added benefit, by asking for advice in a way that promotes mastery of a higher-level skill, you'll benefit from a positive feedback loop: you'll be more equipped to handle related problems that arise, which will make you more confident in your own abilities and committed to your organization, which in turn can make your peers and supervisors think more highly of you.

By this point, you should be noticing a trend. The more impactful the potential advice or feedback, the more favorable the advice giver is likely to react. Relatedly, and as a cautionary note, you'll want to make sure not to present yourself as a low-performer who needs help in your request for improvement-oriented advice. Doing so signals that the advice is less likely to be utilized (and thus will be less impactful).

While I know it can feel intimidating to take the initiative and ask experts for their advice, we generally underestimate the positive feelings people associate with helping. Across six experiments with more than two thousand participants, psychologists Xuan Zhao and Nicholas Epley found that participants consistently "underestimated how positive[ly] helpers would feel about helping, and overestimated how inconvenienced and annoyed helpers would feel." Additionally, beyond just making an advice giver feel useful, your request can also act as a sophisticated and more authentic form of flattery, because it shows you respect their expertise. In a study that involved over one thousand top managers, CEOs, and directors, advice-seeking was shown as an effective influence strategy to assist top managers in gaining appointments to board of director positions.

For advice-seeking to strike just the right notes of acting as effective flattery and making the advice giver feel important, your request needs to be personalized to the person you are reaching out to. A Harvard Business School study found that those who were attempting to get the "wisdom of crowds" by asking the same question of multiple experts offended the advice givers and caused them to personally distance themselves from those seeking advice. These kinds of mass requests signal both that you don't particularly care about the people you are reaching out to, and that the degree of positive impact they could have is likely to be limited. Another quick "buyer beware" is that if you ask for advice, you should be prepared to implement it. The same set of Harvard Business School studies also found that when advice seekers didn't follow advice they were given, the advice givers became offended and a large portion of them removed themselves from the relationship.

Building on these research-based strategies, in my own practice I'm more likely to answer requests via virtual communication (and subsequently form relationships with those people) when the sender: 1) clearly put time into the request and personalized it (e.g., has read at least some of my research relevant to their question), 2) has a strong rationale for requesting my specific help (e.g., they couldn't have just found the answer online or asked any management professor), and 3) would meaningfully benefit from my advice (i.e., my response would feel helpful). The idea here is that it's important to put in the effort and be authentic in your advice requests, a topic I'll cover in more detail in Chapter 5.

The other side of the advice-asking coin, of course, is giving it. Similar to the research I just highlighted, studies have found that when you respond to someone asking for your help, the person seeking your advice is likely to react more positively than you would predict. And no, I'm not suggesting you respond to every cold email that finds its way into your inbox. Using the criteria I noted above can help you separate the spam from messages worthy of a response.

The next time you respond to an email in which a new acquaintance (or a colleague you've never directly interacted with) is asking for help, instead of thinking about how much time it will take to reply, take a few minutes to respond and then pat yourself on the back. You're doing more for your relationship with that person (and your career) than you'd even expect. In the immortal words of Robert Van Winkle (aka Vanilla Ice), "Alright stop, collaborate and listen [. . . ice, ice baby . . .]."

You Had Me at Hello

When I was sixteen and undergoing a bone marrow transplant, I spent almost an entire year in isolation. For the first month, I was confined to a hospital room where friends and family could only visit one at a time during specific hours. Even once I was back at home, visitors could only come in our house if they donned gloves and a face covering to make sure I wasn't exposed to anything my weakened immune system wouldn't be able to tolerate.

Needless to say, it was a strange year.

About six months into my year of isolation, when I was just about losing my mind from boredom, I received an email from another student in my town. I remember my mom printed out the email and brought it to the hospital, since I didn't have access to a computer in my room. The email was from a guy named Jeff. He was a year younger than me, and we'd never had a conversation. I barely knew him well enough to match a face with the name.

The email wasn't anything extraordinary—just a few sentences in which Jeff updated me on lunchroom gossip and a tennis tournament he was thinking about entering. The content was so mundane that there was no reason I should have remembered it years later. And yet, the email had a profound impact on me. Not only had Jeff chosen to get in touch, but he'd made me feel less like I was missing out.

After that, Jeff continued to send weekly emails. He even visited me a couple of times. After my treatment and return to normal life, he became one of my closest friends. Almost a decade later, I was a groomsman at his wedding.

When I asked Jeff why he sent that first email, he said he'd thought about not sending anything since we weren't friends at the time, but he figured it couldn't hurt and I'd want to know what was happening at school. To him, it was a small effort barely worthy of recognition. Yet it was the impetus for one of the most meaningful friendships in my life.

I share this story for two reasons. First, because I know how easy it can be to talk yourself out of reaching out to someone you barely know, especially in a virtual context. It just feels weird to send someone an unexpected email or text out of the blue, whereas if it were in person, informally asking how things are going would feel like no big deal. Second, when we're not interacting in person, there is a tendency for your awareness of others (and vice versa) to fade. Out of sight, out of mind, in a sense. Thus it can often feel easier not to reach out at all. But there's a good chance you're underestimating how much taking that small step will be appreciated—and how far it can go toward establishing a relationship that withstands the test of time.

As part of a research study, University of Chicago students were asked to send an email to someone on campus they knew of but hadn't previously contacted, and who they believed might be facing a difficult time and thus could use some additional support. After writing the email, these students filled out a survey in which they rated how awkward they believed the recipient would feel, and how sincerely their message would be perceived to be.

By this point in the chapter, you should be able to predict what happened.

After writing and sending the message, these student participants said they felt better than normal. They also (surprise, surprise) underestimated how positively their message receiver would feel upon reading their email. The students who reached out to someone they had a more distant relationship with also believed their email would be received less well than if they'd had a closer relationship with the person. In fact, this effect was only in the email writers' heads. The email recipients didn't judge the message any less positively when it came from a distant relationship than from a close one.

Lending support from a distance via virtual communication often feels too cringy to be worth the bother. But it's a necessary first step to having a profound impact on both you and the message receiver. By leveraging virtual communication to connect with someone they might never have interacted with, these students not only were able to improve someone's day, but they opened a doorway to a new relationship.

If you need further proof, put yourself on the other side of this equation. If you were going through a difficult time, would you feel any less positive about receiving a supportive email from a distant acquaintance compared to a close colleague or family member? I'm guessing you would say the same as me: that it's the effort that matters rather than how close you previously felt to the person. If anything, getting support from someone you don't expect can violate expectations in a positive way, and end up being more surprising and impactful as a result.

Whether you're using virtual communication to begin a conversation asking for advice, offering support, or another reason, once you've taken the initiative to do the actual reaching out, there arises a question about mode—namely, which to choose. Email is undoubtedly easiest in terms of degree of effort, but as you've already learned, the easiest approach isn't always the right choice. When trying to start a new relationship off on the right foot, is it worth trading out the convenience of email for a more potentially awkward phone or video call?

Tiny Frames, Strong Connections

We're all intimately familiar with the experience of sitting through a cameras-off video call where we're staring at a tiny thumbnail image of our conversation partner(s) that may or may not have been taken ten years prior (no judgment, just an observation). There are plenty of arguments to be made for why cameras-on interactions are less than ideal. As I discussed in the last chapter, you can end up looking a little cross-eyed if you're trying to keep eye contact with your webcam when the other person's face is in a completely different part of your screen. You also need to consider whether your attire is appropriate, or if there's something in the background of your screen that might be off-putting to whomever you're talking to. With all of this additional time and effort, it would ostensibly make sense to skip the cameras altogether and just have a phone call. Or better yet, send an email.

There are certainly situations when phone and/or email is the right choice. But for the purposes of digital relationship-building, there are some real benefits to having short one-on-one video interactions with cameras on. To get to the bottom of the communication mode question,

I partnered with a digital collaboration analytics company named Vyopta to analyze 48 million remote meetings from ten large global organizations from 2020 through 2022. This was during a time when many executives and news outlets argued that workers were becoming less and less connected with each other due to remote work and burnout.

Despite this perspective, we found the opposite was true: virtual meetings increased by 60 percent from the start of the COVID-19 pandemic lockdowns in 2020 through 2022. In other words, the more time that passed since the beginning of COVID, the more (rather than fewer) people connected with their colleagues via video tools. Notably, as time went on, the types of meetings evolved to have fewer participants on average and last for less time, decreasing in length by 25 percent. These findings indicated that people were increasingly using short video check-ins as a means of staying engaged with each other.

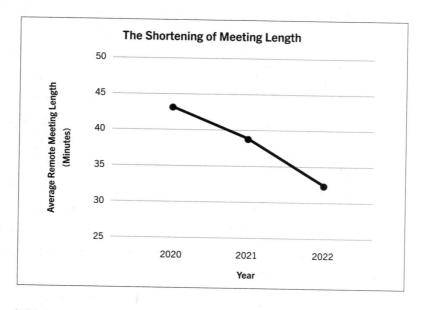

Additionally, meetings became more spontaneous over time, with the number of unscheduled ("meet now") one-on-one meetings increasing over time compared to calendar-invite meetings.

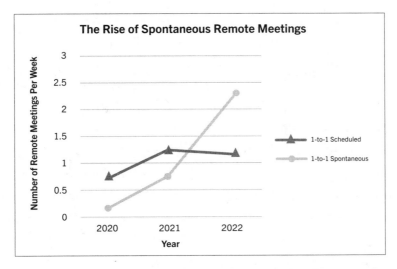

As workers settled into virtual interactions following the COVID-19 pandemic, the proportion of spontaneous (unscheduled) remote meetings increased.

While many have argued that virtual interactions and remote work have led to decreased human connections and loss of spontaneous connections, my research actually found the opposite: workers seemed to be engaging *more* with their colleagues via video meetings as they got more experience with video communication platforms. A study published by Stanford professors in 2023 highlighted the relational value of these short video meetings. Through examining nearly four thousand people engaging in video meetings, they found that shorter video meetings with fewer participants were more effective for increasing how connected people felt to one another. The reason is that longer video meetings that involved more people resulted in participants feeling greater exhaustion, or "Zoom fatigue" (more broadly referred to as videoconferencing fatigue), which limited their ability to engage with each other. In this case, the goal of being more productive (i.e., having shorter meetings) is well aligned with improving relationships.

These types of meetings can act as a requisite foundation for new relationships to build on, as people generally don't feel connected to someone unless they feel familiar with their appearance and mannerisms. For this reason, the visual aspect of video meetings is useful for feeling like we "know" the other person.

Many people incorrectly assume that if you're not colocated with your colleagues, it doesn't matter if you can see their face or not. I've fallen prey to this misconception myself, with one of the most memorable examples involving my interactions with the chief people officer of an organization I was conducting research with. For months while the study was being set up, we solely communicated via email. The CPO was just a faceless name. Then, in our first video meeting prior to the study launch, we saw each other for the first time. To our collective surprise and delight, we realized we were both sporting the exact same hairstyle (well, in our case, it involved having no hair whatsoever, but that's beside the point). Suddenly, we had something to bond over that felt familiar. That mutual discovery led to more small talk and other similarities we might otherwise never have unearthed. From that point forward, it began to feel like we were building a true relationship.

When it comes to video meetings, timing matters. The earlier you have these kinds of richer meetings in a relationship, the stronger your foundations will be. Don't underestimate the importance of establishing trust early on, as first impressions play an essential role in guiding your relational trajectory.

Ears Wide-Open

Up to this point in the chapter, we've looked at using virtual communication to forge connections early in your relationship. But perhaps there's a former colleague you haven't been in touch with for a while, and you think reconnecting with them could be beneficial. Rebuilding that relationship could be a great way to put these strategies into practice.

For these connections, it would be just too bizarre to send them a video meeting request out of the blue. On the other hand, email feels a little impersonal. There are costs and benefits to deciding which communication mode you should choose to minimize hassle and discomfort, and maximize your connection to the other person. The third category of options is using audio modes, like a phone call. But is this a good choice?

Another professor in my business school, Amit Kumar, asked this exact question. He directed study participants to reconnect with old acquaintances using email, video, or phone.

It turns out the interactions involving audio (e.g., telephone, video chat, or voice chat) were far more effective for rekindling old connections than text-based methods (e.g., email and text chat). For those who fear that a phone call will be too uncomfortable, audio ended up not being rated as any more awkward after the fact (even though participants had predicted it would be more awkward than text).

Thus far in the chapter, I've focused on the added benefits of leveraging video in the context of new professional relationships. But Kumar's team found that video offered no benefits beyond audio interactions between people who'd had a prior relationship that had fallen by the wayside. In other words, the visual component of video didn't matter. Instead it was the sound of the person's voice that caused strong feelings of connectedness. In situations where you have a relationship history with someone, you already know what they look like and can picture their nonverbal mannerisms. In these instances, there is less value added to using video in addition to audio (especially when you consider the extra hassle of getting "camera-ready"). The synchronicity, or having a real-time conversation, is more important than the mode richness.

Sometimes you just need to hear a person's voice.

While it might be tempting to let some of your old contacts stay buried, there is value in rekindling them. Daniel Levin from Rutgers

University and his research collaborators found that when MBA students reached out to dormant contacts for help on a work project, they produced final products that were more novel. Why is this the case? Levin's team theorized that these dormant connections had acquired new information and experiences since the participants last communicated with them. Whereas our current colleagues might offer familiar ideas, renewed connections can provide fresh perspectives due to their diverse experiences. And, counter to what you might expect, the study participants didn't experience any negative relationship costs from reaching out after such a long period of silence. In a sense, the participants were able to pick back up where they left off. These findings contradict the oft-stated advice that it's necessary to regularly communicate with any social connections we hope to engage with in the future.

Just one caveat: be mindful of the other person's schedule and degree of busyness so you don't catch them at a bad time. Ideally, it is best to schedule these conversations in advance to avoid calling at a time when the other person might be busy. For instance, you could send a quick text or email saying, "It feels like it's been forever since we connected, and I'd love to catch up if you aren't too busy. Is there a time that would be good for you for a short call to reconnect?"

You don't want to try rekindling a stale professional relationship while the other person is in a meeting with their divorce lawyer, for instance. (This definitely *never* happened to me. Okay, one time. And yeah, it was weird . . . and did not result in a renewed friendship.)

Paving the Digital Road to Friendship

The concern with establishing nascent relationships virtually is that the person on the receiving end of your message isn't receptive. Even if this worst-case scenario happens (which research tells us isn't as likely as we think it is), then you wasted ten minutes of your time, and they'll likely forget about you even more quickly. After all, do you remember all the people you barely know who have reached out to you with a mediocre message? I bet not. On the other hand, if your message is well received, then it opens the gateway to a new relationship. You'll thus expand your network, help yourself professionally, and possibly even pave the way to a new friendship at work. Not a bad risk-reward analysis.

Virtual communication provides us with the necessary tools to forge connections with people whose paths we might never have crossed otherwise. By taking the initiative to reach out, and choosing the right mode to fit your goals, you'll broaden your network and invite unexpected opportunities.

KEY LESSONS
Perspective Taking

✦ Research shows that people overestimate how much others think about them (i.e., "spotlight effect") and how awkward it will be to reach out to cold contacts or contacts that have fallen out of touch. But consider how, from their perspective, your message might come as a welcome surprise. Take the plunge and reach out, because it really is the thought that counts.

✦ When others reach out to you to seek your advice or help, consider how the relatively small time cost of responding to their inquiry will have a much bigger impact on the requestor than you even realize.

✦ When reaching out to ask for advice, think about what requests you would be more likely to respond to. Craft your messages in a way that will make the person you're seeking advice from feel useful rather than just a tool to expand your network.

Initiative

✦ When trying to virtually start a relationship by seeking advice, be sure to make an effort to personalize your message (i.e., make it clear why you're seeking their expertise in particular), rather than mass-emailing and seeking the "wisdom of crowds" by sending the same message to multiple people. And if you seek someone's advice and they take the time to share their insights, make sure to follow through and implement their suggestions. This will prevent potential offense and safeguard the relationship you're trying to cultivate.

✦ Taking the initiative to reach out to old contacts you've fallen out of touch with can give you new insights that you wouldn't gain from colleagues you regularly communicate with.

✦ Lost touch with someone from your life? Give them a call. They'll appreciate it. Just make sure to schedule in advance to avoid interrupting them or catching them at an inopportune time.

Nonverbal

✦ When you're reaching out to a completely cold contact, choose richer communication modes (e.g., video) to help the other party feel more familiar with you.

✦ If you're reaching out to weak connections you already know but want to strengthen, audio can be just as good as video. These individuals already know what you look and act like, so it's the mode synchronicity that's more important than the richness for building strong bonds.

✦ Short one-on-one video calls work better than longer or group video calls for building and strengthening new relationships, as the latter cause more fatigue, which gets in the way of engagement.

Goals

+ If your goal is to connect virtually, make sure you put in time and effort (e.g., write a well-researched and personalized message), as cold communication is easier to ignore virtually.

+ If your goal is to build the foundation of a strong relationship, choosing a richer—yet less productive—interaction tool may make the difference between creating a lasting impression and the other person completely forgetting about you.

5

Removing the Virtual Mask

How to Present Your Most Authentic and Likable Self

He spake, and into every heart his words
Carried new strength and courage.
—HOMER, THE ILIAD

In 2020, the real estate market was booming. Better.com, one of the major online mortgage companies, saw their profits soar as everyone snapped up houses like they were going out of style. In 2020 alone, the company garnered over $24 billion in mortgage originations. Better even went so far as to call it "the year of the home," and highlighted how they were looking forward to more growth in the years to come.

But what goes up must come down. By 2021, Better saw their revenue plummet—a harsh blow, especially after the banner year they'd just had. As consumers were reading about how mortgage companies were assuming the boom would last forever and hadn't made sufficient contingency plans, Better read the writing on the wall. They decided to start taking steps for when the market inevitably cooled even further.

On a December day in 2021, nine hundred employees of Better.com joined a video call with the CEO of their company.

If you don't already know what happened, I'm sure you can guess where this story is headed.

Put yourself in the shoes of one of Better's employees. For you, it should be a normal workday. Except you were invited to attend a video meeting because the CEO of your company has news to share. The meeting subject line was vague, so it could be either good or bad news. You're concerned.

You brew your morning beverage of choice, settle yourself in front of your computer, and join the meeting. At exactly the hour mark, the CEO of your company appears on your screen. His expression is grave, and your worry from earlier grows into an unpleasant knot in your stomach.

"I come to you with not-great news," the CEO announces without preamble.

Your hands start to get clammy.

"This isn't news that you're gonna want to hear."

Your heart rate picks up because you know . . . you just know. . . .

"Ultimately, it was my decision, and I wanted you to hear it from me," your CEO continues. "I do not, do not want to do this. The last time I did it I *cried*. This time I hope to be stronger."

Really?! you shout internally. *I'm probably about to get fired and you're crying about how hard it is for* you?

"If you're on this call, you are part of the unlucky group that is being laid off. Your employment here is terminated effective immediately."

And the rest of the speech feels like a blur, because you just lost your job.

You need to figure out how to tell your spouse and children that you won't be going on that family vacation to Walt Disney World you'd all been looking forward to. Instead you need to look for a new job, figure out how to pay your mortgage, and all the rest. Because you're unemployed.

As you can imagine, this video meeting didn't result in a smooth outcome. A recording of the video call layoff ended up being one of the most viral business videos of 2021, and not for positive reasons. Former employees noted the CEO's "lack of humanity," and that his delivery was "very callous" and "excruciating." Another former employee said, "We're all left gutted, and like just heartbroken before the holidays." Yet another said the layoffs were a "kick in the gut," before asking, "Is this capitalism at its worst?"

You get the idea.

Overall, this all seems like a really bad look for Better's CEO, right?

Given we are all armchair CEOs, let's take a step back before passing judgment. This CEO made the decision to communicate difficult news directly to employees, rather than delegating it to someone else. He was clearly very torn up about the decision and didn't take it lightly. The easy route would have been to communicate the layoffs in a scripted email like his fellow executives at Meta, Tesla, and others. Instead, he chose the richest mode of communication to speak as directly with employees as possible.

Given the situation, and all things considered, Better's CEO was a whole lot more caring in this process than the vast majority of executives. Many of us would be lucky to work for someone who felt so terribly about layoffs that they'd go off script and admit to crying in front of nearly one thousand employees.

But instead of being praised, Better's CEO was lambasted.

What went wrong?

Because Better's CEO chose to announce the layoffs via a video call, it left him open to a slew of criticisms that would have been modulated if he'd used a less rich medium. With video, his delivery was less scripted and more off-the-cuff, which isn't ideal for such a high-stakes conversation. Additionally, using video resulted in more distractions and details for him to monitor, which meant he was less attentive to every one of his nonverbal cues, like his tone of voice, facial expression, and even his posture. That left more room for other people to interpret (and criticize) his body language. Perhaps even worse, the logistics of a video layoff made it easier to circulate, watch, and ultimately go viral for all the wrong reasons.

Here's the other problem. However well-meaning a person might be, sometimes you just can't be authentic enough. Short of the captain going down with the ship (which, in this case, would have probably required Better's CEO to quit and donate his entire net worth to the laid-off employees—something that, to my knowledge, no CEO or manager has ever done), it's not possible to demonstrate enough authenticity to remedy the situation.

Further, in speaking from the heart, Better's CEO discussed how difficult a decision this was for *him*. He even went so far as to note that he cried during the last round of layoffs and hoped to be stronger this time. This was a strange admission of vulnerability—usually a quality I admire and try to practice. But here, this type of vulnerability backfired because it was focused on his own difficulties, while the act itself involved laying off others. It's hard to be sympathetic for the boss when he's the one responsible for taking away the livelihood of his employees. This self-focus is even more difficult to escape when using virtual communication, especially when our own emotions are strong. We don't have another person standing directly in front of us, and thus there's nothing to draw our attention away from our own thoughts and feelings.

If Better's CEO had put himself in the mindset of employees being laid off and taken their perspective—rather than focusing on his own emotions—he might have crafted his message in a way that felt more authentic.

Whether or not laying off employees is something you'll ever have to face, this story and all the lessons that come with it are directly relevant to experiences we all have on a daily basis. The same emotional dynamics (and subsequent fallout) play out similarly even in mundane interactions. There are a lot of times throughout the day when it's not appropriate to display the exact emotions we're feeling, especially in the context of our jobs.

Say you're about to pitch a new marketing campaign to your boss, but mustering the enthusiasm needed to get her approval is nearly impossible because you got in a fender bender that morning. Or maybe you need to deny a customer a loan. It's a bummer, to be sure, but you're flying high because you're going on vacation the next day. You're probably going to want to hide those positive emotions when speaking with your customer, unless you want to upset them more than they already are.

The bottom line is that if you want others to view you in a positive light, being perceived as authentic and likable is vital. And being able to do so from behind a computer screen is not a straightforward task.

Be You . . . Just a More Authentic Version of You

Last chapter, we explored the best ways to initiate new relationships virtually. Here, we're going to look at the relational side of self-presentation in virtual interactions. If you're going to have the maximum impact and ensure your messages come off as intended, then you need to show authenticity—in other words, be perceived as acting in line with your own feelings and values. When customers, coworkers, leaders, or subordinates perceive you as being inauthentic, research shows that they tend to like you far less and be less satisfied with your job performance.

Coming off as authentic is especially important in the virtual communication world. Because you already feel disconnected from the person you're speaking with, it's not easy to get a strong sense of their underlying motives and personality.

How many times have you gotten an email or text with *Haha* or a smiley face, and thought to yourself that maybe those weren't genuine representations of the other person's emotional state? I mean, how often are we really laughing out loud when we type *lol*?

This is the type of challenge we're all up against in the virtual world. When we're not in the same physical space as the person (or people) we're talking to, we make assumptions about how truly authentic they're being. To complicate matters further, your communication partners are making the same assessments about you.

The question, then, is how to use virtual communication in a way that demonstrates your authenticity and humanity. And that's what we're going to be looking at throughout this chapter.

Earlier, I explained why video was the wrong choice for Better's CEO. The obvious question that follows is, What's the *right* communication mode to use in these sorts of situations?

After seeing how Better's CEO was crucified, many of you might be thinking that email would be a safer choice. And you wouldn't be alone. It's certainly easier—and less awkward—than video for the person conducting the layoffs. But email has its own downsides. On the whole, it can come off feeling inauthentic. Do you really want to be fired (or given life-altering news of any kind) over email? It just seems uncaring, especially when the same form email was sent to thousands of others.*

In the words of the general and diplomat Colin Powell, "It is the human gesture that counts. Yes, medals, stock options, promotions, bonuses, and pay raises are fine. But to really reach people, you need

---

* *Some of you may be wondering why it matters how a CEO conducts layoffs in the first place, since these employees no longer work for the company. Aside from the obvious being a good human argument, there are other, less sentimental reasons for conducting layoffs with consideration. First, your ex-employees will become emissaries of your company, and their experiences will play a role in shaping your company's reputation. Second, the way you conduct layoffs isn't just sending a message to the people who lost their job. You're also communicating with the surviving employees. If the surviving employees witnessed their colleagues being treated unfairly or without compassion during the layoff process, then they'll expect the same for themselves (and your top performers will quickly find employment elsewhere). Beyond layoffs, these same dynamics hold true for the vast majority of interactions and relationships. Leaving good impressions not only benefits you in a specific moment, but it can also result in people, some of whom you may not even know directly, hearing about you. You never know when you'll be reaching out to someone for advice, new customers, or a job and discover they already know of your reputation.*

to touch them. A kind word, a pat on the back, a 'well done,' provided one-on-one and not by mob email."

As I'll show, it's possible to get that human connection virtually. You just have to craft your message by considering the recipient's perspective and ensuring the emotions you're attempting to convey are, in fact, the ones coming through.

Virtual Savior or Saboteur?

In her memoir, *Lean In*, former Meta COO Sheryl Sandberg emphasized that "leaders should strive for authenticity over perfection." *Authenticity* is one of those words that are universally understood to be good things. That being said, some days it's easier to be authentic than others, especially when we're all expected to bring our A-games to work. From needing to provide "service with a smile," to being expected to congratulate coworkers for an accomplishment, there are countless times throughout your career when you'll need to express emotions you might not be authentically feeling.

Contrary to what you may read elsewhere, that's okay.

If you broke a treasured keepsake while rushing around to get ready, or had a fight with your significant other, you shouldn't be expected to be completely excited about every interaction you're having that day. And it isn't unreasonable for you to want to hide your unrelated lingering frustration from earlier in the day in order to avoid offending your boss or coworkers. Not wanting all of your emotions to "leak" into your work interactions is entirely reasonable, and in many cases also better for the person you're interacting with (e.g., should your response to your friend who just got their dream job really be, "I wish I could be fully happy for you, but I got a flat tire this morning")? Thus, the need for inauthenticity. The problematic result is a phenomenon called emotional or nonverbal "leakage," of which there are two types.

The first is *spontaneous leakage*, which encompasses inadvertent reactions that occur when we display something without making a conscious decision to do so (like the raising of an eyebrow or a grimace). The second is *overload leakage*, which occurs when we are so focused on managing multiple factors simultaneously (e.g., body language, facial expressions, tone of voice, and wording) that something accidentally "leaks" through that we didn't intend. For instance, we might make a statement we didn't mean, simply because we are focusing on too much else to carefully attend to our word choice in that single moment. The risk of leakage is much smaller with email, because the only factor we need to monitor is the text itself (no one is looking at our face as we're writing the email), and the message can easily be rewritten before being shared with its intended recipient.

Beyond whether you leak emotion, people also interpret your choice of communication mode (e.g., did they send me an email or call me) as a signal of your authenticity. Google CEO Sundar Pichai used email as his mode of choice when he laid off twelve thousand Googlers. His message was crafted in a way that expressed his deep regret at losing talent and acknowledged he was aware of how the layoffs would impact his ex-employees' lives. It even included a section that described, in detail, how Google would support the laid-off workers while they searched for a new job. Yet the mode choice prevented Pichai from infusing real emotion into the message. To many recipients, it likely just felt cold.

Worse, shortly after the email was sent out and twelve thousand Googlers found themselves out of a job, news broke that Pichai's compensation for the year was $226 million. This bad timing, on top of the email's dubious initial reception, spelled a public relations nightmare for him.

The situation led to a host of memes, such as likening Pichai to Lord Farquaad from *Shrek*, alongside the fictitious villain's infamous words: "Some of you may die, but that is a sacrifice I am willing to make."

The CEO and founder of Zoom, Eric Yuan, showed initiative in avoiding this particular failure in authenticity. When laying off employees, his email said:

> As the CEO and founder of Zoom, I am accountable for these mistakes and the actions we take today—and I want to show accountability not just in words but in my own actions. To that end, I am reducing my salary for the coming fiscal year by 98% and foregoing my FY23 corporate bonus. Members of my executive leadership team will reduce their base salaries by 20% for the coming fiscal year while also forfeiting their FY23 corporate bonuses.

This shows perspective taking and initiative, the first two elements of the PING framework. The problem? It fails to feel personal. The email also included these words:

> If you are a US-based employee who is impacted, you will receive an email to your Zoom and personal inboxes in the next 30 minutes that reads [IMPACTED] Departing Zoom: What You Need to Know. Non-US employees will be notified following local requirements. For those Zoomies waking up to this news or reading this after normal work hours, I am sorry you are finding out this way. . . .

Can you imagine how it would feel after having loyally worked at a company for years to get only a template email notification that you were laid off?

The other, and perhaps more glaring, issue for Yuan was the fact that he unironically used email to lay off employees who worked for Zoom, a company whose core product is video communication.

These are not isolated events. Meta, Wayfair, Twitter, and others have conducted layoffs over email, with varying degrees of success. And it's not like in-person layoffs are necessarily a panacea either, as many organizations are now remote and hybrid (i.e., people don't even have a traditional office to come into), and bringing ten thousand employees into a room together to be laid off sounds like a recipe for disaster.

When it comes to expressing sentiments we might not be feeling, we're left with a virtual communication paradox. On the one hand, we have less rich modes, like email. These modes are perceived to be an inauthentic means of communication, yet they are the best at masking inauthenticity. Richer modes (like video) are more authentic but often expose nonverbal behaviors we had no intention of showcasing and which leave us open to criticism.

In the course of my own research, I was curious to discern if there was a way to use virtual communication to positively address the inevitable mismatch in underlying emotions and authenticity. First, I wanted to identify which mode is best (and worst) when our attitudes are truly authentic—and thus no contextually irrelevant emotions are sneaking into the conversation—yet there is some concern that your emotions might be interpreted as inauthentic. Such instances could include when we are purely excited for a coworker's success or genuinely disheartened about a customer's bad situation.

To test this idea, I recruited over four hundred managers for a study to gauge how they would react to a specific scenario. Their task would be to evaluate a message from a coworker who was congratulating them on a promotion. The awkward part: the person congratulating them had worked for the company four times longer, really wanted the promotion, and would now be the participant's subordinate.

The purpose of this scenario was to make participants a little suspicious that the emotions being expressed by their coworker (their future subordinate) might not be 100 percent authentic. For this first study, I was *only* examining how the communication mode altered the managers' perceptions of the sender's authenticity, so I kept the message identical across all conditions. The only difference was that participants were told that the message was communicated either via email, phone, or in person.

The message was simple:

> I just heard the news about your promotion; I am very happy to hear you will be our manager. You really earned it. I am looking forward to seeing the direction you take our team.

Here's what I discovered. Despite the message being identical, the mode in which it was relayed mattered. In-person was seen as the most authentic, followed by telephone, with email ranking as the least authentic. Why? Because email—due to it being less rich and easier to fake emotions with—was perceived as the least effortful method of communication. Thus, if you're not worried about emotional leakage, choose the richest mode possible (e.g., video or in person) to appear most authentic and avoid being seen as picking the low-effort option.

Your Child Is Special. He's Also Failing.

It's just reality that sometimes our underlying feelings don't match the situation we've found ourselves in. What should you do in the times when there's a mismatch between how you're feeling and the message you need to express? In other words, you have to worry that unintentional nonverbal cues may leak through. Maybe you are concerned that you may unknowingly smile or grimace at the wrong time, or your voice may crack or pause, signaling more than you intend.

That's what I set out to answer in a follow-up study.

The study I previously discussed was useful for identifying how inauthentic emotions are perceived across the various communication modes in a vacuum. However, I was interested to see how these effects would play out in an actual workplace context, along with all the messiness that can't be controlled for outside the lab. So, that's what I did. Specifically, I aimed to study what researchers refer to as "surface acting," or displaying emotions to fit a work context, when your true underlying emotions don't exactly match what you are displaying.

To tackle this question, I conducted a study of teachers in eleven international private schools in Vietnam. To get a sense of their workday experiences, picture the following. You're a teacher in one of these international schools, which is attended by both local students and expatriates from English-speaking countries. Also of note: the families pay *a lot* for their children to attend your school. As a teacher there, one of your objectives is to nurture good relationships between the school and your students' parents. You're expected to respond to communication from parents promptly, as well as reach out whenever something noteworthy happens regarding their child. If a child did well on a test or lends a helping hand, you're expected to let the parents know.

The rub, as you might have already surmised, is that it's much easier to foster easy relationships when you're sharing good news. And when it comes to a roomful of thirty or so children, some less-than-flattering moments are bound to crop up. A student forgot his homework? Got into a fight? Failed your class? All those unpleasant headlines need to be communicated to parents. And you need to do it in a way that is warm and optimistic.

I specifically chose teachers as the subjects for this study because, like many of us, teachers are expected to show primarily positive emotions at work. This is especially true when they need to inform a student's parents about how abysmally their "angel" has performed in class. This need to surface act (e.g., provide "service with a smile") can be quite difficult and, if done frequently, leads to stress and burnout. As one teacher I interviewed pointed out, "If I'm not perky every time I talk with a parent, they immediately assume it's because I don't like them—or worse—their [child]. It's exhausting, but necessary unless I want to get labeled as the *mean* teacher."

Let's say you need to display this kind of positive affect, but you aren't feeling the "right" emotions. Which communication medium should you choose?

To answer this question, I surveyed both teachers and parents at this set of schools. Teachers were asked to share how much surface acting they engaged in when interacting with parents. They quantified how well their feelings were reflected in statements like "I just pretend to have the emotions I need to display to students' parents" and "I put on a 'mask' in order to display the emotions my supervisor wants me to display." In other words, how much they were needing to "fake it" in their communication with parents.

On the parent side of the survey, I asked questions about their experiences with one of their child's teachers (whom I randomly selected to evaluate to avoid biases skewing the results). Parents were asked questions that allowed me to see how much they believed their child's teacher was surface acting, or being inauthentic, in their communications.

There were several interesting findings from this study. First, there wasn't a significant relationship between teachers' ratings of their own surface acting and parents' corresponding ratings of those teachers. Sometimes parents guessed correctly, but other times they were completely wrong. Their accuracy depended on a single important detail: the mode of communication.

I found that teachers who engaged in higher levels of surface acting also tended to be more likely to use email relative to other modes. This is not wholly surprising, as email is the least effortful and seemingly best option to hide your true emotions. However, the second finding was that parents perceived teachers to be the most inauthentic when they communicated via email, regardless of whether that teacher was truly authentic or not. Just like in the previous study, email communication tends to come off poorly insofar as demonstrating authenticity in emotional contexts.

Face-to-face interactions worked great for truly authentic teachers but backfired for those who needed to engage in surface acting. It's tough to be a teacher having a difficult conversation with a parent, while trying to stay positive, despite knowing the student will likely never pass the class. The parent is asking tricky questions about what they could be doing better to help their child, with the teacher needing to come up with answers on the spot. On top of that, the teacher needs to make sure nothing in their body language, facial cues, or tone of voice gives away how hopeless they feel the student's chances are. It's easy to see why, during these kinds of conversations, it can be next to impossible for surface actors to prevent unintended cues from leaking through.

Okay, so if a teacher needs to engage in surface acting to do their job, and knowing that email is bad and in-person/video is bad, then what's left? What I discovered is that using audio (like phone or video calls with cameras off) can actually be a "sweet spot." Audio interactions have a couple of benefits. First, they avoid the huge penalty of seeming uncaring, which can occur when you choose to communicate via email. Further, audio interactions only necessitate monitoring your voice as opposed to face-to-face interactions, which require the surface actor to be cautious of even slight nonverbal cues from their facial expressions. For the teachers in my study, audio turned out to be the optimal choice for surface acting because it can hide cues of inauthenticity far better than face-to-face and video interactions, yet it still seems like a reasonably high-effort approach to communication, especially when compared to email.

Beyond my own research, other work and communication research have shown the benefits of audio. In a study of job interviews, a team led by Berkeley professor Juliana Schroeder discovered that recruiters evaluated job candidates as more "competent, thoughtful, and intelligent" when they could hear their voice, as opposed to reading their candidacy proposal. Interestingly, there was no added benefit to candidates using video (including cameras) compared to audio. The reason why? Through a different study, researchers determined that vocal cues are enough of a signal for others to feel confident judging mental abilities.

Before I go any further, let me address the virtual elephant in the room . . . since I can hear shouts from the ether, "But in Chapter 3 you said webcams-on makes you seem more present!"

If you were one of those virtual voices, then you're absolutely right. In Chapter 3, we were considering the best option to demonstrate engagement and productivity. If your goal is to seem present, video is generally going to be your best choice. But when it comes to authenticity, your goal might be less straightforward. In terms of managing your expressions, and potentially leaking your underlying emotions, there's a risk to using video.

Beneath the Surface (Acting)

Returning to the case of Better's CEO, the choice of video made his degree of self-focus on his own emotions abundantly clear. If his priority was to appear caring and authentic, it likely would have gone more favorably if he'd instead opted for a company-wide telephone/audio call. The call would have seemed nearly as personal as if it were done via video. It also would likely have saved the CEO from leaking unintended information—such as facial expressions that didn't match his words—since his face wouldn't be visible and he'd be able to focus more on his words rather than his body language. As an added benefit, audio calls are less likely to go viral, as the richness of video is part of what makes it so interesting for outsiders to watch. Would you really listen to a ten-plus-minute conference call if it had nothing to do with you? Possible, but unlikely.

Not only is audio often better for improving the apparent authenticity of a person relaying negative news, but it also can be beneficial for the person on the receiving end of that news. After all, if you just learned that you lost your job, do you really want to have to worry about your facial expressions? A flurry of tech layoffs in early 2024 brought this question into focus. In a story that went viral, it was claimed that a former employee from Amazon was required to turn his camera on during the call that ended his job. Even though he requested that the conversation be had via audio-only (as he knew what was coming), his manager still required that he turn on his camera. As his girlfriend noted in the viral video, "Since we work from home part-time, are we not allowed to be humiliated just on the floor of our closet?" Getting bad news is hard enough; having to worry about making sure your boss doesn't see you cry (or display angry facial expressions) makes everything worse.

It's unlikely that the manager described in this video intended to be cruel—maybe they thought it would be more authentic to have the conversation face-to-face. The problem was that they didn't take their soon-to-be-ex-employee's perspective. When communicating unpleasant news, it's especially important to ask yourself, *If I were on the receiving end of this communication, would I want the other person to see my face?*

To take it a step further, an even *better* (see what I did there?) approach to the layoffs would begin with a CEO leveraging one-on-one audio meetings to tell a subset of people about their layoffs (as meeting one-on-one with all nine hundred employees wouldn't have been feasible). Meanwhile, the CEO might direct managers to similarly handle the remainder in one-to-one meetings, so each employee would have a chance to ask questions and feel heard.

After these one-on-ones, the CEO could have had a group audio meeting with all those laid off, where he indicated his appreciation for the work those employees did to help the company, and what he and the company would be doing to help them with their transition going forward (making introductions at other companies, extending health care, etc.). At this point, it would be especially important for the CEO to perspective-take and consider how their message may come off to employees being laid off, as the framing can mean the difference between supporting and incensing those who have lost their jobs.

Let's say audio or video isn't an option for some reason and you do need to send an email or text in a situation where authenticity is a concern. How do you avoid the mode undermining your goals? Simple: by explaining that the mode was not your choice, or that you made the choice for an authentic reason. The reason why you're penalized for choosing text is that others perceive that you made a low-effort choice. If you didn't have the option to use other modes, then you can't be blamed for your choice. For instance, if you are emailing someone a sensitive message, you could say something along the lines of "I'm emailing because I wanted to reach out to you as soon as I heard, and didn't want to interrupt with a call. That said, whenever you want to talk, I'm here."

Zappos's CEO, Tony Hsieh, effectively used this strategy when he chose email to announce that Zappos was acquired by Amazon—a move Hsieh knew many employees might not be happy about. He started the email with the following:

> Please set aside 20 minutes to carefully read this entire email.

On its own, that seems cold, right? However, the text that immediately follows is:

> (My apologies for the occasional use of formal-sounding language, as parts of it are written in a particular way for legal reasons.)

And, later in the email, Hsieh wrote,

> We will be holding an all hands meeting soon to go over all of this in more detail. Please email me any questions that you may have so that we can cover as many as possible during the all hands meeting and/or a follow-up email.

By adding in the initial disclaimer that explained why he was using a scripted means of text-based communication (he was required to for legal reasons), and then clarifying that there would be an all-hands call where employees' questions would be addressed (i.e., a richer, synchronous interaction), Hsieh prevented his email from seeming cold and unfeeling.

When it comes to your day-to-day conversations, which virtual communication mode to use might seem like an inconsequential decision that doesn't really matter. But there is a buildup effect over time that, if not properly managed, will harm your relationships. Loss of trust, decreased customer satisfaction, and suboptimal negotiation outcomes are only a few of the ways that mismanaging your inauthentic emotional displays will harm you personally.

Up to this point, I've predominantly discussed strategies for choosing the right communication mode to be seen as most authentic and likable. But what about the messages themselves? At first glance, it might seem like you should ensure they're completely perfect and error-free. But, as you'll see, being perfect isn't always best.

I Am Not a Cat

You may or may not have seen the infamous "I am not a cat" video that went viral on both social media and national news in 2021. Allow me to set the scene.

Imagine a judge and two lawyers on a videoconference court hearing. It's all very formal, except for one detail:

One of the lawyers' faces has been replaced with a sad-kitten filter.

The judge, in a serious voice devoid of blame, says, "Mr. Ponton, I believe you have a filter turned on in the video settings."

At that point, the sad kitten appears downright morose as the lawyer-presenting-as-a-cat informs the group, "I don't know how to remove it. I'm here, live, I'm not a cat."

The judge's bemused expression says it all. Lawyers are usually stereotyped as boring and argumentative to the point of unlikability, and yet this video evokes feelings of warmth and amusement.

This isn't an isolated incident. There was also that time when Congressman Tom Emmer accidentally flipped the image of himself on-screen while speaking during a House Financial Services Committee meeting via video. Amid the titters of his colleagues, the meeting chairwoman paused the (otherwise unremarkable) conversation and said, "I'm sorry . . . Mr. Emmer? Are you okay?"

Someone else added, "You're upside-down, Tom."

Emmer's response? "I don't know how to fix that."

In what would have otherwise been a dryasdust meeting with nary a smile, this one had people chuckling good-naturedly. I have no evidence of it, but I'm willing to bet everyone left that meeting feeling warmer toward Emmer—even those from the opposite party—than they had before the upside-down incident.

There are endless examples of humorous moments when our rapid shift to virtual interactions resulted in, shall we say, adjustments.

It seems contradictory, but while leaking unintended emotional cues has a negative effect, making errors that are unrelated to the situation can make a person seem more human and likable. Seem far-fetched? Consider the last time you felt as warmly amused by either a lawyer or politician's run-of-the-mill daily proceedings. I rest my case.

The Beauty in Our Blunders

Three professors undertook the task of discovering how our clumsy—and inevitable—mistakes influence the way other people see us. While the urge to perfect your messages can be strong, these professors discovered that doing so might not be as helpful as you'd think.

They developed a study in which subjects were given recordings of what they believed were student tryouts for a college quiz bowl team. And the fifty quiz questions the supposed students had to answer were *really* (intentionally) hard. After listening to the recordings, the study participants were asked to share their impressions of the student.

Simple enough.

The tapes used were all the same, except on two dimensions: ability and blunder.

For the ability group, two different tapes were used. One of the tapes, called the "superior ability," had the student answering 92 percent of the quiz questions correctly. As one additional detail, the tape included an interview with the student in which he noted he had been an honors student, yearbook editor, and track team member in high school. In contrast, the second tape, which they called the "average ability," had the student answering only 30 percent of the questions correctly. In his interview, he stated he was a proofreader for the yearbook and had tried out for track but didn't make the team.

Unsurprisingly, listeners rated the "superior ability" student as more competent. But they also rated him as not very likable.

Why would that be?

Think back to school and recall that one student who raised their hand for every single question and got all of them right. If you're like most of us, I'm guessing you didn't really like that person. After all, no one appreciates a know-it-all. (Just ask elementary school me. Let's just say I wasn't the most popular second grader on the playground.)

These study findings reinforced that, in fact, we don't like people who seem too perfect, as they seem unrelatable. Alternatively, the contestants who got some questions wrong came off as much more likable, but also (unsurprisingly) less competent. So how can you be both competent and likable?

By spilling coffee on yourself.

As the study showed, making a blunder—or "pratfall"—that isn't core to the domain of your expertise or isn't situationally relevant can actually make you more likable without hurting perceptions of competence.

Let me explain.

The research team added another condition—the blunder. These tapes went just like the other two, with one difference. Near the end of the interview, the student (after getting the same number of questions right) spilled a cup of coffee on himself. On the tape, listeners hear a lot of noise and commotion, as well as the student's "Oh my goodness, I've spilled coffee all over my new suit."

After listening to the whole interview, followed by the coffee-spilling debacle, the researchers asked the study participants to describe their impressions of the student on the tape, including how intelligent they thought the student was.

The listeners actually rated the person who spilled coffee on themselves as more likable than the non-coffee-spilling know-it-all. For the coffee-spilling "superior ability" condition, the student in the tape was rated as both competent *and* likable.

Shouldn't spilling coffee make someone seem less, rather than more, competent?

As we saw in Chapter 3, making errors when they matter—from email typos to blunders in video calls—can incur severe costs. However, making mistakes unrelated to your work, such as spilling coffee on yourself, can make you seem both competent *and* likable. The idea here is that minor mistakes can make us seem more human and relatable. So, actually making one every so often—or as a more natural approach, simply not worrying so much about appearing "perfect" in your interactions—can end up helping you. Just make sure your errors aren't directly related to the purpose of your interaction. The reason why spilling coffee didn't make the student seem less competent is that being clumsy has nothing to do with answering trivia questions correctly. It did, however, increase their likability because it made them seem even more authentic.

The only downside might be some extra dry-cleaning costs.

This concept is particularly relevant to virtual communication. Because it's so easy to hide these types of blunders in virtual interactions (such as keeping the mustard stain you acquired during lunch out of the camera's view), most people choose to do so. The result, however, is that our virtual communication lacks these innately human aspects, leaving us feeling like we're talking to a robot rather than a person.

As an example of what this might look like in the context of normal work, it may benefit you to casually mention—rather than hide—a blunder of yours that was non-task-related. For instance, you might mention in an email to a teammate that, earlier in the day, you didn't look at your phone's caller ID and accidentally answered a call from your mother by telling her you were sending her that marketing slide deck. Or being in such a rush that you took your son's Pokémon lunch box instead of your own.

Taking the initiative to incorporate these instances of openness into your virtual communication can be a good way to lighten the mood and make you seem more approachable. So don't worry too much about perfecting your messages beyond what matters directly to that interaction, because as you've seen, it's the little errors that make us seem human.

Cracking the Authenticity Code

What's clear is that our virtual communication choices have the potential to say just as much about us as the content of the message itself. Emotions, intelligence, and warmth are part of the story we're telling with even a simple email or phone call. Research has also shown that not only is the choice of mode important for communicating your most authentic virtual persona, but it can also mean the difference between success and failure in your career.

When you approach interactions, think about whether your goal is to be perfect or likable. By considering both mode and message, you'll be able to better craft how you'll be perceived by others. You'll also be way ahead of the curve now that you know that others will use your communication mode, nonverbal behaviors, and message content to determine how much effort they feel you put into the interaction.

KEY LESSONS

Perspective Taking

✦ In virtual interactions, what feels authentic to you may not seem authentic to the person you're interacting with. Make sure to pause to consider how your communication choices and message will come off to others.

✦ Especially when you're communicating bad news, it's important to craft your message so it's focused on the impact on the other person, rather than you. It will make the bitter pill of whatever news you're communicating easier to swallow.

Initiative

✦ Don't choose text-based communication solely because it seems easiest. In situations where seeming authentic is key, choosing less rich communication will result in your message coming off as inauthentic.

✦ If you provide a reason why you're using a low-richness communicationn mode, it can make it more likely that others will view your message as more authentic. (E.g., "I'm emailing rather than calling because I know you're with your kids right now. Feel free to call me tomorrow to discuss everything further.")

✦ If you are being truly authentic, the richest modes (e.g., video or in-person) are best for being perceived as more likable.

Nonverbal

✦ When you need to present emotions that are different from the ones you're feeling (surface acting), choose audio to get the best balance between demonstrating effort and preventing nonverbal leakage. You'll seem more authentic but won't have to worry about your body language showing something you didn't intend.

Goals

✦ Consider whether your goal is to be seen as perfect, or authentic and likable. If it's the latter, letting some blunders sneak through into your virtual communication, as long as they aren't work- or situationally relevant, can make you seem more human and likable.

6

Building Bridges, Not Firewalls

How to Build Trust and Foster Long-Lasting Virtual Relationships

When the trust account is high, communication is easy, instant, and effective.
—STEPHEN R. COVEY, *THE 7 HABITS OF HIGHLY EFFECTIVE PEOPLE*

Consider the following social media posts from two different people that take a *slightly* different approach. Don't worry, there won't be a quiz after. But I will be curious to know which author seems more trustworthy and like someone you'd want to be friends with. Ready? Here we go.

Kimberly's most recent social media post displays a staged family photo with her husband and two children. They're all wearing white and standing against a blank wall. The text below reads: "I would like to thank my family for their constant love and support."

Taking a different approach, Kristen posted an image with a pile of children's toys scattered all over the carpet. Her caption reads, "This is a picture of both the floor of my house and the interior of my brain."

Before you rush to judgment, let's look at two more posts from the same people.

Kimberly posted an image on her Facebook account of green, rolling hills dotted with grazing sheep and the caption, "New Zealand is the most beautiful place in the world."

Kristen shared a video that she deemed "worth watching because it's embarrassing." In the slightly wobbly and out-of-focus frame, she's curled on her bed and sobbing. She isn't sad, though—she's thrilled, because she just learned that a sloth from a local zoo would be making an appearance at her birthday party. The video ends with Kristen sitting bolt upright in bed and asking, "He's coming for the party?!"

Consider the posts I just described. Simply judging from these tiny snapshots of Kimberly's and Kristen's lives, who do you feel more connected to?

The answer, I presume, is Kristen. Her posts are funny and, more importantly, relatable (okay, maybe less so with the sloth one). You get a clear sense of who Kristen is behind her posts, whereas Kimberly could really be anyone. In fact, and in the spirit of full disclosure since this chapter is all about building trust, let me clarify that Kimberly is a made-up person. Kristen is real, as are the stories I told above.

Some of you might have even recognized one of the above posts from Kristen, since that particular video has been viewed more than 30 million times and her Instagram has 15.6 million followers. I'm referring to the acclaimed Broadway, TV, and film actress Kristen Bell. Among other roles, she was the voice behind Anna in *Frozen*. (If you have kids, you can probably start singing some of the movie's songs right now. If you don't have kids, you can probably start singing some of the movie's songs right now.) Bell also played a pharmaceutical saleswoman in *The Good Place*, a private detective in *Veronica Mars*, and—my personal favorite—an electricity-wielding villain in the TV series *Heroes*.

Most celebrities seem unapproachable and unrelatable. Bell, on the other hand, has used virtual communication to present herself as someone you could really trust, even though you've likely never interacted with her directly. In fact, she has built several successful companies based on her down-to-earth brand. Dunshire Productions, a studio and production company she cofounded, notes on their home page that "[m]oms usually like us if that tells you anything." Instead of a lot of industry jargon in the "How we make our content" section of their website, Bell and team give the following breakdown: "6% internet cats, 10% intellectual acuity (with mediocre dexterity), 60% communication degrees from mainly state universities (minors in Philosophy), and 24% mom jeans."

These minorly self-deprecating and personality-laden tidbits make you feel like you already know Bell, and thus can trust her. She's broken down the [virtual] fourth wall, preventing her behind-the-screen communication from appearing robotic or insincere.

Perhaps sharing a video of you crying from excitement about a sloth isn't the fastest way to engender feelings of trust with your colleagues (unless you happen to work at a zoo). But there are lessons from Bell's virtual communication that we can all implement on a daily basis to strengthen our interactions.

Trust Is Like Wi-Fi. It's Invisible, But You Know When It's Not There.

In the last chapter, I focused on how impressions are shaped from singular interactions. While authenticity is important for one-time interactions, this chapter is going to focus on arguably the single most important attribute to building long-lasting relationships: trust.

In person or virtual, it doesn't matter—trust is paramount to maintaining successful relationships. The difference is that, when communicating virtually, trust is harder to cultivate and maintain. As a result, many people come to the incorrect conclusion that in-person communication is the only possible solution. However, just because trust doesn't occur as naturally in virtual relationships, that doesn't mean it's unattainable.

Trust isn't just vital to developing strong friendships; it's a necessary component of successful careers. If you want to get ahead in the workplace, obtain information that might not be readily available, and/or have successful long-term relationships, trust is needed. Further, trust in the workplace doesn't just impact employees themselves. For an organization to succeed, employees need to trust each other. Without trust, employees won't put as much effort into their work. They'll avoid taking risks that could be tremendously beneficial for the company, such as innovating or presenting an idea that diverges from what was previously implemented by executives. They'll play it safe.

If you want to succeed as an employee, manager, or business owner, trust is a vital ingredient. And this chapter will show you how to form lasting trust via virtual communication.

The Evaporating Water-Cooler Culture

While writing this book, I spoke with my former student Elena about her experience getting her first full-time job.

Elena had been ecstatic to land her dream position at an amazing company. Her new office was a comfortable nine-minute drive from home, and she'd be working with a top-notch international team that was collaborating from offices spread across three continents. Since she was the only employee on her immediate team working in her city, she would be interacting with the other members virtually. Elena told me that her bubble burst during her third week, when she finally met her new supervisor via video.

Elena was based in the US and her supervisor was in Australia. As a result, due to time zone differences, most of their communication over the first couple of weeks occurred via a flurry of emails. And Elena wasn't completely sure how to approach these messages. For instance, should she use happy-faced emojis or exclamation points to show her excitement, or would that come off as childish? Should she share personal information so her manager could learn more about her, or would that be weird to do over email?

To avoid the risk of appearing unprofessional, Elena played it safe.

The unintended consequence of all those messages was that she ended up feeling like she never really got to connect with her manager. She was relieved when, weeks later, they were finally able to meet via video during a time when they would both conceivably be awake.

While Elena had high hopes for the meeting, their first conversation seemed cold. Elena didn't know what would be appropriate to say to bond with her boss, so she mostly just listened. The video meeting ended up seeming more like a lecture than a two-way conversation.

Elena felt similarly disillusioned when she met with her other team members, mostly via email and instant messaging. She wanted to express her excitement about the new job and convey her strong commitment to the projects she'd be working on, but she didn't feel like text provided the ability to do so in an appropriate way.

Elena is still working through the kinks of her new job, but suffice it to say, it's been a rocky beginning.

If you recall the examples of Kimberly and Kristen from earlier in the chapter, you can imagine why Elena was so disheartened by these interactions. They weren't personal in the way a good first meeting might be. It was difficult for her (and presumably her supervisor and teammates) to trust the person on the other end of the connection.

Elena's experience is one many of us can relate to. The more that workers communicate predominantly via electronic means with their coworkers, the more they often struggle to build feelings of trust and "fit" with their colleagues. This challenge includes employees who work in person, since a significant portion of communication that previously occurred via dropping by a colleague's desk has switched to instant messaging or email. As a result, even for office workers, there is often a decreased level of personal connection. The simple fact is that for workers who engage in some—or all—of their communication electronically, there are fewer casual "water-cooler" conversations, which are key opportunities for bonding.

All that isn't to say that trust in the workplace is a thing of the past.

Although at first glance it appears that communication technology is the cause of these problems, it can also be a solution when properly leveraged. It's possible to establish the same degree of trust virtually compared to in person, and virtual communication provides the additional benefit of being able to strengthen relationships across cities and continents. To be successful, we just need to make some adjustments and embrace new methods that make sense in a virtual context.

Schmooze Operators

In 1964, Nelson Mandela was arrested and sentenced to life imprisonment in South Africa's most infamous prison, Robben Island. He'd been clashing with the government for decades over his fight to establish a racism-free society. His teachings were banned in an effort to maintain the status quo. Mandela didn't give up. Even during his imprisonment, he continued his fight to end apartheid.

The world took notice. By the 1980s, Mandela was "one of the world's most quoted public figures." He became the embodiment of South Africa's anti-apartheid struggle. Unable to ignore Mandela's international popularity, then-president F. W. de Klerk held a secret meeting with Mandela to discuss their country's future. The prison wards even needed to scrounge up a suit for Mandela to wear instead of his prison uniform. It was the start of what would become a yearslong conversation.

In 1990, Mandela was released from prison. Years later, when tension in South Africa had reached a pinnacle, Mandela ended a speech by holding out his hand to de Klerk in a demonstration of his willingness to work peacefully with the president. After decades of violence, this handshake was seen as momentous. The winds were shifting. Hope was renewed.

The iconic image of the two men clasping hands came to be heralded as a symbol of Black South African citizens standing beside the white president as equals. It was the first of many handshakes that would play a role in shaping the country's future, especially after Mandela became the first democratically chosen leader of South Africa.

In fact, Mandela became so renowned for shaking hands with everyone—from world leaders to food servers—that people flocked to his speeches in the hopes of receiving one themselves. At his divorce trial in 1996, Mandela even shook his newly ex-wife's hand.

Mandela understood how a gesture as seemingly simple as a handshake can inspire trust and a willingness to cooperate. There's even research showing that people with firmer handshakes tend to be rated more favorably by interviewers.

The problem, of course, is that handshakes necessitate being physically colocated. Any efforts to attempt a handshake virtually won't have the same effect (let's face it—a GIF of two hands shaking just doesn't inspire the same feelings of goodwill).

It's not just the physical connections that are lost in virtual contexts. Small talk, the back-and-forth that naturally occurs in office hallways, doesn't lend itself to virtual interactions. As my student Elena found, the difficulty with making small talk virtually resulted in all of her interactions feeling stiffer and less personal.

To tease apart the differences between email and face-to-face communication, Columbia Business School's Michael Morris and his colleagues studied participants who engaged in a simulated negotiation. Half of the participants conducted the negotiation through email, while the other half were in person.

A stark difference between the two conditions emerged. Email negotiators only spent a third as much time discussing non-negotiation issues as the face-to-face participants. In a similar vein, the email negotiators asked their opponents only a fifth as many questions about non-negotiation-related topics. Compared to face-to-face, virtual negotiators were less likely to share truthful information and less adept at preventing negative feelings from escalating.

This is seemingly bad news for those of us who have seen a huge uptick in our virtual interactions in recent years.

So, how can you create that same rapport when communicating electronically?

The answer, as Morris and his colleagues discovered, is through schmoozing—or briefly exchanging personal information prior to tackling the task. Schmoozing, so often seen as a time-waster,* can make tense conversations go more smoothly and enhance feelings of trust on both sides.

Next, we'll examine ways to help *schmooth* (sorry) the way for virtual schmoozing.

TMI: True Moments Illuminated

I'm going to give you two hypothetical scenarios. Both are asking for donations to a charity that assists homeless people. I'd like you to decide which you'd be more likely to donate to.

Scenario #1:

We are a nonprofit charity that is deeply committed to providing assistance to homeless individuals throughout the United States. We work to provide mental, financial, and educational assistance to help individuals and communities in need. Last year we helped over 200 people get off the street and into their own homes. Let's work together to end homelessness in our country. Please donate today, and help make a difference.

---

* *That's because small talk can also be a distraction that reduces productivity. Thus, in order to optimize your communication-productivity equation, you need to clearly define your communication-outcome goal. If expediency is of the utmost importance, then it will make sense to limit small talk. If, however, your goal is to build trust, then the extra time spent socializing can prove valuable. In order to make the right choice in each situation, you need to gauge which goal is most important.*

Scenario #2:

> Hi everyone, I'm reaching out because I'm a single father with beautiful twin girls and recently lost my job. My partner died in a car accident last year, and since then, we've been trying to scrape by. Now that I've lost my job, we got kicked out of our apartment and are living in our car. My girls, Annie and Cally, sleep squished up in the back of my old van. We leave the windows cracked at night, but it's still getting into the 90s and they can't sleep. Any help you could give would be so appreciated.

Below the second post, there's a photo of his daughters, Annie and Cally, in the van they're living out of.

Both of these scenarios are asking you to donate money to help with homelessness. But if you're like most people, you'd be rushing to give your money to the individual person from Scenario 2, despite the fact that the charity in Scenario 1 likely has greater resources and is able to leverage economies of scale to potentially help more than just a single family with the same amount of money. Why, then, would you give your money to the single family? Because that story felt more personal. You got a distinct picture of exactly who you'd be helping with your donation. You almost feel like you know them.

This feeling of connectedness to the more personal story is supported by research. One study found that charity donations more than doubled when, instead of just being asked to donate to a general charity working to relieve the severe food crisis in southern Africa and Ethiopia (in this case, the organization Save the Children), participants were additionally provided with an image and description of one of the children helped by the charity. In theory, finding out about a single individual the organization helps shouldn't meaningfully alter the donation decision (as the charity helps more than 100 million children). However, something just feels different when it's more personal.

This effect is known as the *identifiable victim effect*, whereby people are more likely to help an identifiable victim (one particular starving child) rather than a statistical victim (millions of starving children). This effect is relevant to virtual communication because when interacting virtually, we become more anonymous beings. Think about it this way. When you're in person, there is a strong motivation to be aware of how the other person might react to what you say, because another identifiable human is clearly standing in front of you. But when you communicate with someone virtually, because you're interacting with your computer or phone and the other person is not standing in front of you (at most, you are just watching a video of them), you're more removed (both physically and figuratively). Thus, you're going to be less attentive to the fact that another individual person is on the other side of the digital conversation. This is the same reason why individuals are willing to speak more negatively to others on the internet and via virtual communication than they would if the person were standing right in front of them. A lack of physical proximity leads to less perspective taking.

To counter this effect, you need to remind others that you are more than an anonymous robotic email response by highlighting who you are as a person. You can see how Kristen Bell's social media would be a whole lot less compelling if the only posts on her accounts were filtered, professional photos of her at movie premieres. And yet, it's understandable why so many people feel more comfortable with only taking a very scripted and solely professional approach to their virtual relationships. Especially when you consider the longevity of your online activity and the oft-cited advice to keep personal and professional separate, many people are reasonably hesitant to put anything out there that isn't edited, polished, and the best version of themselves. I'm not suggesting that you should make your life an open book in each interaction. Rather, there are ways to share personal tidbits through virtual communication that are foundational to developing trust. And sometimes it's the details you least expect to share that end up having the greatest impact.

A Tale of Two Selves

Professor Robert Kelly learned about the power of sharing personal details firsthand when he got a surprise visit from his toddler during a video interview with BBC News. In a recording that has been viewed ten million times, viewers can see Kelly's toddler dancing behind his chair while he's discussing South Korean politics. As he's trying to gently nudge his daughter out of the camera's view, his baby comes wheeling into the office in a baby walker, followed by his wife, who is frantically trying to herd the children out while ducking out of the frame.

As an anchor from ABC News noted, "Never before has an interview on Korean politics gotten this much attention for all the wrong reasons." After featuring the clip on her talk show, comedian Ellen DeGeneres said, "I've never laughed so hard at a video about North Korea in my life."

This scenario might not be the most professional look for Kelly, but it certainly inspired feelings of warmth and familiarity for everyone who viewed it. We've all had that moment when a pet, kid, spouse, or woodpecker at the window (true story) interrupts an important meeting. Instead of wishing you could undo the last ten seconds and somehow eliminate the interruption, embrace it as an opportunity.

I've inadvertently put this strategy into practice every time Minnie, my fourteen-pound dachshund-mix (who is convinced she's a huge guard dog), starts maniacally barking at birds that dare fly near my window while I'm in a meeting. Instead of apologizing and fumbling for the mute button as my instinct tells me to do, I turn what could have been an awkward interruption into an opportunity. By calling Minnie over and introducing her to whoever I'm meeting with, I can give the person I'm interacting with more insight into who I am as a human being (rather than just a video on the screen). Afterward, the conversation almost always ends up turning much lighter and more personal.

When we're communicating virtually, and because we can't always rely on our dogs/children/surrounding wildlife to inject personality into a conversation, it's up to us to add that sense of humanity (and familiarity). If you're feeling overwhelmed by the prospect of revealing deeply intimate details about yourself just to make your virtual communication seem friendlier, let me offer you some reassurance. Self-disclosing personal details doesn't require you to halt a conversation in its tracks so you can share a deeply held secret in the hopes of getting the other person to trust you. Instead, it's a matter of subtly integrating personal tidbits throughout our day-to-day interactions.

For example, when sending a message to a coworker you already have an established relationship with, something as small as sharing an interesting anecdote from your weekend (and asking the other person what they were up to) can strengthen feelings of closeness and trust. Or, you could talk about the vacation you recently took and maybe share a picture or two. You could even do something as simple as mention a new recipe you tried over the weekend that failed miserably but was fun to cook nonetheless (cauliflower fried rice, anyone?). You get the idea.

Another option that gets around the out-of-sync aspect of email is a quick pre-email phone call. It might seem like a waste of time; however, researchers discovered that having a five-minute phone call before an email negotiation took place meaningfully increased feelings of rapport and trust, resulted in fewer negative personal impressions, and led to better outcomes for the negotiator. If you find yourself in the position where email is the optimal negotiation mode (rather than just the easy one), having even a brief phone call before a text-based negotiation occurs can increase the likelihood of reaching a deal by over 20 percent.

Not a bad payout for ten minutes of your time.

If you are in a similar position to my former student Elena, where your relationship is newer and you're concerned about professionalism norms, there are still ways to build trust during your conversations without it feeling forced. In Elena's case, she could have asked for a quick call with her boss to get some clarification (i.e., using a business reason to initiate the conversation). Her message might be something as simple as:

> Hi X, The project you mentioned sounds really interesting, and I'd love to take it on. I have a few questions just to make sure I execute it properly, as I'm still learning the ins and outs of our company. If you're available, I figure it might be quicker to have a short call to get your advice, rather than send a bunch of emails back and forth. If that sounds good to you, let me know when would work best. I look forward to connecting!

Then, during the course of the subsequent conversation, Elena might infuse a personal anecdote into the conversation like "I was in the middle of weeding my tomato garden on Sunday, when I came up with a great idea for the project." This offhanded comment shows enthusiasm for a work initiative, provides a nice introduction to the reason for the conversation in the first place, and humanizes her at the same time.

The idea here is that it's advantageous to take initiative to "fill back in" the parts of in-person interactions that are missing into virtual interactions. At first, this can feel a bit odd to do digitally, but it's a learned skill. And it will enhance your work experience on the whole beyond just improving your relationships. Over time, you'll find that these small efforts to virtually self-disclose can improve your well-being and result in better performance evaluations.

However, sharing information about yourself is only half the equation.

Swipe Right

Imagine you're a single thirtysomething who is feeling unlucky in love. So, you decide to take a break from the apps and try something different: speed dating.

You enter a room full of tables and eager-for-love singles. As the person running the event explains the rules (you'll have five minutes for each conversation before switching to a new partner), you glance at the strangers milling around. Panic starts to take hold as you wonder what you could possibly say in five minutes that will make you seem like second-date material.

As it turns out, it's not about finding the right words to say—it's about asking the right questions.

Rather than looking at how people interact in stuffy offices, a group of Harvard researchers led by Karen Huang decided to explore their research question in the *slightly* more appealing context of speed dating. Their findings? That people who asked more questions during a speed-dating session were more likely to get asked on a second date. For every 10 percent increase in follow-up questions, the likelihood of getting a date went up by approximately 6 percent.

These findings have direct applicability to people you interact with at work. Asking questions gives the other person permission to talk about themselves. We all like talking about ourselves. When you give others that opportunity, not only do they enjoy the interaction more, but they are likely to attribute those good feelings to you. As an added plus, you'll discover more about them, which you can use to generate more personalized small talk with them in the future.

Win-win-win.

Question-asking is a highly underestimated tactic for building trust. And, unlike handshakes, it works just as well virtually as it does in person. The next time you are having a video, phone, email, or instant-messaging conversation with someone you'd like to build trust with, ask them a question that will give them the opportunity to self-disclose. It can be as simple as asking how their family is doing, how their newly adopted kitten is getting along with everyone, or what they did on their recent weekend getaway. Because these questions don't arise as naturally in virtual communication, you need to take the initiative to raise them. But it will be worth your time. This small effort will go a long way toward strengthening your bond. And you might just learn something new in the process.

One quick caveat. Like all strategies in this book, handle question-asking and self-disclosures with discretion and in contextually appropriate situations (i.e., perspective-take on how others might receive your message). I once received an email from an employee at a Fortune 100 company where I was doing research. He started the email by telling me and the five other people on the chain about the stomach flu he'd gotten over the weekend.

There were two paragraphs of excessive detail. Needless to say, his self-disclosures didn't inspire feelings of trust (mostly just a loss of appetite). So, proceed with caution.

Now that we've covered what you should say (and ask) to elicit self-disclosures that can lead to trust, let's go down a level and take a closer look at the best ways to actually word messages themselves to build trust with others. And if you're already thinking of methods to make sure your messages stand out from the virtual pack, don't. As you'll soon find out, you don't need to be anywhere near as creative as you might think.

Be a Conversational Chameleon

If you know anything about sports in England, you know that football (soccer in the US) is a big deal. One of the biggest rivalries in the sport is between two teams: Manchester United and Liverpool. People born in the two cities have different accents and identities that are rooted in history and integral to people's sense of self. Being a Manchester United or Liverpool fan isn't confined to who you cheer for on the football field; it's a statement about your whole persona. Fans take this rivalry so seriously that there have been violent clashes between the two fan groups. Talk about superfans.

Making use of this strong identity, researchers from Lancaster University and St. Andrews University came up with an idea to test how far this team loyalty actually went. They recruited university students who identified as Manchester United fans and told them they'd be participating in a study about football clubs. Once selected, the participants were asked to walk a short distance to continue the experiment. As they were making their solo trek across the path, they caught sight of someone nearby who—unbeknownst to the study participants was an actor—fell over clutching their ankle and groaning in pain.

The twist? The person who fell over was wearing one of three outfits: a Manchester United shirt, a Liverpool shirt, or a plain shirt that didn't represent any football team.

The results were staggering: when the actor was wearing a Liverpool or plain shirt, only about 30 percent helped the fallen individual, but when their shirt matched the study participant's favorite team, over 90 percent of participants stopped to help.

The point here, which has been replicated in a variety of settings with different groups, is that we feel a connection with people who seem similar to us. And we're therefore more likely to help them out.

Like the Manchester United shirt-wearers, finding commonalities with your virtual communication partner can enhance feelings of trust and familiarity. The same mechanism applies to your background during video calls. For instance, a set of studies found that for interviewees, having visual signals that you are a parent (e.g., having a visible "#1 Mom" or "#1 Dad" mug) resulted in higher ratings of warmth and higher overall interview performance ratings. When having a video meeting with a die-hard New York Yankees fan, consider wearing your Yankees cap while on the call (provided casual attire is appropriate). Additionally, cues indicating political affiliation in the background (e.g., a "Proud Democrat/Republican" hat on a bookshelf or a "Vote Democrat/Republican" poster on the wall) tended to improve interviewer ratings of candidates' warmth and interview performance when they had similar (as opposed to differing) political party affiliations. If you don't know your communication partner's political affiliation, don't run the risk of offending them by having political swag in your frame, as you'll completely undermine your goal of finding common ground.

Beyond your video-call background, mirroring someone else's nonverbal behavior can be beneficial. A study leveraging a job-offer negotiation simulation over instant messaging found that those who mimicked their negotiation partner's behavior style (e.g., using similar words and nonverbal behaviors) improved not only their individual outcomes by 39 percent, but also the combined joint outcomes by over 30 percent. Beyond just their outcomes, mimickers' partners indicated that they felt the negotiation went more smoothly and they got to know their counterparty (the one engaging in mimicry) better. In other words, participants who "became a chameleon" and mimicked others not only did better than those who did not, but also improved outcomes for their counterparty as well.

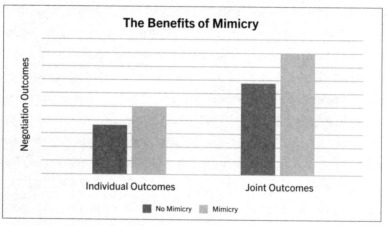

Mimicry improves negotiation outcomes.

If you're instant-messaging with someone who uses a lot of abbreviations, try mirroring their shorthand. Likewise if they use particularly (in)formal language, tend to ask questions, include lots of emojis or exclamation marks, or always include/exclude salutations/closings.

The point here is that similarity matters, even if it's just perceptual. It's human nature to trust those who are like us. When others mirror the same mode we originally chose, not only do we feel more comfortable, but we also assume they are more competent because they are making the "right" choice.

For this strategy, timing is important. The benefits of mimicry are strongest when they're used early in the relationship, when trust is lacking and it matters most. Researchers studying virtual communicators in Thailand, the US, and the Netherlands found that across each of these cultures, "negotiators who actively mimicked their counterpart's language in the first 10 min of the negotiation obtained higher individual gain compared to those mimicking during the last 10 min."

As always, there can be "too much of a good thing." Your communication practices shouldn't turn into a grown-up version of Simon Says. Instead, the idea is to be attentive to how the other person is communicating, and model your practices off theirs.

I recognize it's easy to talk about language mimicry in isolation, but it can be difficult to visualize what that actually looks like when your boss sends you an email full of exclamation points and smiley emojis.* Wouldn't it seem weird if you responded in kind?

I had this exact conversation with Colonel Everett Spain, head of the Department of Behavioral Sciences and Leadership at the United States Military Academy at West Point and a senior adviser to the Army Talent Management Task Force. Due to his Army service across the world, Colonel Spain has received dozens of awards, including the Soldier's Medal, Purple Heart, Combat Action Badge, and the Secretary of the Treasury's Honor Award. When I had the chance to interview Colonel Spain about his communication habits, he shared an interesting story that involved mimicry.

Colonel Spain told me about an interaction he had with a lieutenant general he'd met a few times in the passing. One day after briefly crossing paths, Colonel Spain received a text from the retired lieutenant

---

* *Emoticons are symbols made up of punctuation marks to resemble human expressions (e.g., :-)), while emojis are the pictograms (e.g., ☺). Given using emojis and emoticons often lead to similar outcomes, for purposes of simplicity, I'll default to using the term "emoji" to describe both.*

general. It went something like "Hey Everett! Great to see you," followed by six colorful and happy emojis. "They were all different," Colonel Spain recalled, "and they were just positive emotions stuff—smileys, American flags, that kind of thing."

When I asked Colonel Spain about his thoughts after receiving this message, he told me he had two simultaneous reactions. He explained, "I wouldn't expect a three-star general to have colorful emojis in his or her text, right? It's just not that fitting. But, on the other hand, I was like, man—it made me smile. And maybe if it does that to me, I can do that for other people that I care about."

Because of his positive—albeit surprised—reaction, Colonel Spain responded in kind, sending back an array of emojis. The short text exchange made him feel closer to someone he'd previously thought of as a casual acquaintance. The two don't communicate on a regular basis, but when they do, their messages are full of emojis. In a sense, they cultivated a private language through the use of emojis—and enhanced their personal relationship at the same time.

Not all mimicry will be this obvious; it may be as subtle as a management consultant opting to use similar abbreviations for industry-related terms as a client. But by mirroring the use of the other person's language behaviors (e.g., exclamation marks, formality, business jargon, paragraph structure, or emoji usage), you'll be perceived more positively.

Using mimicry is an effective means of increasing comfort when you're interacting digitally rather than face-to-face. Beyond mirroring the other person's communication style, a secondary benefit of engaging in similar nonverbal behaviors is that it can make you seem more trustworthy.

Who Says We Don't Judge a Virtual Book by Its Cover?

In Chapter 3, we looked at how details like attire, camera angle, lighting, and video-call backgrounds can impact perceptions of competence and professionalism. Here we're going to go further and examine how everything in your video-call frame affects the way others are evaluating your trustworthiness.

I'm going to take a dive into analyzing the highly varying information that is relayed in a variety of backgrounds, and how these seemingly innocuous choices inform others' perceptions about our warmth, likability, and trustworthiness. The images are all from video calls that Rosalind Brewer, CEO of Walgreens Boots Alliance (the parent company of Walgreens), has leveraged during her virtual interviews. As you'll see, her backgrounds range from providing limited information to painting a detailed picture of her preferences and accomplishments. Still the same person—just a very different message being shared via her video background.

Background #1

This first background is bland, yet professional. Note that Brewer isn't surrounded by a messy room, wearing pajamas, or lounging by the pool. She's also staring directly at the (correctly positioned) webcam.

This background is successful in preventing any distractions (there's very little to look at besides her); however, there's nothing in her background that creates a direct feeling of connection or trust.

Background #2

This background seriously ramps up the warmth. Now we have Christmas trees (who doesn't like twinkling trees?). The celebratory spirit is palpable. It's Christmas, after all. This is the type of person you can connect with. You both enjoy holidays (not necessarily the same ones), and you both like to celebrate. Cheers. This background is likely to create a kind of emotion-based trust known as *affective trust*.

Background #3

Here's Brewer in a much more business-oriented setup. She's sitting in front of paintings of Walgreens stores and offices, and she's wearing a blazer. The message she's sharing here is company loyalty and commitment to her job. You see this and you want to up your professionalism game immediately. This kind of background highlights her competence and is likely to generate a more thoughtful kind of trust known as *cognitive trust*.

Background #4

Finally, we have Brewer demonstrating high power and accomplishment. In the background, you can see what appears to be a marble bookshelf, with an expensive-looking sculpture of a woman taking a powerful stride. You can also see her wine refrigerator in the bottom right of the screen.

While she does a great job of demonstrating status and power, this background may decrease feelings of emotional connectedness (unless you happen to have a wine fridge in your home office, in which case, all the more power to you). But while she may lose out on connectedness, she's clearly exuding confidence and competence. This is the image of a high performer.

When it comes to virtual communication, generating (or curtailing) trust isn't just about what we say and how we say it. It's also about what's around us when we say it.

Radio Silence or Overload?
Finding Your Dialogue Groove

Have you ever gotten into an awkward text or email exchange where you're basically going back and forth with some variation of *Sounds great, looking forward to it,* or *Thanks again for all your help*? It's the text communication equivalent of "No, you hang up first. . . . No, *you* hang up first. . . ." On the one hand, it can seem rude to let a message go without a reply. On the other, it might feel like you're annoying the other person by crowding their inbox with a simple "Thanks for the attachment." Virtual communication has made it so easy to get in touch with each other that, paradoxically, sometimes we end up communicating less. Everyone's in-boxes are full, and no one wants to be known as *that person* who keeps a conversation going after everyone else is finished.

Generally, you should worry less about sending superfluous mes-sages after a conversation might be over than not responding—and then discovering later that you offended the other person by seemingly ignoring their message. In a set of studies of business leaders and their employees, researchers found that undercommunicating actually made leaders seem the least qualified because they're seen as less empathic.

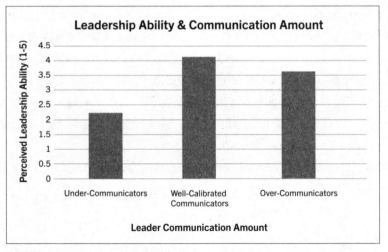

Although it's best to be well calibrated in terms of amount of communication, undercommunicating is punished more strongly than overcommunicating.

While it may not feel necessary to send an email saying, "Got it; I'll read through this and update you as soon as I'm finished," you'll be better off sending a quick message to show you're attentive and acknowledging the other person's communication. If you choose not to reply at all, you run the risk of violating the other person's expectations because they anticipated a response.

Perspective taking here is key because, even though you know you're attending to an email (or text or phone conversation), the other person doesn't necessarily have that same insight. Just by replying to the message, you'll show that you are "listening," which can help build trust and prevent you from violating the other person's expectations. If you're in a video meeting and happen to be checking your email simultaneously (not that I've ever done that, mind you), then something as simple as nodding your head in acknowledgment will go a long way toward showing the other person you're paying attention. Adding in that one extra behavior might seem unnecessary, but when we're missing much of the nonverbal cues present in face-to-face interactions, it could mean the difference between ensuring clarity and inadvertently disrespecting your interaction partner.

More Is More

LeBron James is without question one of the best basketball players of all time. To achieve his level of skill on the court, one would assume he spends all of his time and focus honing his basketball skills. You might be surprised to learn, therefore, that he also puts in effort to foster trust and cohesion with his teammates . . . off the court.

How does he do that? By taking the initiative to send periodic texts to his teammates.

Quinn Cook, one of James's past teammates, was inspired enough by James's texts to mention them to a reporter. Cook shared that James texted his teammates messages like "Miss you guys" and "Can't wait to get back on the floor with you guys, finish what we started."

Sometimes it can be the smallest of communications that make the biggest difference. By taking the initiative to reach out to his teammates, James demonstrates warmth and caring, which enhances his team's cohesion even when they're not together. These small efforts help build trust (and are likely a contributing factor to the team's on-court success).

If you're worried that in reaching out you might inadvertently say the wrong thing, don't sweat it. A set of studies found that even negative book reviews of more unknown authors in the *New York Times* led to increased book sales. This is because overarching familiarity and awareness is "stickier" in our memory relative to more fine-grained information. In the context of communication and trust, this means that people are generally more cynical and distrustful of people they don't know than those they've interacted with regularly, even if not all of those interactions have been positive. That's not to say people are going to forget a truly terrible conversation in a hurry. But an interaction that is even moderately negative may increase trust, as feelings of familiarity can be more important than the actual outcome of the interaction.

When in doubt, err on the side of reaching out (hey, that rhymes). The cost of sending an instant message or text every so often is relatively minor, especially when you consider how easily it can help maintain and strengthen your relationships.

Caught in the Carbon-Copy Crossfire

You and your colleague Jan have been working on an important deliverable for a client. When you start getting toward the end of the project, you decide it might be a good idea to loop in both of your bosses, so they'll know what you're planning before the client meeting next week. You compose an email that includes your updated proposal, cc your bosses, and send it off.

Both of your bosses respond positively and give their stamp of approval. You're feeling pretty good.

The day of the client meeting arrives. Jan doesn't greet you and responds to your small talk with one-word answers. As soon as the meeting is over, Jan leaves without acknowledging you. You get the sense that you did something wrong . . . you just don't know what it could be.

Many people assume that, when in doubt, you should include more people on email or instant message chains to keep everyone up to date. Similarly, I've seen a number of employees who are quick with their trigger finger when it comes to cc'ing, since it seems like a good way to maintain a record of evidence that can be used later. While they aren't wrong, the inadvertent secondary consequence is that they've harmed their relationship with their colleague. Here's the problem. When you cc someone outside of the initial conversation, you may be unintentionally signaling that you either feel the need to loop in additional recipients because you don't trust the other person, or you are trying to take credit for whatever you're discussing in the message. Both interpretations lead to less-than-ideal outcomes.

When it comes to including more participants in a conversation, there's a trade-off between transparency ("covering your butt") and maintaining trust. Ghent University professor Tessa Haesevoets and her colleagues discovered that while using cc can help increase the former, it negatively impacts the latter. They found that workers who often cc their boss are seen as less trustworthy by their colleagues. Further, use of cc makes people feel less comfortable expressing themselves and can lead to a culture of fear in the organization, because it's viewed as a controlling move. It can even go so far as to feel unethical. These researchers found that, in some contexts, the simple act of cc'ing your boss on messages can reduce trust by up to 50 percent.

That's pretty extreme.

Virtual communication experts are more cautious with using cc and adding extra people to email, instant messaging, or text chains, particularly when their goal is to enhance trust. When they choose to cc, they note a specific reason why they added the extra individual(s), so it's clear they aren't making the choice out of a lack of trust for the person already on the message. An alternate and even more proactive approach would be to ask the person you're communicating with if they think it's worth adding your boss (or whoever) onto the message chain.

If you're a manager, you can make this decision easier for your employees by being straightforward about when (and why) you want to be included in messages. This will have the added benefit of avoiding a distrustful culture where everyone feels the need to cc you even when it's not necessary. As an extra bonus, it'll keep your inbox emptier.

We've established that cc'ing one or two extra people onto a message chain can potentially harm your relationships, but what about when you want to communicate something to a much larger group? Hint: there's another risk to adding lots of recipients, which I found out the hard way.

Reply All-pocalypse

During high school, I spent a summer interning for my uncle at his storage business. One of my most important tasks was to help with his book launch—specifically, composing and emailing the publication announcement. Seemed like a simple enough task. So, I wrote the message introducing the book (using his brand-new AOL email address), proofread it about a thousand times, and then sent it out to four hundred of my uncle's contacts. I bcc'd everyone on the email message so they'd think they were getting a more personalized email.

I went out for lunch with a few other employees before returning to the office, eager to see if anyone had responded. I booted up my hefty desktop computer, opened AOL (iPhones weren't a thing yet) . . . and stared. There were already fifty email replies.

Before I could start congratulating myself on writing such a reply-worthy email, I noticed a disturbing detail—the messages weren't sent just to me. They were reply-alls. And, instead of congratulating my uncle on his forthcoming book, most of the emails were some variation of *Please remove me from this email list.* These were followed by a flurry of reply-all emails that less politely demanded that everyone else stop replying-all (the hypocrisy of using reply-all to stop others from replying-all was apparently lost on them). A couple of people used the email list as an opportunity to pitch their own books or services, which incited new rounds of "stop replying-all!" that got progressively more belligerent.

How could this happen? I wondered. *No one on this email list should be able to respond to anyone except me.* After a few more seconds of frantic investigation, I realized my mistake.

I remember sitting across from my uncle, my face tomato-red, as I explained to him that I had accidentally cc'd (rather than bcc'd) everyone on the email list.

As you can imagine, my uncle was not pleased. This email was supposed to feel like a relatively personalized announcement coming directly from him. Instead, because of my blunder, everyone recognized it as a form message that had been sent identically to four hundred people. It definitely didn't feel like an intimate conversation between a limited set of people with a preexisting relationship. Not to mention, everyone's email inboxes would be cluttered with reply-all messages for weeks and weeks. And my uncle got a funny story about me that he would retell for many Thanksgiving dinners to come.

Years later, I felt better after realizing that even large companies make similar errors. The news media firm Reuters had its own "reply-all" situation, when someone named Vince also forgot to use the bcc field and sent an email to thirty-three thousand Reuters employees. Everyone's inboxes then got flooded with messages—hundreds of which were reply-alls telling others to stop replying-all (when I shared this story with my uncle in the vein of *see, it happens to the best of us,* his response was that whoever started that chain was probably getting yelled at by his uncle too). The Reuters email chain even earned its own hashtag: #ReutersReplyAllGate.

A *reply all-pocalypse*, if you will.

Whether there are thirty-three thousand or eight people on your message chain, the effect is similar: your recipients feel like just a number. The subtext here is that you don't know the other people well enough (or have a strong enough relationship) to contact them directly. It feels a lot more like spam and gives the impression that you, as the sender, didn't have any regard for the message's recipients (thereby undermining trust).

I'm not going to tell you to unconditionally avoid mass communication; sometimes it just makes sense when you need to contact a group at once and individual messages are neither practical nor sensible. However, there are some steps you can take to avoid these negative impressions (aside from the obvious of correctly differentiating among To, CC, and BCC). First, by putting yourself in your message recipients' shoes (perspective taking), you'll get a better sense of how your communication might be coming off so you can address any potential concerns before they arise. Then, provide a reason for why you're including everyone together (e.g., "I figured it would be better to share this news with everyone at once, since I know you all were waiting for more information before moving forward on the project"). Finally, leave the door open for a more personal one-on-one conversation (e.g., "I'd love to chat individually with all of you about your thoughts. Feel free to put some time on my calendar this week to discuss further."). In this way, you can balance the need to send out messages to an entire group for efficiency's sake with the occasional direct contact to show you care.

Mind the Gap

Rome wasn't built in a day, as the saying goes. And trust takes time to develop and maintain. Trust is even harder to come by in virtual interactions, because when executed thoughtlessly, the human element gets lost more easily. When we take the time to ask a coworker something about themselves, send personal messages, or take the initiative to call someone following a group email, it shows there's a human being behind the message. It proves we care. Playing it safe and keeping your communication to the bare minimum won't do you any interpersonal favors. You have to, as many a parent has told their children, "put yourself out there."

Is your goal to save time and cover yourself, or are you trying to foster warm feelings that will grow your relationship over time? This isn't a trick question, and there's no right answer. The point is that you're going to have to make choices about what primary goal you're trying to achieve through your virtual communication. Once you have that established, and you've considered how your message might be interpreted, you'll be in good shape. Trust me (see what I did there?).

Taking the time to send a couple of messages or spend a few minutes chatting at the beginning of a video call won't significantly hamper your work output. It can, however, go a long way toward developing trust in an environment where genuine relationships can be more difficult to cultivate.

KEY LESSONS
Perspective Taking

+ Realize that when others are communicating with you virtually, they're staring at a screen, which makes it easy to forget there is an actual human behind that text or video display. Bringing that personal aspect back into virtual communication is key to building trust.

+ You might be aware that you've read someone's message or are listening to them speak during a video call, but they don't have that same insight. Ensure that you send or display a reaction to what they're saying, so they know you care and are paying attention.

- By putting yourself in your message recipients' shoes, you'll be able to envision how your communication might be interpreted, so you can head off any misinterpretations before they occur.

Initiative

- Small talk—a foundation of building trust—is often lost in virtual interactions. Go out of your way to self-disclose information about yourself and ask questions about the person you're interacting with. This personal sharing will help strengthen your connection.
- Taking the time to initiate a brief, pre-email-interaction phone call can increase feelings of rapport and lead to better outcomes. This tactic can be especially useful when you're going to engage in an interaction that could become contentious, like a negotiation.
- If you want to build trust, interact more frequently. When it comes to virtual communication, the tendency to undercommunicate can reduce trust and weaken relationships. When in doubt, err on the side of overcommunication.

Nonverbal

- Engage in virtual language mimicry (use similar emojis, jargon, punctuation, etc.). By using language and nonverbal patterns that are similar to the person you're communicating with, it will make your interaction partner feel that you are more familiar and trustworthy.
- When you are aware of (and share) your communication partner's preferences (e.g., favorite sports team, political affiliation, or status as a parent), consider displaying evidence of these similarities during video calls. Because we're drawn to those who share our interests, you'll set the stage for a more amicable conversation.

Goals

+ There are goal trade-offs when it comes to building trust. Strengthening trust and relationships via virtual means requires making an extra effort (through additional time spent communicating) and being willing to take risks to show you trust the person you're interacting with (e.g., avoiding self-protective behaviors like cc'ing).

+ Be thoughtful about how the details of your video call, from your outfit to the objects in your background, will communicate information about yourself. Based on your goal (e.g., communicating professionalism or casualness/informality), you'll want to adjust accordingly.

7

The Virtual Wrecking Ball

How to Effectively Manage Digital Conflicts and Emotions

People may hear your words, but they feel your attitude.
—John C. Maxwell, author of *Everyone Communicates, Few Connect*

At 8:10 a.m. on a January day in 2013, Hawaii's Emergency Alert System sent out a dire text message to the cell phones of residents of the entire state.

⚠ EMERGENCY ALERTS   ✕

Emergency Alert
BALLISTIC MISSILE THREAT INBOUND TO HAWAII. SEEK IMMEDIATE SHELTER. THIS IS NOT A DRILL.

Can you imagine the immediate and visceral panic you'd feel upon seeing this message pop up on your phone?

Throughout the state of Hawaii, residents and tourists scrambled to find safety. A tourist in Waikiki noted, "I was just putting on my makeup when this popped up and I got the biggest fright of my life." An international gymnastics tournament devolved into pandemonium as hundreds of people fled in search of safety. At the University of

Hawaii, students raced for a fallout shelter on campus, only to find it locked. Some two hundred students took refuge in an empty classroom. "It just kept filling up and filling up and filling up," one student remembered later. "People were screaming, 'You have to shut the doors! Time's running out!'" Other students gathered as many belongings as they could and sprinted down the road as they sobbed.

Residents who thought they were living the last moments of their lives called loved ones to say goodbye. A man who was golfing when he received the alert recorded a final message to his family: "If you're watching this video, that means I didn't make it. I just parred the last hole and I hit the shiz-nick out of my ball. I love y'all, but I'm playing golf, and that's the last thing I'm gonna do."

Calls to 911 wouldn't go through, and panicked messages flooding into the Federal Emergency Management Agency went unanswered. Phone lines and data services went down, which meant many people couldn't get any additional information beyond the emergency alert. A man even had a heart attack after getting the alert and having what he thought would be his last conversation with his children (thankfully, he survived).

Turns out, all the hysteria was for naught. Thirty-eight minutes after the initial alert went out, a second message followed that said—and I'm paraphrasing here—*whoopsie*. Richard Rapoza, a Hawaii Emergency Management Agency spokesperson, later admitted, "Someone clicked the wrong thing on the computer."

I'll say.

I've heard many people argue that email and other forms of text-based virtual communication are devoid of emotion. Yet, with just a three-sentence text message, the entire state of Hawaii was sent into a sobbing, heart attack–inducing state of panic. Quite the emotional response, albeit a warranted one, from a brief virtual message. The fallout from this message is enough to convince even the most hardened skeptics that virtual communication can evoke the same reactions as in-person communication.

Communication Missile Crisis

Whether a message is sent in error (like the Hawaii missile alert debacle) or interpreted differently from the way the sender intended, the results can be less than ideal. And you don't need to send an entire state into survival mode to experience repercussions from your communication. For instance, you might send a thumbs-up emoji to one of your colleague's suggestions for a new initiative, only to learn later that they interpreted that thumbs-up as you volunteering to complete the entire project. Or you might send your colleague an email offering them feedback on a presentation, only to discover later that the person interpreted your message as sarcastic and condescending.

The challenge with virtual communication isn't conveying emotions; it's communicating (and interpreting) them as intended—especially in interpersonally complex situations. The stress, relational, and career ramifications resulting from virtual miscommunication can be enough to make you want to hole up in an isolated, internet-free hideaway. Fortunately, there are less extreme measures that can help you to avoid virtual communication misinterpretations from occurring.

In this chapter, I'll explain why miscommunication runs rampant in virtual interactions, and why it can be harder to ensure your emotions come across as intended. You will learn why something as seemingly innocuous as inserting an emoji can be a risky decision. By recognizing how to anticipate the ways your virtual communication might cause an unintended reaction, you can avoid the most common (and potentially problematic) emotional impacts of virtual misinterpretation. I'll highlight strategies to avoid miscommunication and achieve your ideal outcome, whether you're engaging in an email negotiation or conflict resolution in a video call. By following these steps, you'll increase your chances at having a conversation that transforms conflict into cooperation. Not an easy feat, particularly when it comes to virtual communication—but I know we're all up for the challenge.

Lost in Translation

HSBC, one of the world's largest banks and financial services groups, decided it was time for a virtual makeover. They spent $10 million rebranding, including a new catchphrase of "Assume Nothing." The problem was that "Assume Nothing" was translated in several countries to "Do Nothing."

Doesn't quite have the same motivational ring, does it?

HSBC was forced to switch to a different headline and call their $10 million failed experiment a loss.

Because of a seemingly simple mistranslation, the message changed from taking action to doing nothing at all—and in the process lost any hope of a positive emotional reaction. A lack of understanding of cultural nuances and missing context from text-only communication led to a costly, botched large-scale rebranding effort.

I don't expect your virtual miscommunication will regularly carry a $10 million price tag. However, it's a near certainty that you will have at least a few instances in your career when you'll communicate something with a specific intention in mind, only to have your message recipient interpret your email (or text or voicemail) completely differently.

Being a high-powered CEO doesn't shield you from these communication breakdowns, either. Marc Benioff, CEO of Salesforce, sent a company-wide Slack instant message to the members of his organization questioning the effectiveness of remote work. He crafted the message in a way that he likely thought would make a serious topic feel a little lighter. He included a common meme (joke) in which you pretend that, rather than asking a question for your own benefit, you're seeking the information on behalf of a friend. In his Slack message, Benioff wrote, "New employees (hired during the pandemic in 2021 & 2022) are especially facing much lower productivity. Is this a reflection of our office policy? . . . Asking for a friend. . . ."

In sending this message, Benioff was trying to downplay the seriousness of a controversial topic. Unfortunately for Benioff, his message came across as critical and condescending. Salesforce employees responded with sarcastic pro-work-from-home statements, requests for references for applying to jobs outside of Salesforce, and less-than-supportive emojis. Benioff's message was made public and went viral against his wishes. He later chastised his employees for sharing his internal communications with the media, which likely didn't help repair his relationship with employees.

Benioff's message garnered the complete opposite reaction to what he intended. So, what went wrong?

The issue is that people are chronically bad at accurately relaying and interpreting emotions in less rich modes of communication (e.g., text and email), where we don't have the added information that nonverbal and audio cues provide. Worse, most people don't realize this near-universal shortcoming. The result of this misalignment between expectations and outcomes can lead to conflict and even ruin relationships.

Right now, I want you to think of a song that you're confident most people would know. Once you've chosen your song, tap it out on the nearest hard surface without singing it out loud.

Done?

If you were to find someone and tap out that same song again, how likely do you think it is they'd be able to identify it?

In her dissertation at Stanford, Elizabeth Newton studied this exact scenario and found that participants who tapped out a song the way you just did predicted that about 50 percent of listeners would be able to correctly guess the title. Here's the interesting part. After playing out the scenario, the actual accuracy rate was 3 percent.

What accounts for such a big difference between predictions and actual outcomes?

When you're tapping out the song on your desk, you're singing it along in your head. It seems completely obvious which song you're tapping, because you can "hear" it. But put yourself on the other side of this experiment. See if you can guess what song I'm tapping:

Taaa-p tap-tap tap tap. Taaa-p tap-tap tap tap....

Did you get it?

It was "Happy Birthday," of course!

When you know which song I'm tapping, it makes sense. When you just read or hear the taps without musical accompaniment, you're missing the critical context necessary to make an accurate guess.

A similar effect occurs when you're communicating with someone via text. You may think your message unambiguously relays your sarcasm, enthusiasm, or humor. But the person receiving your message doesn't have the same insight into your intentions. They're missing the information that has led you to assume your emotions are clearly displayed on the [virtual] page. Thus they're going to interpret your message without understanding the motivations and emotions that inspired you in the first place. Further, without being able to read your facial expressions or hear your tone of voice, text miscommunication can quickly spiral out of control.

If I write an email to one of my research assistants that starts with "Thanks for the first draft," there are a variety of ways they can interpret it (e.g., genuine, sarcastic, encouraging, dissatisfied). If I'm standing in front of them and say the same words, they can hear my intonation and see my facial expressions. Without that additional information, there is a lot more guesswork about the intentions behind an email or instant message. As a result, more nuanced emotions are harder to accurately convey and interpret.

Research led by New York University professor Justin Kruger applied the song-tapping concept specifically to emails. Kruger's team gave participants a list of twenty email sentences that had been written by someone else in the study, and asked them to identify whether each statement was sarcastic or not. The initial sentence writers were asked to predict how likely it was that their sarcasm (or lack thereof) would be correctly identified.

By now, you probably have a good idea about what happened.

Like in the song-tapping study, participants turned out to be over-confident that their (non)sarcastic statements would be correctly interpreted. There was too much guesswork involved because participants were missing necessary context, such as verbal emphasis on certain words, eye rolls, or knowledge about the message sender's personality.

When we are overconfident that others will correctly interpret our emails, we are making assumptions that our message recipient has the same knowledge we do. The worst part is that we don't even realize it's happening. Even though people may understand, in general, that text-based communication can lead to misinterpretations, they tend to assume it is just related to messages written by others because they're overconfident in their own abilities to clearly compose a message. To this point, a survey found that, on average, employees believed their coworkers needed additional email training, but that they themselves did not. It turns out that *egocentrism*, which embodies the challenge of separating oneself from one's own perspective, is the culprit behind a lot of virtual communication breakdowns.

Kruger's team took their findings a step further, asking a group of participants to write an email, but before they sent it, to read it aloud using a tone that was different from their intended meaning. That meant that sarcastic messages were read in a bland way, and vice versa. This exercise made sarcastic messages sound less sarcastic, and nonsarcastic messages sound more acerbic. Simply changing their tone of voice made the participants realize the statements they had written were ambiguous, since reading them in a different tone could completely alter their meaning. And, just as changing tone could alter a statement's meaning, a complete absence of tone could similarly cause misinterpretations. This exercise decreased participants' overconfidence and more accurately calibrated their expectations of a recipient's ability to properly interpret their message.

If you're not sure whether your message is explicitly conveying your intended emotions, try reading it aloud in an inflectionless voice, and consider whether the meaning would change if you used a more enthusiastic or sarcastic tone. I'm not saying you need to start narrating all of your text-based messages in different voices (although it could be entertaining); I am suggesting that you consider that the "voice" you hear when you're writing an email or instant message may not be the same one your recipient uses when reading.

Here's the other problem we're all up against when trying to get the emotional tone of a message right: work-related emails tend to be interpreted more negatively than intended. Syracuse University's Kristin Byron highlighted two biases related specifically to email message interpretations: the neutrality and negativity effects. Due to the neutrality effect, people don't readily notice positive emotions in email and are more likely to perceive them as neutral. Even less ideal, the negativity effect means that people interpret negative emotions in email as more intense than they actually are. That means we're starting from a deficit when it comes to conveying positive emotions in emails.

In order to offset these effects, remember that message senders probably aren't as upset as their emails might make them seem. When you're the sender, keep in mind that positive sentiments will come off a little less strongly, and negative ones will be even stronger than you intended.

To reduce the risk of your emotions being misinterpreted, increase the amount of clarity and feedback you're providing. For instance, instead of writing "Good work on the project so far. Let's move on to the next milestone," try something like "Excellent work on the project so far! I really liked how you did X, but could you add more detail about Y? When we move on to the second milestone, let's keep the approach the same as it's great. Thanks everyone!" By reducing the ambiguity in your messages, there will be less room for (mis)interpretation. When you're on the receiving end of work-related text messages, in addition to keeping the neutrality and negativity biases at the top of your mind, similarly beware of making assumptions about what the sender was feeling.

One of my mentors used to reply to many of my emails with an ellipsis (. . .) at the end of each of his messages. For instance, he'd reply to my message about a proposed study with

> That's a good idea . . .

Given that I was concerned he wouldn't like my ideas, I "heard" that kind of response in a somewhat sarcastic and unimpressed voice. The mere presence of the ellipsis made it unclear to me (the recipient) how my mentor really felt about my work. Months later, while we were on a call, I finally decided to ask what he meant by including the ellipsis at the end of his messages.

His response—and I remember, because it was such an *aha!* moment for me—was "It doesn't mean anything; it's just how I end most of my emails to indicate that the conversation is ongoing."

You can imagine how ridiculous I felt hearing that after I'd spent months worrying about the emotional subtext of his ellipses. When I stopped overinterpreting those three little dots, I found that his messages suddenly started seeming much more positive.

Instead of making assumptions, just ask. Much like the song-tapping study, without the audio and other nonverbal context clues, what you see as obvious emotional displays might appear to your recipient as nothing more than a series of taps. You therefore need to be overly explicit with your emotions in low-richness virtual communication. Beyond reducing emotional misinterpretations, it can save you a whole lot of needless worrying.

Head and Heart

We're all guilty of operating within the boundaries of our own egocentric preconceptions. The challenge, therefore, is to take the initiative to put ourselves in others' [virtual] shoes.

LinkedIn CEO Jeff Weiner did an excellent job at engaging in perspective taking when writing an email to LinkedIn employees to announce its acquisition by Microsoft:

> No matter what you're feeling now, give yourself some time to process the news. You might feel a sense of excitement, fear, sadness, or some combination of all of those emotions. Every member of the exec team has experienced the same, but we've had months to process.

Here, Weiner avoided making assumptions about how others felt and recognized there would be a diversity of views. Further, he managed to both show an understanding of employees' emotions ("the exec team has experienced the same"), while still managing to avoid appearing inauthentic by noting how his position was benefited in the situation ("but we've had months to process"). Weiner was attuned to the fact that the rest of the organization wasn't operating under the same facts and assumptions as he was, and he gracefully acknowledged that everyone would react to the news differently and would need time to process. This is a prime example of how, if we want to avoid egocentrism leading to virtual miscommunication, perspective taking is key.

When it comes to perspective taking, however, there can be *too much of a good thing*. You need to be wary about crossing the line over to empathy, which can cause your efforts to backfire.

Let's say you're the owner of a gas station. You've done relatively well for yourself, but now you're looking to sell the business. You have one interested buyer whom you're in the process of negotiating with. You've reached a slight snag in the communication process because the lowest price you're willing to accept is slightly higher than the amount your buyer, let's call them Cheapskate, is willing to pay. You're about to walk away from the deal when Cheapskate happens to mention something that piques your interest: they want to hire you back as a manager once the deal is completed. That aligns with your goals, because if you're going to pay off the sailing trip you're planning to take, then you will need a steady income. If Cheapskate hires you back as a manager after the deal closes, then you don't need to capture as much value for the sale of the gas station. You agree on a price and terms to hire you as the manager once you return from your sailing trip. You shake hands (virtually) and close the deal. Good job—now, go get packing for your sailing trip!

This scenario (with some minor embellishments on my part—ahem, Cheapskate) was created by a research team led by Adam Galinsky at Columbia Business School to test the degree to which perspective taking led to a successful deal. The catch was that the participants needed to identify their overlapping interest about managing the gas station through the course of their communication (i.e., it wasn't stated in their negotiation role sheets).

The study participants were split into three groups. The first group was the control condition, and they were simply given their role instructions and told to focus on their own goals. A second group of participants took on the perspective-taking role. They were given these additional instructions: "In preparing for the negotiation and during the negotiation, take the perspective of the service-station owner. *Try to understand what they are thinking, what their interests and purposes* are in selling the station. Try to imagine *what you would be thinking in that role.*" The final group—the empathy group—was given the following instructions: "In preparing for the negotiation and during the negotiation, take the perspective of the service-station owner. *Try to understand what they are feeling, what emotions they may be experiencing* in selling the station. Try to imagine *what you would be feeling in that role.*" Note the shift from "thinking" in the second group to "feeling" in the third group. After the negotiation, participants were asked to rate how happy they were with the way they were treated during the conversation.

While it shouldn't be surprising that the perspective-taking group reached more deals than the control group, there was a very unexpected finding. The third group, who went beyond perspective taking into empathy, was less successful than the second group. The reason was because the empathetic negotiators actually experienced an emotional response to their negotiation partner's experience.

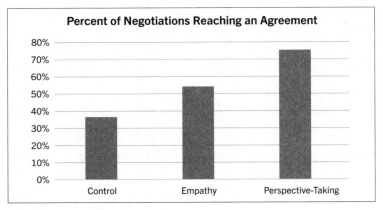

Perspective taking improves negotiation outcomes compared to empathy, due to the tendency of individuals engaging in empathy to detrimentally overlook their own interests.

Perspective taking reduces the egocentric bias (which is faulty evaluation due to overreliance on your perspective), helping us to avoid making assumptions that can lead to miscommunications on the other end of our text (or email). When you're perspective taking, you're considering the other person's motives and how they feel. At the same time, you still have your personal objectives and interests in mind. In other words, you're not losing sight of your own goals, even if you are attentive to the person (or people) on the receiving end of your communication. Empathy, on the other hand, takes this consideration of your communication partner to a whole other level. When you're being empathetic, you're actually experiencing the other person's feelings and motivations as though they were your own. While in many cases it's commendable to be selfless and put other people's needs before your own, empathy can be problematic when it causes you to sabotage your self-interests. For instance, consider a startup founder who is trying to sell his product to a multibillion-dollar company. Because the startup founder really cares about the feelings of the company representative he's been communicating with, he offers his product at a massive discount. A deal is made, and everyone at the company is thrilled. The representative from the multibillion-dollar company gets a hefty year-end bonus, and the startup goes bankrupt and has to fire all their employees due to cash-flow issues stemming from the deal. These types of selfless decisions can be harmful both for the business and the empaths themselves.

All that said, when it comes to empathy in virtual communication, you have to consider the possibility of competing goals. Generally, going beyond perspective taking into empathy won't help you from a purely economic sense, but it can help you to build long-term relationships. If your goal is to make the other person feel satisfied, then empathy may be a good bet. But if you're looking for the optimal (and most creative) personal or joint virtual communication outcomes, perspective-take without tipping over into empathy territory.

Mind (Reader) over Matter

Once you start considering all the ways your virtual emotions might be misinterpreted, it's easy to fall down a rabbit hole of worrying that you'll need to clarify every sentence and perspective-take for even the simplest messages. There is one piece of good news, however. You don't have to be as concerned about getting into other people's heads when you're interacting with a person or group you have a longer-term relationship with. To explain why, let me give you a couple of examples.

Let's say you just received the following email from a colleague you barely know: "I don't know what you did. It's broken." The message seems like it might have some emotional undertones. Is the other person angry? Annoyed? What are they even talking about? In this situation, you likely won't feel confident in your interpretation of that person's intentions while they were writing the message. In contrast, imagine receiving the same message from your spouse or close friend. In this case, you'll likely know exactly what the other person meant at a quick glance—no extra interpretation needed. Whereas with strangers it's hard to "read between the lines," there is no need to engage in this process with closer friends and colleagues, because you already have all the information you need. You know their perspective almost as well as you know your own.

The research theory that provides evidence of this phenomenon is known as Channel Expansion Theory. The core idea behind this theory is that the richness of virtual communication modes isn't solely objective to the technology itself (e.g., email is always lower richness than phone), but rather the richness of the mode is also dependent on contextual factors related to familiarity: To whom and about what are you interacting? For instance, communicating over email with your closest colleague may effectively be "richer," in that more emotion can be relayed and properly interpreted, than interacting with a complete stranger via an audio call. Despite the latter mode allowing for tone of voice interpretation, the lack of familiarity would still leave more room for confusion and miscommunication. Thus, the more you interact with someone over a given mode, the richer the interaction will become. If your team communicates predominately over email, you'll all begin to develop a better understanding of each other's intended meanings, such that the need for perspective taking and being overly explicit will become less necessary with time.

When it comes to the choice of communication mode, there may be no downside to using "leaner" communication media (e.g., email and instant messaging) for established groups who already have a good rapport. However, when meeting team members for the first time or working with new clients, a richer mode—such as phone or video—can ensure interactions flow smoothly without the danger of conflict-inducing misinterpretations.

One question I often get from business leaders is: Do I really need to consider all of these factors—if there's potential for confusion, can I just add in an emoji?

Smiley and the World Smileys with You. Or Does It?

A flaxseed farmer in Saskatchewan, Canada, found himself in a seedy (pun intended) dispute with a customer who hadn't received the flax he'd ordered. The problem was that the grain buyer thought the contract had been accepted due to a text exchange between them. The farmer disagreed.

The issue was that the buyer had sent a contract via a text message. The farmer responded with a thumbs-up emoji. The question that remained was whether emojis counted as an acceptance of the contract.

Their dispute made it to the courts, where a judge determined that, yes, the thumbs-up meant the contract had been accepted. The farmer was subsequently ordered to pay almost $62,000 USD in damages.

That's one rye-diculously expensive emoji.

In his written opinion, Judge T. J. Keene wrote, "I am satisfied on the balance of probabilities that Chris okayed or approved the contract just like he had done before except this time he used a 👍 emoji."

It seems difficult to take a decision summary seriously when the court ruling used twenty-four emojis itself, but there you have it.

This court-directed decision to count emojis as comparable to written statements wasn't an isolated event. A twelve-year-old student in Virginia was charged for posting emojis of a gun, knife, and bomb to her Instagram. A man in France was imprisoned after texts to his ex-girlfriend that contained a gun emoji were deemed threatening.

The issue with emojis is that they convey a great deal with just an image, yet there is too much left open to interpretation. This ambiguity can get emoji senders into trouble. Similar to our wording choices in virtual communication, we tend to be overconfident that our emojis will be correctly interpreted.

The solution doesn't necessarily require reducing your emoji count (heaven forbid) to improve emotion interpretation. Rather, you need to make the implicit explicit—in other words, be overly explicit with your emotions in virtual interactions to avoid misinterpretations. Before you start thinking that you'll need to qualify every thumbs-up with a "This emoji means I like your idea but am not officially agreeing to it," let's take a deeper dive into the science of using emojis to digitally communicate emotion. Knowing how your text-generated emotions compare to the real thing will help you make an informed choice about which mode to choose depending on your communication goals.

Psychologist Ella Glikson and her team set out to discover whether a smiling-face emoji is an acceptable replacement for a genuine in-person smile in business contexts. Specifically, they asked: Are smileys received as warmly in first impressions as a real in-person smile?

To test the impact of actual smiles, smileys, and no smiles whatsoever in first impressions, participants were split into four groups: "(1) a photographed neutral face, (2) a photographed smiling face, (3) a greeting text without smileys, and (4) a greeting text with smileys."

The research team measured how each of the conditions stacked up on the dimensions of warmth and competence. As you'd expect, when someone smiled, they were seen as the most warm and competent. Smileys, on the other hand, only increased warmth a slight amount and—here's the really interesting part—*reduced* how competent readers perceived the message sender to be compared to the message that contained text sans smileys.

When you use an emoji, you're signaling casualness, which results in more negative first impressions about your work competence. And it gets even worse. Not only did smileys in initial interactions reduce first impressions of competence, but due to this worsened perception, the study found that people were less willing to share information with those who used emojis in their initial interaction.

On the bright side, Glikson's team found that for first impressions in more informal work contexts (e.g., asking a question about a social gathering of coworkers), using emojis increased warmth and had no impact on perceived competence. Note that these results are about first impressions rather than established relationships, the latter of which are less likely to be negatively impacted by emojis (since by that point, impressions are fairly established). It's first impressions in more formal business contexts where the smiley can lead you astray.

When in doubt about whether you should use an emoji, revert to a strategy I shared in Chapter 6 and engage in language mimicry. If your colleagues pepper their messages with emojis, then you can respond in kind without sacrificing perceptions about your competence. If you only get formally worded, emoji-free messages from a coworker, then probably save the smileys for another time (or text).

Ketchup-gate. Or, Take Caution Before Sending a *Saucy* Message.

Now let's consider what happens when virtual conflicts go awry.

Awhile back, a London legal secretary named Jenny spilled ketchup on one of her boss's pants (or trousers, if you will). The lawyer then sent the following email to Jenny:

> Hi Jenny, I went to a dry cleaners at lunch and they said it would cost £4 to remove the ketchup stains. If you'd let me have the cash today, that would be much appreciated. Thanks

After Jenny failed to promptly reply to the email, he had a colleague leave a Post-it note on Jenny's desk to reiterate the debt. Upon finding the note, Jenny replied to her boss's email. She also cc'd hundreds of law firm employees onto the message:

Subject: Re: Ketchup trousers.
With reference to the email below, I must apologize for not getting back to you straight away but due to my mother's sudden illness, death and funeral I have had more pressing issues than your £4.

I apologize again for accidentally getting a few splashes of ketchup on your trousers. Obviously your financial need as a senior associate is greater than mine as a mere secretary.

Having already spoken to and shown your email and [colleague's] note to various partners, lawyers and trainees in ECC&T and IP/IT, they kindly offered to do a collection to raise the £4.

I however declined their kind offer but should you feel the urgent need for the £4, it will be on my desk this afternoon. Jenny.

Clearly not a great look (ketchup-stained or otherwise) for this lawyer. Now, it's entirely possible that this lawyer is normally a very affable boss—maybe he'd had a bad morning and getting ketchup on his pants was the last straw. Whatever the case, that message ended up going viral after it was shared, making him a subject for ridicule worldwide. And that's the point.

I know it can be extra tricky to rationally consider your communication mode when you're feeling emotional, but it's worth remembering that anything you put in writing can be shared or made public without your knowledge. Before sending this kind of text or email, ask yourself: *Would I be okay with this message being shared with everyone in my company?* If the answer is no, then a rewrite (or choosing a different mode altogether) will be in order. After all, no one relishes (sorry—I couldn't resist) becoming a laughingstock because of a message they sent in the heat of the moment.

The advice of *don't send a message when you're upset* may seem obvious, and yet emotions push us to action rather than thoughtful deliberation. As you saw with the GlaxoSmithKline data-hiding scandal I described in Chapter 1, even CEOs fall prey to DWI . . . or digital writing impulsivity. And that is not something you want on your record, driving or otherwise. From high school students to executives, none of us are immune to acting before thinking. When it comes to virtual communication, these rash choices can become permanent, which is why they need to be approached with the utmost care. That's not to say you should never put an emotional or emotion-provoking message in writing. Sometimes getting your message out there is the best way to reach your goals.

Emotion-omics

Dave Carroll, a member of the Canadian band Sons of Maxwell, was flying United Airlines with his band and their guitars during a one-week tour. During a layover, passengers saw the baggage handlers roughly tossing around the guitars. When Carroll arrived at his destination, he found that his Taylor guitar, worth $3,500, was badly damaged. After months of back-and-forth with United representatives, Carroll was eventually told that United wouldn't compensate him for his loss. Frustrated, Carroll performed a song about his experience and shared it on YouTube, where it garnered over 22 million views.

In the refrain, set to a catchy (guitar-led) tune, Carroll sings,

> I should've flown with someone else
>
> . . .
>
> 'Cause United breaks guitars.

As the viral video continued circling the internet, a reporter claimed that the song was responsible for United's recent tanking stock, which equated to a loss of about $180 million. There's a great deal of debate about whether (and how much) Carroll's viral video can be attributed to United's financial downswing, but it didn't stop several variations of the news headline from appearing elsewhere. What's clear is that the attention Carroll's song garnered certainly didn't do United any favors and was likely one of several contributing factors to the drop in stock price.

In this case, Carroll effectively channeled his anger and frustration into a public video that caught overwhelming attention. And he probably helped his own band's international recognition while he was at it. The lesson here is that sometimes it pays to choose a permanent, easily shareable communication mode when you're trying to have a big emotional impact. You just want to make sure the mode you choose is aligned with your goals, and that if your message does go viral, you're prepared for the potential consequences.

Collective emotions in virtual communication have the power to destroy and revive reputations, as evidenced by an online community that managed to send all of Wall Street into a panic. GameStop, a brick-and-mortar videogame retailer, had been slowly failing for years. But in January 2021, something inexplicable happened: its stock jumped 2,000 percent over the course of a single month. Shares that had been selling for $18 were now worth $350.

GameStop hadn't made any big announcements or done anything dramatic. Instead, the gains were all due to a small group of amateur day traders who congregate on the social and discussion website Reddit. The Reddit group, "wallstreetbets," collectively decided to exploit hedge funds that were "short selling"—a risky bet that involves selling "borrowed" shares of a stock and then purchasing them at a future date (in hopes that the price will go down in the meantime)—GameStop's stock. By quickly driving up the stock price, the short sellers would lose all the money they'd "bet" on GameStop's prices falling even more.

What was the goal of this endeavor? For many, it wasn't profits, as you might rightfully suppose. Instead, wallstreetbets was motivated by something more emotional. In a word: anger.

Frustrated that the large financial institutions were making enormous profits while individuals struggled, the members of this Reddit group displayed "stick-it-to-the-man" energy by quickly driving up the price of GameStop's stock. The result was a $20 billion loss in a single month for Wall Street hedge funds that were short-selling the stock. Author Kurt Andersen described it as "almost a kind of collective work of satirical art."

The cumulative anger of this Reddit forum gained traction and resulted in a very real financial ramification. And there are plenty of other examples of people rallying together on text-based communication modes to effectively express and spread strong emotions.

A group of researchers led by Arik Cheshin at the Israel Institute of Technology examined *emotion contagion*—the unconscious process whereby individuals "catch," or begin to feel, emotions another individual is displaying—in text-based communication modes. They discovered that both happiness and anger can spread via text similarly to the way it occurs in person. However, given that text provides fewer nonverbal cues to judge this information, they found that people tried to identify their communication partner's emotions from their behaviors. In their study, Cheshin's team showed that when virtual team members displayed resoluteness (i.e., stood their ground), they were perceived by others as angry. In contrast, when flexible behaviors were displayed (i.e., a willingness to cooperate), teammates were seen as happy. With these findings in mind, it's important to be aware that virtual emotions are inferred not only from our words and emojis, but from our broader behaviors as well.

So, to summarize: If you're seeing (ketchup) red, be wary of putting your thoughts down in writing. When we're emotional, we tend to be doggedly convinced we're in the right. If you find yourself in that position, take a moment to breathe and look past your emotions long enough to rationally reflect on how your message might be perceived. Consider first running your message by your accountability partner (Chapter 2) to get their impression of how you will be perceived by others outside of the interaction itself, who may have limited context, before sending it in a way that could be shared with the world. Seeking out someone to play devil's advocate can also give you much-needed perspective before hitting the send or post button. If you are sending an emotional message via an easily shareable platform, it should be because you have a compelling reason for using that particular mode (e.g., you intentionally want it viewed by lots of people and know without a doubt it will be interpreted as you intended).

Boiling Points and Virtual Chill Pills

Beyond purely emotionally driven messages, there's another interaction category that gets even thornier with virtual communication: negotiations. Negotiating is an inescapable—and often stress-inducing—part of our jobs and lives. Actress and writer Carrie Fisher once said that "Everything is negotiable. Whether or not the negotiation is easy is another thing." Whether you are participating in traditional negotiations as a customer or vendor, trying to negotiate a salary raise with your boss, or engaging in more informal negotiations with your loved ones (or hey, trying to sell a book ☺), having the skills to tackle these tricky interpersonal situations virtually isn't just valuable—it's a necessity.

Negotiating is difficult enough in person, but when done virtually, the number of choices (e.g., which mode to use and how to best communicate your meaning) can be overwhelming. Let's say you've taken on enormous new responsibilities at work and have gotten great performance evaluations. You know the next promotion cycle is coming up, and you're confident you've done the work necessary to get a title upgrade and significant pay raise. Here's the rub: your immediate supervisor isn't the easiest person to get along with. You know them to be aggressive, quick-talking, and generally unwilling to budge from their immediate gut instinct.

If you're like most people, this scenario would be pretty intimidating. And when we get nervous, many of us default to choosing email over richer communication modes, since it gives us a feeling of safety and prevents a rapid back-and-forth negotiation that can be flustering and cause us to say things in the heat of the moment that don't serve our purposes.

The problem with this logic is that research shows that in negotiations, choosing email and other forms of text-based virtual communication over richer modes generally leads to more impasses, lower profits, and less collaborative behavior—especially when there isn't a preexisting relationship. In a meta-analysis of over thirty studies that compared face-to-face versus virtual negotiations, the former were found to be less hostile and generally more successful in reaching a better joint outcome. When the person you're negotiating with is in front of you, there's more humanity (and less anonymity) to the interaction, which prevents your negotiation partner from thinking of you as nothing more than words on a screen. Furthermore, more synchronous modes allow you to quickly identify when the conversation is going downhill (e.g., mistaken assumptions, miscommunication, or negative affect) and change course before the damage is done.

When you're engaging in negotiation or conflict resolution, even though it might feel less "safe," it's usually best to choose a richer communication mode, such as phone or video. That's not to say, however, that you should always avoid email. In some specific situations, it can be exactly what you need.

Steve Jobs, known as one of the premier negotiators of the twenty-first century, was a master at using email to navigate incredibly high-stakes deals. One such email conversation was between Apple and News Corp. Jobs, then CEO of Apple, was negotiating with News Corp executive James Murdoch on several issues simultaneously as the two sought a partnership for eBook distribution. Specifically, Apple was planning to announce the launch of the iPad, and they wanted users to be able to purchase e-books right on the tablet. Several of the major publishers were already on board, but HarperCollins, which was owned by News Corp, was holding out until several of their requests were met. In a nutshell, HarperCollins wanted to set the e-book prices themselves.

Over the course of several email exchanges, Jobs pushed back on HarperCollins/News Corp's requests.

From: Steve Jobs <sjobs@apple.com>
Date: January 24, 2010 11:31:24 AM PST
To: James Murdoch [REDACTED]
Cc: Steve Jobs <sjobs@apple.com>
Subject: Re: HarperCollins

James,
Our proposal does set the upper limit for ebook retail pricing based on the hardcover price of each book. The reason we are doing this is that, with our experience selling a lot of content online, we simply don't think the ebook market can be successful with pricing higher than $12.99 or $14.99. Heck, Amazon is selling these books at $9.99, and who knows, maybe they are right and we will fail even at $12.99. But we're willing to try at the prices we've proposed. We are not willing to try at higher prices because we are pretty sure we'll all fail.

As I see it, HC has the following choices:
1. Throw in with Apple and see if we can all make a go of this to create a real mainstream ebooks market at $12.99 and $14.99.
2. Keep going with Amazon at $9.99. You will make a bit more money in the short term, but in the medium term Amazon will tell you they will be paying you 70% of $9.99. They have shareholders too.

3. Hold back your books from Amazon. Without a way for customers to buy your ebooks, they will steal them. This will be the start of piracy and once started there will be no stopping it. Trust me, I've seen this happen with my own eyes.

Maybe I'm missing something, but I don't see any other alternatives. Do you?

Regards,
Steve

In this one email, Jobs employed a few interesting strategies that helped bridge the gap on various issues. By providing a comparison with Amazon, Jobs made the terms he was offering (and News Corp was challenging) seem more favorable. He was also using time to his advantage; because the iPad announcement was only days away, the News Corp representatives knew they needed to make a quick decision.

Jobs clearly laid out all the issues in his email, making the different pieces of information visible and impossible to miss. He also took a hard, yet well-reasoned stance. He refused to bend to News Corp's requests by providing precise reasoning for each of his points. By ending his email with a question, and basically putting it back to his negotiation partners to find an alternative solution, Jobs effectively transformed adversaries into collaborators. The subtext in this case was that, failing to offer up a superior alternative, the News Corp team would have to default to Apple's proposal. Which they ultimately did. One day before Apple announced the iPad, the two reached an agreement.

There are a couple of reasons why email worked especially well in this case, and which you can use to inform your choices about when to use it during a negotiation. When you have a lot of points that you want to lay out explicitly, as Jobs did, email can be better than phone or video. If you have a particularly strong position (as Jobs did), emailing your negotiation terms will give your opponent time to fully process your relative strength. The asynchronous nature of email can also be advantageous when you're on the right side of a high time-pressure situation. In Jobs's case, he likely knew that the deadline for a deal was fast approaching (and since the deadline coincided with a publicly announced product launch, there was no chance of extending the timeline). The News Corp team presumably didn't know exactly when Jobs would respond to their message, so they were under additional pressure to resolve all the issues in a single message rather than going back and forth on individual issues.

Beyond the more practical rationale, there are also more emotion-driven reasons why email can sometimes be the best option. Jason Fried, cofounder of Basecamp—a project management tool that centralizes communication—sat down to talk with me (virtually, of course) about a time when text communication actually helped him to salvage a deal that had gone south. He told me about a negotiation he was conducting for a high-priced domain name. The negotiation got heated, and the deal fell through.

Jason took some time away from the conversation and reflected on what had happened. The next morning, he wrote a follow-up email:

> Hey [Name],
>
> My competitive spirit got the best of me. I slept on it and thought about it this morning, and I'm sorry. Can we start this over?
>
>   Jason

This concise message served a few functions. First, it reopened the channel of communication. When I asked Jason why he chose email over phone, he explained that he wanted to give his negotiation partner time to process and decide if he wanted to continue their conversation where it had left off. In this one short email, Jason effectively took his counterparty's perspective and realized that, even though he'd had a chance to think through their prior conversation, it was possible the other person hadn't. By using email (rather than phone or video), he gave the other person space to similarly consider what they wanted and whether (and how) they wanted to move forward. Because of this thoughtful approach to communication mode, the two started their negotiation again and were ultimately able to complete the deal. In this case, email's asynchronous nature provided enough time for everyone's tempers to cool so they could move beyond their differences. This extra time gave both parties a way of saving face by allowing them to "leave" and "come back" to the negotiation table. Additionally, the time lag of emails enables negotiators to come up with creative solutions that likely wouldn't be considered in a more synchronous conversation. Lastly, as an added benefit, research on less rich modes of communication has shown they can be more beneficial in situations that are likely to involve high levels of conflict. The reason is that lower-richness modes mask conflict-reinforcing negative nonverbal behaviors. In other words, over email you can't see someone angrily glowering or rolling their eyes at you, which can help make interactions more cooperative than they would have been otherwise.

As you saw from Jason's story, having an argument over email may seem like an awful idea (re: Ketchup trousers), but in some cases, email can be best because it provides an opportunity to walk away from the conflict—at least temporarily—thereby deescalating "hot" emotions.

In sum, it's generally best to default to richer modes for negotiations, except in cases when there is a particular benefit to asynchronicity (e.g., leveraging time pressure) that meaningfully outweighs the advantages of more synchronous and richer modes (ease of information exchange, being able to better observe counterparty nonverbal behaviors, etc.). However, regardless of which mode the interaction occurred over, a virtual communication best practice (indeed, this strategy also applies to in-person conversations) is to send a thank-you email after the conversation. This strategy will serve two functions. First, thanking other people for their time and input is just polite, and it will help in your relationship-building efforts. Second—and this is one of the strongest benefits of digital communication—it will create a record of the conversation. A key strategy I often recommend to MBA students taking my negotiation course to combat the reality of different recollections (whether inadvertent or intentional) is to follow up any negotiation with a thank-you email (which should be the apparent primary "purpose" of the message). In this message, I suggest including a brief summary of the agreement (which is actually the main purpose of the message). Having this text-based record of an agreement gives you the paper-trail advantage of email even if it wasn't the mode over which you negotiated, and it can save headaches resulting from having to renegotiate potentially millions of dollars due to a misunderstanding.

Digital Diplomacy

In his book *Working with Emotional Intelligence*, Daniel Goleman writes, "We're being judged by a new yardstick: not just by how smart we are, or by our training and expertise, but also how well we handle ourselves and each other." Even when we're not standing face-to-face, we're communicating information about ourselves and our emotions. The danger is that, with a lack of other information to clue us in to how our communication partners are feeling, we make assessments based on the information available. And research shows that the choices we make in virtual communication—from emojis all the way down to our punctuation—communicate information that others will use to pass judgments about our mood and intentions. It's up to us, therefore, to make sure the emotions we're expressing over virtual communication are the ones we truly mean.

Is your goal to seem warm or competent? If your communication got spread around to others, how would that make you look? These are the questions that you need to ask yourself. Because if you don't, there's the danger that you're "saying" something—emotionally speaking—that you didn't intend. Now that you know how virtual miscommunication occurs, you can avoid the most common emotion and conflict pitfalls. Better yet, you'll be able to use emotions in your virtual communication to connect, persuade, and get ahead in your career.

KEY LESSONS
Perspective Taking
+ To avoid assuming your communication partners are operating under the same information and assumptions as you (egocentrism), put yourself in their shoes. Try reading your messages aloud before sending them. Does the meaning change if you keep your tone inflectionless versus adding sarcasm? With this practice, you'll convey your emotions more clearly and leave less room for misinterpretation.
+ If you want the best outcome for all parties, be careful not to cross the line from virtual communication perspective taking to empathy. You don't want to lose sight of your own interests in your quest to understand your communication partners.
+ When interacting with someone you know well, you don't need to worry as much about mode choice or being explicit about your intended emotions. The other person will already know your perspective and communication style well and be able to read between the lines.

Initiative
+ Instead of making assumptions about what a message sender meant, take the time to ask them. Chances are they were falling prey to the egocentric bias and never considered there might be other possible interpretations beyond their own.

Nonverbal

+ The lack of nonverbal cues in low-richness communication modes makes it difficult to accurately relay and interpret emotions. To avoid the misinterpretations, be explicit about your intended emotions.
+ Work-related text communication is interpreted more negatively on the whole, so it is useful to be overly positive in cases where you want your enthusiasm to come through.
+ In formal contexts, using smileys can make you seem less competent in a first interaction and make the other person less inclined to share information with you. On the other hand, using emojis in informal work contexts can make you seem warmer. If you're not sure whether or not to use an emoji, engage in language mimicry and do as your interaction partners do.
+ When interacting with someone you don't know well, using a richer mode will add back in the nonverbal cues (including tone in audio and facial expressions in video) that will provide needed emotional context.

Goals

+ When you find yourself in an emotional virtual communication situation, take a minute to breathe and try to examine your options rationally. Whether your objective is causing a stir or reducing conflict, you should choose your mode and message when you're in a cool state.
+ In general, richer communication modes are better for negotiations because they allow you to quickly iterate and identify if the conversation is headed south. Times when choosing a less synchronous mode is ideal would be when: 1) you are on the right side of time pressure (e.g., Steve Jobs), 2) you have a meaningfully stronger position that you want to clearly lay out and allow the other side to fully process, or 3) you want to give both sides time to cool down.

✦ To get the best of all worlds, in the context of negotiations, follow up with a thank-you email that contains a summary of your agreement. This way, even when negotiating via audio or video, you still create a written record of your deal while simultaneously increasing the odds of future cooperation.

8

We All Know What Happens When You Assume . . .

How to Use Communication Technologies to Reduce Stereotypes and Interpersonal Biases

We will all profit from a more diverse, inclusive society,
understanding, accommodating, even celebrating our differences,
while pulling together for the common good.
—Ruth Bader Ginsburg, US Supreme Court justice

When she joined Uber as a site reliability engineer (SRE) in 2015, Susan Fowler was ready to embark on a new challenge. There was a lot going on at the company, and Fowler was eager to roll up her sleeves and apply her engineering skills. After completing her initial training at the company and getting acquainted with her team, her experience at Uber took a turn for the weird.

During one of her first days, Fowler described conversations with her manager over the company chat in which he solicited her for sex. She said that he shared details about his open relationship and noted that "he was looking for women to have sex with."

When Fowler presented evidence of sexism and harassment to HR, she said she was given the brush-off and told that, because her manager was a high performer, he wouldn't get anything more than a warning.

In another instance, Fowler noted that the company purchased leather jackets for all the male engineers on her team—but refused to buy any that would fit the women in their organization. When she inquired further, Fowler recalled being told there weren't enough women to "justify placing an order."

When Fowler started working at Uber, the organization was more than 25 percent women. By the time of the leather jacket incident, it was less than 6 percent.

After documenting a number of sexual harassment issues, Fowler said she was told she might be the one responsible for instigating these problems, given that she was the "common theme" in each of her reports.

Fowler finally decided to cut her losses and get another job. Two years later, she wrote a blog post titled "Reflecting on One Very, Very Strange Year at Uber," which detailed her experiences with sexism at the company. In her post, Fowler noted a series of encounters that ranged from ridiculous to downright horrifying. Her blog ended up being shared twenty-two thousand times on X (formerly known as Twitter) and ultimately read by six million people. Six months before the #MeToo began, Fowler's post made other women in tech feel comfortable enough to share their own stories. That year, she was among those featured on the front cover of *Time*'s Person of the Year issue, alongside the text "The silence breakers: the voices that launched a movement."

There were two separate investigations into Uber, which resulted in hundreds more complaints about sexual harassment and bullying coming to the surface. The CEO resigned and other top Uber employees were fired. The company committed to revamping its policies in order to support sexual harassment and bullying victims like Fowler, and establishing a more inclusive culture.

Months after dealing with the fallout from Fowler's post, Uber found itself at the center of another sexism scandal that went viral. As part of a promotion, a local Uber Eats social media account shared a message reminding husbands that it was Wife Appreciation Day, and they should let their wives "take a day off from the kitchen" by ordering from Uber Eats (and they would receive an approximate $1.56 discount).

As you can imagine, the virtual backlash was swift and cutting. The message garnered reactions such as "Sorry @uber but why do you think that only the 'wife' needs to be at the kitchen!" and "Thank you @Uber for defining gender roles in India. Of course women are meant to slog it out in the kitchen & the men need to BUY us freedom." Uber swiftly reacted by removing the promotion and apologizing, saying, "This was totally inappropriate."

This seems like a particularly unflattering look for Uber, especially in light of the Susan Fowler blog post. But there's a detail of this story that muddies the waters a bit. The promotion was run in Bangalore, India, where there was very little reaction to the messaging. Most of the locals who were asked about the promotion hadn't even heard of it. Due to differing social and cultural norms at the time, there weren't any attention-worthy social media reactions or news headlines within the Bangalore community. It was only when the international community got wind of the promotion that it went viral. As BBC journalist Ayeshea Perera said, "If Uber is to be taken seriously, it will have to be careful to avoid carelessly worded messages like this one and come up with something more imaginative."

It's entirely possible Uber's message was posted by a local social media intern who was unaware of how foreigners might perceive it. And while it's likely no harm was meant by this promotion (the goal was likely to make money, not stir up controversy), it showcases one of the challenges of virtual communication—namely, that we can write messages that offend others without intending to (or even realizing what we've done). Because it's more permanent and easily shareable, virtual communication can be a megaphone both for discriminating against others and reducing discrimination. When a story like Fowler's is read by six million people, or a single promotion gains international traction on social media, the impact is exponentially greater than if it had been shared without virtual communication. Whether we're sending messages to someone from a different culture or making assumptions due to a lack of cues, there are additional considerations when virtually communicating with someone who is different from us.

Building Virtual Bridges, Not Barriers

Across the world, there have been ongoing conversations about the impact of virtual communication on more visible stereotypes, such as race, country of origin, gender, age, and disability. For those who don't visibly "fit" into the majority, the consequences of stereotypes are likely all too familiar. When it comes to communication technologies, which provide the safety of communicating behind a screen, a key question is whether these modes act as a "great equalizer" or worsen stereotypes. On one hand, it's possible that visible differences in our appearance (e.g., skin color) become less salient in virtual communication. In text, email, and phone, the other person's appearance is invisible altogether, and in video, the impact of physical differences is diminished because other people aren't standing right in front of us and drawing all our attention. Thus, physical differences may be less likely to alter how we treat each other virtually. On the other hand, it can be easier to marginalize others and be more aggressive in a digital environment due to the physical separation. Just because we can't readily see differences when we're communicating virtually doesn't mean we're not still making assumptions about our collaborators, and these interpersonal biases have the potential to aggregate over time.

To some extent, we're all impacted by biases whether you are from an underrepresented minority or not. For example, imagine you're a hiring manager for a computer programming position and you're presented with two candidates who have nearly identical résumés. The only difference between the candidates is that one is sixty-five years old and the other is thirty-five. Or consider a situation where you might be looking for a virtual health-and-wellness coach, and your two options are a male body builder versus a four-foot-nine transgender woman. In both scenarios, you probably have an image in your head of which person better fits the job description right off the bat. In many cases, our choices are impacted by preconceived notions about the traits a group is "supposed" to embody. We treat each other differently based on these expectations, which can work against us whether we're part of an underrepresented minority or a majority group. For instance, men who negotiate on behalf of someone else often achieve worse outcomes than women because being communal (i.e., helping someone else) is viewed more as a female rather than male quality. Biases and prejudgments have wide-reaching implications for the workplace and will influence others' impressions of you before you've had a chance to differentiate yourself—whether you're male, female, nonbinary, young, old, Black, white, Asian, wheelchair-bound, overweight, short, or tall.

In this chapter, we'll investigate how virtual communication has tremendous power to worsen or improve outcomes related to inclusion and equity. We'll examine how various modes can be used to reduce being personally impacted by biases and how to handle the most precarious of these situations. I'll offer advice both for making others feel more included and helping you to free yourself from others' negative expectations. You'll also learn which communication mode to choose to reduce the potential of biases, and how to use your virtual communication toolkit to enhance accessibility for others. When it comes to stereotypes and inclusion, virtual communication isn't unilaterally good or bad. It's up to us, therefore, to use communication tools to enhance inclusivity in the workplace.

Virtual Smoke and Mirrors

In 1993, a *New Yorker* cartoonist named Peter Steiner submitted an image that would become the most reproduced cartoon in the magazine's history. At a 2023 auction, it also became the most expensive single-panel cartoon ever sold. With eight words, Steiner—or rather the dog drawn sitting at a computer—became a meme that would resonate decades later as a symbol of the bright and dark side of online anonymity: "On the Internet, nobody knows you're a dog."

"On the Internet, nobody knows you're a dog."

Although there are benefits to the potential anonymity provided by virtual communication (which I'll get to shortly), there are downsides. We're more likely to unknowingly offend people we can't hear or see because we don't realize they're different from us—or because they don't realize we're different from them. Because virtual communication allows us to reach people more easily across the globe, there are more mistakes that result from our—often incorrect—assumption that the people we're interacting with are like us and have similar backgrounds and viewpoints. Additionally, because of the ease of shareability of most virtual communication, unintended audiences may end up interpreting our actions through differing values and lenses than our own—such as with the Uber Eats promotion fiasco I described earlier. In that case, the person who posted the promotion on a local social media account in Bangalore likely didn't consider how people on the other side of the world would interpret it.

Much like the song-tapping study we explored in the last chapter, it's human nature to assume others have the same baseline information as us, and thus will assess situations and communication similarly. But it's these very assumptions that can get us into trouble. When we're communicating across demographic divides, such misunderstandings and information gaps can be even starker.

There's a fascinating study led by University of Chicago psychologist Becky Ka Ying Lau in which Mandarin Chinese speakers were asked to estimate how well native English-speaking Americans would understand what they were saying in Chinese. The twist was the participants were fully aware that the Americans didn't understand any Chinese. In the study, there were twelve rounds during which Chinese speakers would say something, and the American listeners would try to guess their meaning from four options. Speakers were told to say the phrase in a way that would make it easier for the listener to choose the correct meaning from the options; however, the speaker and listener couldn't see each other (to avoid the complication of "reading" facial features and nonverbal communication). Then, the speakers were asked to predict how confident they were that the listener would select the correct meaning.

Can you guess what happened?

The Chinese speakers vastly overestimated how well the Americans would be able to understand what they were saying, in spite of the fact that they knew listeners had no linguistic knowledge that could help them. Funnily enough, the Americans who were listening also overestimated their understanding of the Chinese speakers. The American participants estimated that they had a 65 percent success rate in identifying the Mandarin phrases. As it turned out, they were only correct 35 percent of the time.

This mutual overoptimism was dubbed the "illusion of understanding," and it carries important implications for helping to reduce the impact of virtual miscommunication when there are culture, demographic, or language barriers. Knowing that your meaning is less transparent than you assume, and that you probably understand less than you think you do, should inspire more question-asking and fewer assumptions.

The Great Equalizer . . . Sort Of

Sociologist Sherry Turkle said that, when communicating virtually, "You can be whoever you want to be. You can completely redefine yourself if you want. You don't have to worry about the slots other people put you in as much. They don't look at your body and make assumptions. They don't hear your accent and make assumptions. All they see are your words." Like in Steiner's dog cartoon. In this sense, it's almost as though virtual communication can transcend visible differences and—in theory—create a space that will shield you from the judgments others make when they can see you. Race, age, attractiveness, socioeconomic status, and even species can become invisible. Virtual communication provides a refreshing ability to reinvent yourself. You can be anyone you want and be judged solely on the content of your messages, rather than the visible differences others use to make judgments before they really know you.

There are two specific ways in which virtual communication can be impactful in reducing interpersonal biases. The first is straightforward: when differences aren't known. In these cases, using low-richness modes like audio or text, as opposed to video, can keep differences hidden and therefore reduce any chances of bias. An example of a visual bias is what researchers identified as the "beauty premium," whereby more physically attractive employees can earn up to 15 percent higher salaries than those who are seen as having below-average beauty. A different study found that taller job candidates were viewed as more competent, and that every additional inch of height may be worth up to $897 extra per year in salary—incidentally why, at the time of the study, nearly 60 percent of Fortune 500 CEOs were men over six feet tall (even though only 14.5 percent of men in the general population are six feet or taller). Considering these findings, it is unlikely to come as a surprise that a study also found that "less physically attractive applicants" are more successful when they conduct their interview via phone rather than face-to-face. As psychology researcher Yair Amichai-Hamburger explains, in-person meetings are impacted by visible features that can "lead to labeling, stereotyping, and other distorted perceptions." This is why many organizations "mask" identifying characteristics like gender, race, and age during hiring, whether it involves utilizing programs to strip out identifying information from résumés, using audio-only interviews (to mask visual characteristics of interviewees), or having separate evaluators who only read the interview transcript after somebody else has conducted the interview. Although complete anonymity is the only surefire way to remove all biases, it is only relevant to a very narrow set of situations (e.g., job interviews) in which the participants don't know each other and building relationships isn't important.

The question then arises as to which communication mode is best for reducing interpersonal bias when differences *are* known. Here the answer is slightly more complex, because it depends on whose biases you want to reduce.

First, let's focus on communicators themselves. Research shows that virtual communication allows people to free themselves from the pressures they feel to conform to society's expectations of their role. For instance, a norm in many societies is that men are "supposed" to be more aggressive, while women are "supposed" to be warmer and more cooperative. In situations such as nego- tiations, which often require competitive behavior, women can be hurt by these societal expectations, as they feel pressure to be more cooperative. A review of thirty-five published research pa- pers revealed that when negotiations occurred virtually, women were more comfortable being aggressive, and thus achieved more successful outcomes. In situations where you or others might feel forced to conform to expectations set by the team, organization, or society, using less rich virtual communication modes can provide more freedom from these constraints.

When looking at how to reduce biases that people have against others, the recommendation flips. Although low-richness communi- cation modes allow people to behave more freely without worrying about others' expectations, they can also lead people to make assump- tions about others when differences are known.

Earlier in the book, I discussed how we tend to unconsciously fill in gaps in our knowledge about another person, and often rely on false assumptions and inherent biases in the process. In a series of studies run by psychologists Nicholas Epley and Justin Kruger, participants were asked to interview a candidate either via email or phone. They were then shown a picture of the person they were in- terviewing, who was either an Asian American woman or an Afri- can American woman. Unbeknownst to the study participants, the communication was identical irrespective of mode (the transcribed answers from audio interactions were the exact text provided in emails). Furthermore, they were actually interviewing a European American woman in all cases (i.e., the pictures were only used to manipulate race perceptions—the interviewee's race was irrelevant). One would imagine that participants would rate interviewees iden- tically regardless of perceived race and mode, since the wording of their messages was the same and all were generated by a white woman. However, Epley and Kruger found that stereotypes of race persisted strongly over email and effectively disappeared when the interviewer and interviewee interacted via audio.

The problem with less rich communication modes is that all the information we might have for a first conversation is that the other person is likely X gender and Y race based on their name . . . along with the few lines of text in their email. As a result, we generally end up picturing a generic person who embodies those characteristics when interacting with them. This unconscious process applies to any underlying stereotypes we may have. When we interact via richer modes, however, we have more information and can begin to imagine the person we are interacting with as an individual human being, rather than a more generic, all-encompassing category.

In sum, if your goal is to reduce stereotypes and interpersonal biases, there are two questions to ask yourself to determine the right choice of mode (which I summarize in the flowchart on the next page). First, is this an interaction in which differences are unknown? If the answer is yes, then choose less rich modes to mask these differences from becoming apparent. If the answer is no, then the follow-up question is whether you are more concerned about individuals being constrained by others' expectations of them, or if you are trying to reduce people's biases of those they're interacting with. If you are focused on the former, less rich communication is ideal once again, since the physical distance and lack of visual cues enable people to feel freer from others' expectations. If you're focused on the latter, then richer communication is ideal in order for people to build fuller pictures of each other as individuals. Whether you're meeting in person or virtually, it's important to be sensitive to biases and aware of the fact that creating an inclusive culture takes effort.

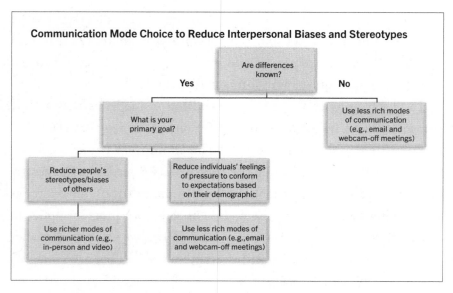

Communication Mode Choice to Reduce Interpersonal Biases and Stereotypes

If your primary goal is to reduce interpersonal bias and stereotypes, choosing the optimal communication mode depends on whether those differences are known and whose biases you want to reduce.

Forgive and Forget . . . but Only If You're Foreign

Let's say you receive the following email from someone in your company whom you've had no prior interactions with:

> Hello [Name],
> Please share the spreadsheat [*sic*] as soon as posible [*sic*]. I need to start inputting data immediately for the client meeting next week.
>
> Most Sincerely,
> [Name]

How do you feel about the person who wrote this email? The message is short . . . even a little demanding . . . and there's two spelling errors in the first sentence. And that "Most Sincerely" seems like overkill—maybe even condescending—especially when there were no niceties in the message body. If you're from North America, this message probably struck you as a bit rude and poorly written. However, the inherent assumption here is that the email writer (and not just reader) is also from North America.

What if I told you the person who wrote the email doesn't live in North America and isn't a native English speaker? Chances are, you'd view this email through a slightly different lens.

Error-free email senders are viewed as more competent, intelligent, trustworthy, and conscientious. Emails with grammatical mistakes or etiquette breaches result in snap negative judgments about those same traits. The exception, as we explored when discussing typos in Chapter 3, is when there is a valid reason for the mistake, such as sending a message from your smartphone or explaining that an emotional event preceded your message. It turns out that differences in culture have this same effect, where mistakes are attributed to background differences rather than competence and are thus less costly. The problem is that, due to the egocentric bias, we tend to be self-focused and often assume others are from a similar background to us unless we have clear evidence to the contrary.

When President Jimmy Carter visited Poland in 1977, he said that he was eager to learn about the Polish people's "desires for the future." His interpreter translated it as he sexually desired the Poles. When Carter said, "I left the United States this morning," it was translated to "I left the United States, never to return." Finally, when he expressed happiness to be in Poland, his interpreter translated it to happiness "to grasp at Poland's private parts."

Awkward.

I don't speak Polish, so I won't try to judge whether the interpreter made a few honest mistakes or was messing with the then-president. Either way, you can imagine how humorous this exchange must have been to the Polish audience. If, however, they didn't realize it was a foreigner who was speaking (say, if the exchange had occurred via text rather than in person), then their impressions might have been very different.

There's a concept in psychology called the *fundamental attribution error*, which explains how people tend to forget about a person's situation or context when judging the reasons for their choices, and instead attribute their actions to that person's underlying personality or abilities. Thus, a spelling error in an email can quickly be internalized as *this person isn't conscientious*. But—and this is a big *but*—that assumption is potentially flawed when you have no knowledge of the other person's background. While it is completely possible that they're a careless communicator, it's also possible that a language or cultural barrier, rather than sheer incompetence, resulted in the error.

While you probably (hopefully?) won't be in the position of accidentally propositioning someone from a different culture in a widely broadcast conversation, there is a decent chance that at some point in your career, you will inadvertently violate a norm when communicating with someone from a different culture. Since it's easier to read into cultural faux pas when communicating virtually due to the lack of nonverbal cues, you might understandably be even more concerned about having one such mistake live on in permanent infamy.

Fortunately for anyone who has made a language or etiquette error, researchers have discovered that when a message receiver knows the sender is from a different culture or speaks a different native language, these communication missteps aren't viewed as harshly. When participants in a study evaluated an email sender who violated language norms (e.g., spelling and grammatical errors) and etiquette norms (e.g., short messages lacking a conversational tone), they rated the person as less intelligent and conscientious. But, when provided with information that the sender was foreign, mistakes or divergences from etiquette norms were attributed to cultural differences rather than lack of ability. The bottom line is that knowing where other people are from provides crucial details that can inform the reason behind their communication choices.

Giving your communication partners this leeway is useful when interpreting their message and will work out better for your relationship in the long run.

The problem, of course, occurs when you're communicating virtually and may not be able to easily see whether your interaction partner is from a different geographic background. If you can't hear their voice, see their appearance, or quickly note their country of residence, how are you supposed to know whether an error is based on cultural differences or just a lack of attention to the communication itself? Missing context about your communication partner's background results in knowledge gaps that the unwary virtual communicator will unconsciously (and potentially mistakenly) attribute to their ability, rather than their background. For example, if you're in an in-person meeting in your company's San Diego office and a client joins your meeting after a long flight from the other side of the world, there are easily identifiable clues that can help provide context for any deviations from your communication norms. Are they speaking with an accent? Do they bow rather than shake hands? Are they dressed differently from you? All these details provide context that we unconsciously factor into our assessment of their behaviors. When we're communicating virtually, many of these cues are missing. Even for high-richness modes like video, the person we're meeting with could be joining the call from the other side of the world or two office buildings over. Most videoconferencing technologies provide no inherent means of identifying where the other person is from (unless they happen to be sitting in front of a window displaying a view of an iconic, location-specific building; even then, there's a chance it's a good background image rather than the real thing). When it comes to low-richness modes, such as email and instant messaging, you're missing all visible context clues about a person's identity. The result is that we often make a fundamental attribution error by believing communication or etiquette errors are necessarily due to another person's intelligence.

Realizing someone is from a different culture makes both parties more forgiving of virtual communication mistakes. While it may seem counterintuitive, being open about your differences (rather than hiding them) may give you extra latitude as you traverse cultural and other demographic boundaries. On the other side of the equation, be wary of assuming someone is incompetent (or unintelligent or untrustworthy) from the errors in their email message, and seek out more information about their context before rushing to judgment. Where you might be attributing errors to their capability and professionalism, it's possible there is a less nefarious explanation. It's also completely possible that someone is a nonnative speaker *and* incompetent, but the whole idea is that you shouldn't make assumptions, particularly when you don't have necessary information about your interaction partner's background. When you're working with people across cultures, it's worth pausing before you leap to judgment based on the content of a single text message or phone call.

Many companies use virtual communication platforms that contain some amount of background information (e.g., country and time zone) that can help inform your impressions. If you're communicating with someone you don't know anything about, it might be worth looking at their work bio if it's available to get a sense of where they might be coming from (literally and metaphorically). If you're the one communicating in a nonnative language, consider highlighting (rather than hiding) your differences in order to create a situation where message recipients "forgive" potential norm violations due to those differences. There are both subtle and direct ways to execute this strategy. Options include mentioning in the passing that you recently visited your immediate family "back home" in [your native country], to directly initiating a conversation that highlights how you may be approaching a task differently due to demographic-related experiences you previously encountered (e.g., "My perception of the market is because of my own experience with X in [location]"). If you're communicating in a nonnative language, you can even preface your message with something as direct as "I apologize in advance for any errors in my message, as [this language] is not my native language."

If you work in a company or on a team that is made up of international members, it's worth having conversations about how expectations for email and meeting etiquette vary. For instance, communication in Western cultures tends to be more direct, and disagreeing with someone's idea over email may be an acceptable and productive means of quickly reaching a solution. Likewise, interrupting another person during a video call might be seen as part of the brainstorming process. However, these same behaviors are more likely to be seen as offensive and counterproductive in Eastern cultures, where there is a greater emphasis on relational harmony. As a result, communication tends to be more indirect and disagreements would be better handled softly via question-asking. Even within a geographic region, there are different etiquette norms that can get you into trouble if you're not paying attention. For example, a research study found that smiling-face emojis are considered disrespectful by younger Chinese communicators, whereas older Chinese generations find smileys appropriate.

By discussing communication norms from the beginning, you can avoid these costly misinterpretations that may—unbeknownst to you—harm your relationships. Explicitly addressing these demographic and cultural differences facilitates more diverse behavior and better understanding, particularly when you don't have the benefit of being colocated. By being more attentive to the possibility of different cultures influencing communication content and style, and more directly addressing how our own differences might impact an exchange, we can prevent others from viewing us negatively due to a lack of cultural awareness.

Culture and geography aren't the only factors that can result in the need to communicate differently. Sometimes, choosing a specific mode or engaging in a particular conversation style is a matter of practicality. Yet we often overlook important signals from our communication partners and make assumptions that can have long-term relationship ramifications.

Picture Imperfect

Stereotypes surrounding disabilities are something I've struggled with communicating throughout my career. Although I don't have a visible disability, my immune deficiency is not wholly invisible. Whether I'm dealing with nuisances like a chronic cough, wearing an N95 mask in public, having to miss group meetings due to frequent doctor appointments, or being the only one to attend a meeting remotely to avoid getting sick, I often find myself in situations where others may build unflattering perceptions of me solely due to my disability.

When I first began working, I was preoccupied with the best way to approach these kinds of sensitive interactions. If I couldn't meet with others in the office, would it be better to use video as much as possible to get more face time, or would it be best to stick to email because that was the default communication mode for most of my peers when not meeting in person? How could I ensure that I didn't inadvertently put one of my colleagues in a position where they needed to use a communication mode that didn't meet their needs?

For individuals with disabilities, there are times when the accessibility of a communication mode may be more important than whether the mode is exactly ideal for a task at hand. Sometimes accessibility is the most important factor. For instance, for cancer patients, those with an immune-related disability, or anyone who has a family member who falls into the former two buckets, in-person meetings come with the risk of catching an infection that would be inconvenient to most people but could prove deadly for that individual. Both from a well-being and productivity perspective, keeping your immune-compromised colleague away from a virus going around the office can outweigh the task-specific advantages that might be gained from having an in-person meeting. Similarly, for people who are hard of hearing or those who are on the autism spectrum (some of whom may benefit from having more time to communicate and/or lower stimulation in their interactions), it may be difficult or downright impossible to communicate via modes that aren't text-based (or at least allow for audio transcription). Less rich technology may seem like it is the safest choice for accessibility, but that isn't always the case. For example, for individuals who are visually impaired and have difficulty reading, richer modes of communication that contain audio may be ideal.

There are countless reasons people might have for preferring one communication mode over another. For instance, parents or those caring for elderly parents might strongly prefer to attend meetings virtually to better balance their home and work obligations. Allowing these individuals to attend meetings virtually can also contribute to an organization's diversity, as caregivers tend to be women. Relatedly, being flexible about cameras-on policies can allow parents to have their child, who stayed home from school because of a snow day, playing in the background while they work. These types of accommodations are especially helpful for one-parent households.

Meta (the parent company of both Facebook and Instagram) discovered that employees who accepted remote job offers were more likely to be from diverse backgrounds—"Black, Hispanic, Alaskan Native, Native American, people with disabilities, veterans, and women." One reason for this effect is that those who might feel uncomfortable being the only visible minority may prefer communicating via less rich modes. Likewise, colleagues who come from a lower socioeconomic status might prefer cameras-off meetings to avoid needing an expensive camera, office background, and fancier clothes. Low-richness communication is also useful for those who are communicating in a nonnative language and favor being able to reread and correct emails rather than needing to meet in real time.

My point is that accessibility looks different based on the needs of each communicator. There is no overarching "best" communication technology for everyone. But there is still a way to identify the best approach to increase inclusion via our virtual communication. Put simply, ask the other person what their mode preference is. When I began asking others their preferences, I discovered that there were far more people who had their own challenges that I might never have discovered if I hadn't simply asked how they prefer to communicate. To avoid the egocentric bias, proactively ask your communication partner if they have any modes of communication they prefer (or would prefer to avoid). If you unilaterally schedule a meeting in a specific communication mode with someone you are unfamiliar with, you may put them in the awkward situation of having to explain why that mode is not ideal for them. While it may seem more complicated to communicate virtually with all these considerations in mind, there is a silver lining. The breadth of communication technologies now available provides access to jobs and relationships that were never before possible for many people.

Partial Sunshine and Pixelated Rainbows

In 2019, Wayfair employees turned to social media to express frustration that their company had sold more than $200,000 of furniture to a detention center for migrant children. Using the #BoycottWayfair hashtag, employees organized their protest and brought widespread attention to the mistreatment of migrant children at these border detention centers. In their message to Wayfair leaders, employees noted that their goal was to make sure Wayfair had "no part in enabling, supporting, or profiting from this practice." Congresswoman Ayanna Pressley reacted to #Boycott-Wayfair with the message, "I proudly stand in solidarity w/ the hardworking individuals at #Wayfair who are walking out in the name of #justice & humanity."

The goal of these (and similar) movements has been to use virtual communication to bring large-scale awareness to injustices and hold decision-makers accountable. Like *Time* magazine's 2017 Person of the Year, which was awarded to a group of women described as "the silence breakers" for speaking up about sexual harassment, people around the globe are using their virtual voices to reduce inequity and increase inclusion. When Susan Fowler was asked why she decided to publicly share her experiences with sexism at Uber, she explained, "I'm just one of many. I'm the small voice in a really big choir of men and women who have stood up and said, 'We have experienced this stuff, too.'"

Communicating virtually doesn't automatically eliminate appearance-related stereotypes stemming from factors such as age, race/ethnicity, gender, and disability status, and without a magic wand, there is no quick fix for eradicating interpersonal biases. But there are ways to employ virtual communication to reduce the impact of interpersonal biases and increase accessibility for everyone. Being aware of the degree to which we all make assumptions based on limited information can help us to choose the right communication mode and check our biases at the [virtual] door. Knowing how you might unconsciously (and incorrectly) fill in missing gaps about another person, and how you can help others form a more accurate picture of you, will get you ahead in your relationships and career.

KEY LESSONS
Perspective Taking
+ To avoid the egocentric bias (especially when accessibility is a factor), proactively ask your communication partner if they have any modes of communication they prefer (or would prefer to avoid). What you think is the best mode of communication for a given purpose may not be the best for others.

Initiative

✦ Taking the initiative to highlight differences, rather than bury them, can help your communication partners "forgive" errors or etiquette breaches in your virtual communication.

Nonverbal

✦ Be wary of "filling in the blanks" with text and making assumptions about your communication partner. Paradoxically, text communication heightens stereotyping due to an absence of nonverbal cues, which results in less personal information coming through.

Goals

✦ If differences *are* known: if your goal is to reduce others' biases, then richer communication modes (e.g., video) are best.
✦ If differences *are not* known: if your goal is to reduce others' biases, then less rich communication modes (e.g., email or instant messaging) can help avoid needing to reduce biases in the first place by masking differences.
✦ If you want to avoid your (or others) feeling the need to conform to societal expectations/pressures of your race/gender/age/etc., choose less-rich modes (e.g., email or instant messaging).

9

Navigating the Noise

How to Thrive in a Digital World

A happy man is too satisfied with the present
to dwell too much on the future.
—Albert Einstein

Peter Hopper, the founder and CEO of a software company, starts his day at 5 a.m. Hopper checks his emails, takes calls with his leadership team while he walks two miles on his treadmill, and uses his commuting time to the office to review data reports. Known around the office as the king of hustle, Hopper has a tendency to work at breakneck speed: he sends near-instant email responses to his team members and takes hurried phone calls while in transit to other meetings. The rest of Hopper's day is a flurry of emails, conference calls, and meetings. He falls asleep well after midnight, his phone clutched in his hand.

One day, Hopper wakes up to find an unwelcome message in his inbox: his investors are assigning him a co-CEO. Apparently, this man—Shelldon Terrapin—has expertise that will help push the business forward and meet shareholder demands.

Well, Hopper thinks as he sits down at his desk to get another hour of work in before breakfast, *I just hope he can keep up.*

Shelldon Terrapin wakes up around 8 a.m., does his daily crossword puzzle, and enjoys a leisurely breakfast. Upon arriving at his office, he sends "Good morning" instant messages to each of his team members before even glancing at his email. At 10 a.m., he opens his inbox. Despite having at least forty emails that accumulated since the previous day, Terrapin only responds to the most urgent ten. He won't check his email again until after lunch. He works at his desk until 4:30 p.m., taking fifteen-minute breaks every couple of hours. For any emails he didn't get a chance to address by the end of the day, he responds with a very brief form message: "I apologize that I am unable to clear out my inbox every day. Please follow up if you require urgent assistance." By 4:50 p.m., Terrapin is on his way home. *Slow and steady* is the mantra that's gotten Terrapin this far in his career, and he doesn't see any reason to change.

One day, Terrapin learns that he's going to become the co-CEO of a software company. He doesn't know much about the company or its founder, Peter Hopper, but he's looking forward to learning more and making new connections along the way.

On their first day as co-CEOs, things get off to a rocky beginning. When Terrapin mentions he rarely answers all his emails and will miss their end-of-day meeting because he needs to get home in time for dinner, Hopper loses patience and jumps all over him.

"You're slower than a turtle," Hopper says with a mocking laugh. "Do you ever get anywhere in life?"

"Yes," replies Terrapin, "and I get there sooner than you'd think. I'll race you in finishing this presentation for our board members and prove it."

Hopper is amused at the idea of competing with Terrapin and agrees.

Hopper sits down at his computer and is soon hours-deep in spreadsheets and emails that will help him finish first. He works non-stop, interrupting his progress every so often to reply to his emails and instant messages as they come in. As time passes, Hopper finds himself making errors and struggling to focus, but he presses on. By the early hours of the morning, he has outlined a presentation that—

once finalized—will secure him the win (and make the company's investors happy). To make Terrapin see how ridiculous it is to try to keep up—and certainly not because words are starting to blur on his screen from so much stress and time spent at his computer—Hopper lays down on his office couch to relax. As soon as he stretches out, his long hours catch up with him, and his eyes fall closed.

When Terrapin gets into the office, he finds Hopper fast asleep. Terrapin takes his laptop into an open conference room and works his way steadily through his presentation, making sure to focus only on the presentation without distractions. *Slow and steady*, he reminds himself, as he takes several breaks outside the office to recharge and brainstorm novel ideas. When Hopper wakes up, Terrapin is near the project goal.

Hopper races to his computer and types his swiftest, but he can't overtake Terrapin in time. When they present to their board members, it's immediately clear that Terrapin more effectively won over his audience both with a cleaner presentation and more creative ideas. Terrapin wins the competition, proving that "the race is not always to the swift."

Winning the Virtual Race

If Hopper and Terrapin's story rings any bells of familiarity, it's because you've almost certainly heard it before. It's one of Aesop's Fables, "The Tortoise and the Hare," with slight modifications to the characters and setting, of course. The classic fable is about a speedy hare losing a race to a slow, but confident, tortoise.

Why would I choose to share a children's story in the final chapter of this book?

One of the most obvious aspects of virtual communication—yet the most difficult to manage—is the fact that it's ubiquitous. Being able to reach anyone at any time in any location means your productivity potential—in theory—is limited only by the number of hours in the day. And with the growing popularity of augmented reality (i.e., the integration of internet access, including virtual communication, overlaid onto the real world via glasses/goggles/wearable devices/brain chips), it will continue to become even harder to disconnect. Instead of devices making a potentially ignorable sound, notifications from our virtual messages can now pop up right in front of our faces. But just because you could be juggling eight different devices like some kind of hyperproductive octopus, that doesn't mean doing so will help you thrive by improving your well-being. In fact, as you saw in my corporate version of "The Tortoise and the Hare," trying to do it all without focusing on your personal well-being is unsustainable. There's also the fact that many of us end up bringing work home in the form of frequent after-hour pings on our personal devices. Thus, setting boundaries and finding a balance in our virtual communication practices has become an essential component of thriving at work.

Have you ever found yourself in the middle of family dinner, or catching up on your favorite TV show, only to jolt to attention when your work phone vibrates in your pocket? If so, you're not alone. This constant connection to work impacts our ability to detach and replenish our mental energies before the next workday because unwanted communication can seep into, and interrupt, every part of our lives. Left unchecked, staying plugged in to work communication leads to stress, fatigue, and ultimately burnout. While most of us can't—nor should we—ban communication technologies from our lives, there are science-based strategies that can help you maximize the upside and minimize drawbacks of virtual communication's pervasiveness.

In this chapter, I'll explain why virtual communication has made it so much easier to stay connected—which simultaneously has the unintended consequence of sucking people in. Amid the seemingly constant stream of incoming messages, I'll answer the question of how frequently you should deal with virtual communication, as well as how to make meetings themselves feel less exhausting. You'll learn how to decide how much blurring between work and home is too much, and how to create better barriers between the two. Finally, I'll show you how to make the most of your time away from the office to replenish your mental energies, even when it seems impossible to unplug. This chapter will show you how to build virtual communication habits to meet your goals, find a balance between work and home, and ultimately thrive in a virtual world.

Running on Empty

In 2013, Moritz Erhardt, a twenty-one-year-old intern at Bank of America Merrill, was found dead in his shower. The cause of his death was found to be an epileptic episode, likely triggered by the fact that he'd come off a seventy-two-hour shift working at the bank. In response to his death, the bank made a rule that intern workdays couldn't last for more than seventeen hours.

Kenji, an employee at a Tokyo-based security company, regularly worked fifteen-hour days and contended with a four-hour commute to and from work. One day in 2009, he was found slumped over his desk—dead from a heart attack. He was forty-two years old.

Unfortunately, these stories aren't as unique as one might hope. By some estimates, the number of lives lost to overwork is equivalent to those who die in traffic accidents. The Japanese even have a word—*karoshi*—that translates to "death by overwork." This phenomenon is legally recognized when an employee worked more than one hundred overtime hours in the month preceding their death. In Japan, if a death is ruled as karoshi, the victim's family can receive up to $1.6 million in restitution.

I'm not sharing these anecdotes to ruin your day or cause you to immediately quit your job. The point I'm trying to make is that while virtual communication provides the convenience of being able to work anytime and from anywhere, there's also a downside. It's frighteningly easy to fall into work communication patterns without questioning whether the rewards are worth the sacrifices. We're so used to answering messages when we receive them, regardless of the hour or day of week, we never stop to think, *Do I have to reply to this message?* Or *Is communicating about this work project the best use of my time and energy?*

Contrary to what we might expect, research has found that scheduling autonomy—or the ability of workers to set their own schedule by deciding when and where to work—doesn't impact employees' job experience and performance as favorably as would be expected. The reason why is that there's an "autonomy paradox," whereby having more freedom over digital connectivity has an ancillary consequence of making employees feel a stronger need to stay plugged in (which results in a feeling of lack of control that grows over time). In the short term, being able to respond to work messages on your chosen device at any time that's convenient provides a sense of heightened control over the process. But it's fleeting. In the longer term, employees increasingly feel an urgency to respond to any and all messages as soon as they arrive in their inboxes. This sense of urgency is stressful and makes it more difficult to carve out work-free time, which in turn makes any sense of autonomy over work and virtual communication feel more illusory.

Have you ever gotten a work call or chat message that you answered right away, before realizing that if you'd taken a few more minutes to consider your response, you would have said something completely different? One of the biggest advantages of asynchronous virtual communication is that it allows us time to process information and think through our responses. The issue is that when we're expected to constantly be "on" and respond to messages as soon as we receive them, that benefit disappears. This pervasive and stress-inducing feeling that we need to reply to messages semi-instantly has been termed *workplace telepressure*, and it reduces the autonomy benefits of asynchronous communication. Additionally, workplace telepressure causes employees to feel that they have less control over their work communication, which increases burnout. Left unchecked, this pattern leads to a culture of "inescapable work."

The less attentive we are to our virtual communication practices, the more difficult it becomes to accurately evaluate our communication choices and react most appropriately to achieve our goals. Without our awareness or consent, work-related virtual communication has a habit of taking over. The challenge, then, is to find a balance that's right for you. To do that, you'll first need to evaluate your behavior in the context of your virtual communication goals.

Goldilocks and the Three Devices

Through a survey of a Chinese pharmaceutical company's five thousand employees, Professor Shuang Ren of the Deakin Business School in Melbourne, Australia, and her team set out to discover how to identify the ideal amount of digital connectivity outside of the workday. After surveying the pharmaceutical company employees, Ren's team found that an inverse curvilinear relationship (i.e., an upside-down U-shaped curve) exists between the amount of time we spend plugged in to work mobile devices after hours and resulting performance.

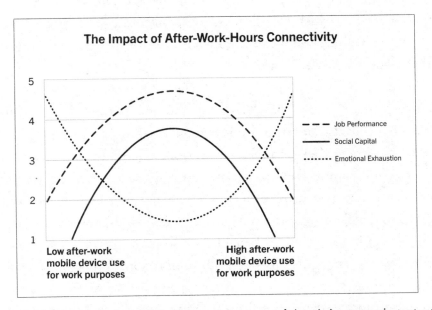

Too little after-work-hours digital connectivity can result in missing out on important relationships, but too much can lead to burnout and undermine your goals.

Up to a point, after-work digital connectivity was associated with accumulating more social capital (i.e., strengthening and building new relationships with work colleagues), which makes sense since more connection with colleagues can lead to stronger relationships. And it was this social capital gained through connectivity that led to improved work performance, since close colleagues often can provide beneficial resources, such as task-relevant advice or information. Further, these kinds of relationships can be emotionally energizing, which can further boost performance. Overdo it, though, and it's as bad as no communication at all (and a whole lot more time-consuming). Once the optimal amount of after-work-hours digital connectivity was surpassed, it tended to lead to greater emotional exhaustion or burnout, which can worsen both job performance and the ability to form meaningful connections. The takeaway here is that, up to a point, staying connected outside of work hours can improve work relationships and performance. When taken too far, however, the extra time spent communicating will result in feelings of fatigue and burnout associated with work . . . which can decrease job performance and motivation. If you've ever received a call from your boss at 8 p.m. on a Saturday night, you know what I mean.

There are a few ways to achieve the Goldilocks *just-right* balance between work connectedness and motivation. First, each person needs to determine for themselves how much time, and precisely when, they will respond to work-related communication. Being deliberate rather than passive in this decision-making process will help you hit the high point of optimal communication and avoid the trough of emotional exhaustion. Keeping this curvilinear graph in mind will enable you to more accurately identify when you're engaging in too much digital connectivity and risking burnout, or too little and in danger of losing motivation and undermining work relationships. Quickly identifying when you're out of alignment will allow you to recalibrate before you hit the wrong part of that curve.

In this regard, it's especially helpful to set expectations with your manager (or your subordinates if you are a manager) and teammates for after-hours communication. After all, there's nothing worse than tucking into a delicious bowl of not-too-hot, not-too-cold porridge, only to have ~~the three bears~~ your manager surprise you with an unplanned call, text, or meeting.

Communication received during the workday, however, is a—forgive me—bear of a different color. Video meetings, in particular, can often be more stress-inducing and depleting than even a dozen after-hours text message exchanges. Thus, managing your after-hours virtual communication is only half the battle. The other half is making your workday interactions feel less exhausting.

Zooming Out

If there's anyone who should be a fan of using video calls, it would be videoconferencing platform Zoom's CEO, Eric Yuan. That said, Yuan admitted to feeling fatigue himself after having nineteen video meetings in a row. After that, he stopped scheduling his meetings back-to-back. In a similar vein, the CEO of Citigroup, Jane Fraser, called out video meetings for "blurring lines between home and work." To combat the time and energy toll, Citigroup instituted video call–free Fridays.

Assuming you don't work at a company that has implemented these types of rules, there are ways to manage virtual communication to make it feel less draining (both in terms of time and energy). In Chapter 4, I discussed the exhaustion that comes from overusing video communication, known as "Zoom fatigue" or "videoconferencing fatigue." If your goal is to reduce stress imposed on you by your video meetings, the simplest solution is to turn off your camera. Research shows that cameras-on meetings are especially draining because they require you to monitor your nonverbal behaviors throughout the meeting.

If you are required to leave your camera on (or if it's useful to achieve one of your other goals), one way to reduce stress during virtual meetings is by dressing more casually. As discussed in Chapter 3, researchers who studied how different clothing combinations affected workers' emotional well-being found that dressing more casually ("home attire") can increase feelings of authenticity, which results in improved work engagement and overall happiness.

Beyond clothing, it is also valuable to consider where your attention is focused during video calls. University of Illinois Urbana-Champaign psychologist Talia Ariss and her colleagues found that people who spent more time staring at themselves than their interaction partner reported higher negative emotions after the exchange. An interesting detail of this study was that it tested whether consuming alcohol improved this effect, since the research team predicted alcohol would make the participants more social compared to self-focused. It turned out (and probably for the best, as I wouldn't want to advocate drinking while working) that consuming alcohol didn't lead to any emotional improvements following the interaction. However, the strategy I shared in Chapter 3 of maintaining greater eye contact with your camera rather than focusing on your own video image on-screen will do double duty: you'll be better able to engage with your interaction partners and you'll avoid hyperfocusing on how you look on-screen. If you're too distracted by your own image, you can temporarily hide your self-view option. As tempting as it might be to fixate on whether you've got a weird expression on your face or salad stuck in your teeth, research shows you'll be happier if you spend more time looking at the other people in your meeting.

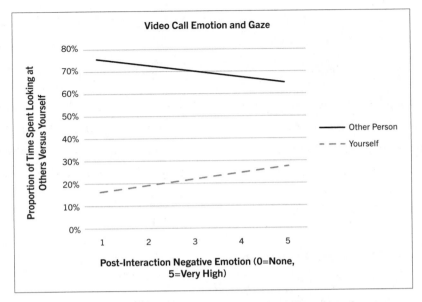

The proportion of time study participants spent focused on themselves versus others was associated with experiencing a higher level of negative emotions.

To further decrease stress during video calls and other forms of virtual communication, it can be invaluable to take other people's mindset into consideration. It's easy to fall into the trap of thinking your interaction partners will analyze your recent video meeting/email/text/phone call for weeks to come, especially when you're interacting with a superior. When you catch yourself in this stress-inducing mindset, take a step back from your own perspective and consider your boss's position. Let's assume your boss gets somewhere in the neighborhood of one hundred emails a day. That means that if your boss were only focusing on their email and nothing else, then the message you've been perfecting and feeling anxious about will only get 1 percent of their attention. That seems pretty minimal. And it gets even less significant when you consider that your boss isn't simply thinking about their email—they're also focused on meetings, their communication with their bosses, their lives outside of work, and any number of other factors. Thus, the odds that your boss is thinking about you (or your communication) long after an interaction are slim to none. Recall the spotlight effect I introduced in Chapter 4, which causes us to assume others are thinking about us (and our communication) far more often than they actually are. This effect also plays a role in how we should evaluate our virtual communication from a time and mental energy perspective. While the way you virtually present yourself will have an additive effect over time, any errors or slips of the tongue you make in a single interaction will be unlikely to move the needle much. As in Ariss's social interaction study, spending less time focusing on your own imperfections and directing your [digital] gaze toward others will make your virtual communication less depleting.

The Great [Virtual] Wall

I recently came across a surefire way to disconnect from work, establish virtual communication boundaries with your coworkers, and ensure that you can take full advantage of a Nordic vacation with a single email . . . that you don't even need to write. In fact, all you need to do is out-*horse* your away message to one of three equine experts from Iceland. After booking your travel, this process simply entails visiting a section of Iceland's tourism website, where you can choose a horse (based on your specific business needs, of course), who will then [literally] bang out an email away message in your name on a giant, horse-sized keyboard.

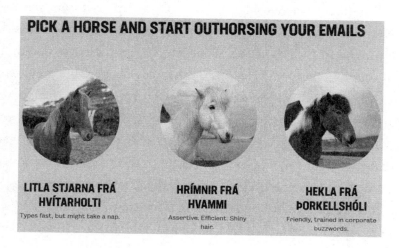

PICK A HORSE AND START OUTHORSING YOUR EMAILS

LITLA STJARNA FRÁ HVÍTARHOLTI
Types fast, but might take a nap.

HRÍMNIR FRÁ HVAMMI
Assertive. Efficient. Shiny hair.

HEKLA FRÁ ÞORKELLSHÓLI
Friendly, trained in corporate buzzwords.

Works like a charm. Take a look:

MESSAGE

Andrew Brodsky is away on vacation and not able to respond to your email. Meanwhile, Andrew has OutHorsed all emails to an Icelandic horse called Hekla frá Þorkellshóli, who is trained in corporate communications.

Here is Hekla frá Þorkellshóli's response:

Aælkj5hbyiu89 n89u ð´ˈl2+ji hð9 u3boæjrk2 n 9089ui qeægj eronbqo ð gnjqergni8h aq fear i

Qñuoq4uhhæ 34 4 4 ædoifuuuuuuuua q34o

This email was composed by an Icelandic horse using a giant keyboard for horses. Seriously.

OutHorse your email at: www.outhorseyouremail.com

Andrew will return to work on February 11, 2035.

This has to be one of the better tourism campaigns I've ever seen (Visiticeland.com even offers suggestions for "Things to do in Iceland while a horse answers your email"), and while hilarious, it points to just how problematic our virtual communication connectivity has become. After all, no one should be worrying about when they'll next be able to check their messages as they're kayaking past glaciers. And yet, our increased connectivity has made the old saying "work to live, don't live to work" all but impossible to maintain in practice.

Other countries have taken a more serious (albeit less adorable) stab at helping to establish boundaries between work and life. France and Spain were at the forefront of legally defining knowledge workers' "right to disconnect" from their job. These countries wrote a law that employees are free to ignore their devices outside of contracted work hours without fear of penalty. Other countries, including Italy, Slovakia, Canada, and the Philippines, have instituted similar amendments to help protect employees' after-work hours and prevent burnout. Germany's employment minister passed a guideline defending workers who choose to ignore messages outside of normal business hours. The code specifies, "Managers should apply a principle of 'minimum intervention' into workers' free time and keep the number of people whose spare time is disrupted as low as possible." These nationwide regulations establish a culture in which employees aren't expected to be "on" at all hours of the day, since there is an expectation that they won't be checking their email or phone during personal time. By protecting workers' right to disengage, these policies help to create a balance between work-related communication and life that is the norm rather than the exception.

Even in countries where there aren't laws (or norms) about disconnecting, some leaders are creating a culture that includes a virtual communication off-switch. At the US Army's Fort Drum in upstate New York, the 10th Mountain Division's commanding general sent out a memo stating that there should be no work-related virtual communication between the hours of 6 p.m. and 5 a.m. Major General Milford Beagle Jr. said that the goal was for soldiers to "have uninterrupted personal time outside the standard duty day."

For many employees, however, there are no company- or country-wide barriers in place to safeguard their time away from workplace communication. That means that many knowledge workers are left in the position where they need to create their own boundaries while still meeting the expectations of the job.

Infinite Scroll . . . or Sisyphus 2.0

According to Greek mythology, Sisyphus was a king who became renowned for transforming his city into a lucrative center of commerce. His contributions to trade and navigation were overshadowed, however, by his deceitful and ruthless nature. He was known for slaughtering travelers who passed through his city, just to demonstrate his power. Because of this, and other offenses to the gods, Zeus took it upon himself to punish Sisyphus. Zeus doomed Sisyphus to push a boulder uphill for eternity. Every time Sisyphus reached the top of the hill, the boulder would roll back down and Sisyphus would need to begin again. Over and over again . . . forever.

Left unchecked, our virtual communication practices start to feel like the modern-day version of Sisyphus—and about as productive as rolling a boulder uphill and watching it tumble back down without an end in sight. While your job may not permit you to entirely stop pushing that [virtual communication] boulder, there are steps you can take to feel more recovered and motivated to keep pushing it back up the hill. When considering how to protect your time away from work, it's worth examining how executives, who are bombarded by a near-constant deluge of virtual communication, manage to stem the tide.

As a founder, CEO, and author, Arianna Huffington is no stranger to virtual-communication-related stress. In 2007, she was at home checking her email when she passed out from sheer exhaustion. She hit her desk on the way to the floor, breaking her cheekbone. Huffington woke up in a pool of her own blood and decided then and there that she needed to make some lifestyle changes. She therefore came up with her own method of creating a clear stopping point to her daily work communication.

In order to signal to herself that she's reached the end of her device-checking day, Huffington literally tucks her devices into bed at night (it's really a charging station that looks like a bed). She explains, "You put your phone under the blanket and you tuck it in and say goodnight." And if you think that's weird, here's an even crazier detail. Huffington's devices sleep *outside* of her bedroom. That means no middle-of-the-night phone checks, last-minute email responses, or flashes of light signaling a new message. And she rests easier—and uninterrupted—this way. This ritual of physically tucking her phone in helped Huffington to build a habit of not checking her messages (or engaging in work) after a certain time at night to avoid slipping back into old patterns.

Alfredo Ramirez cofounded Vyopta, a company that improves virtual collaboration through tracking digital communication metrics. Because he spends his entire workday helping companies use virtual communication more effectively, he's put a great deal of thought into his own uses of communication technology. He told me that one strategy he uses to manage his seemingly endless communication is to chunk his messages by mode. He takes calls first thing in the morning and at the end of his day, and he has four separate periods of time throughout the day allotted to emails. This schedule leaves Ramirez with the rest of his day to focus on high-priority tasks, client relationship-building, and time outside the office. In Chapter 2, I suggested assigning particular times throughout the day for meetings and messages, rather than having them interspersed. Not only does this practice increase your work productivity, but it also allows you to avoid being frustrated because these constant interruptions are preventing you from completing your work and enjoying life.

Famed investor Warren Buffett doesn't even own a smartphone, joking that he uses the "one Alexander Graham Bell gave me." Gyana CEO Joyeeta Das physically removes herself from the temptation to be on her phone by taking twice-yearly deep-sea boating trips where she completely disconnects. Hootsuite's CEO and founder, Ryan Holmes, "declares inbox bankruptcy" when his inbox gets out of control. He simply deletes all his messages, adds a note to his email signature like

"Sorry if I didn't get back to your last email. To become a better communicator, I've recently declared email bankruptcy," and starts over.

I don't expect you'll necessarily be able to (or even should) implement all these leaders' virtual communication habits. Rather, I share them to demonstrate creative approaches to achieving the right balance, and also to emphasize the importance of being more attentive to how work communication patterns encroach on your personal time.

If reducing your anxiety and increasing productivity isn't enough of an incentive for creating boundaries around your digital communication, then consider how doing so can also benefit your significant other. Research has shown that having email "on" and "off" times can reduce conflict with—and improve well-being for—your partner. Because semiconstant virtual communication engagement requires your focus and attention, these interruptions indirectly affect your closest relationships by allowing work communication stress to spill over and cause relational conflict.

I have already discussed chunking your virtual communication time so it doesn't bleed into other tasks, but it's also just as important to make sure you set aside uninterrupted blocks of "life time." It isn't just important for your mental well-being—separating work and life will actually make you more successful at work. Professor Sandy Wayne from the University of Illinois Chicago and her colleagues found that when there is more conflict spillover between the work and family domains, employees are more exhausted and less engaged, which results in fewer raises and promotions.

At this point, you may be noticing that some of this chapter's suggestions are at odds with recommendations elsewhere in the book. No, I haven't suddenly had a change of heart. The reason for these deviations is that, in this chapter, the goal is improving your own well-being. The reality is that some of these strategies may marginally undermine work performance and/or relationships; however, if you're spending all of your time and mental energy on work, then you'll be at risk of burning out. After all, what good is a promotion if you're so stressed in your job that you end up quitting (or being miserable)? Sometimes, self-care trumps getting ahead in your career. At the end of the [work] day, it all comes down to your goals. And it's certainly possible that your goals today will be different from the ones you have next year. The key is to be thoughtful about what you're trying to achieve (and then periodically reevaluate). Establishing firmer boundaries between the office and home, even for a short period, will help you to replenish your energy and avoid burning out. And if deleting your entire inbox or chartering a deep-sea vessel isn't feasible for you, don't despair. There are other less time- and cost-invasive means of detaching that will help you get that balance *juuuust right* and thrive.

Logging Off and Tuning In

When I ask executives what their most limited resource is, they invariably bypass the oft-assumed response of money and instead go straight to *time*. For good reason: people are bringing more work home with them (literally and mentally), and spending more hours at work, both during the week and on weekends. For instance, a quarter of American workers don't get any paid vacation time at all. For the other three-quarters, many employees choose not to use their allotted days off due to time constraints or pressure from their employers. This lack of vacation usage leads to a workforce that is collectively more stressed-out and less happy. The busier we get at work, the more we feel a need to detach (and paradoxically, the less we feel we have the freedom to do so). Sometimes, simply leaving the office (or stepping away from your computer) and hiding your smartphone isn't enough by itself. Instead, you actually have to psychologically detach from work-related communication in order to fully recover and make the most of your free time.

While the problem is obvious—workers should take more vacations—the solution isn't as simple. It would be great to pack up your family and whisk them off to the Bahamas, but that's not a practical solution for many people any time they're feeling an imbalance between work and free time (if it is an option for you, go get those palm trees and turquoise waters with my blessing). For those who can't jet off to the tropics at the drop of a hat whether due to cost or lack of time, there is a far more achievable way of getting that vacationlike feeling (if not the tan) without leaving home. In a study led by Colin West at UCLA, a group of participants who were told, "Treat this weekend like a vacation. That is, to the extent possible, think in ways and behave in ways as though you were on vacation," returned to their jobs on Monday with more positive affect (and fewer negative feelings). They also felt greater satisfaction with their lives overall. By thinking about your weekend at home as a vacation, you will set yourself up to be more successful at your job, engage in more prosocial behaviors, and be less likely to burn out. No flights, hotels, or reservations needed.

What this "weekend vacation" looks like will differ from person to person based on interests and preferences. That being said, there are a couple of categories that, if appealing, can be especially rewarding. If you're someone who enjoys being out in nature, there's evidence to suggest that spending your free time outside will help you feel more energized (and less depleted) than other methods of unwinding from work and virtual communication. This is especially true for workers who spend most of their day indoors. Using free time to volunteer has also been shown to increase "psychological detachment" from work (and work communication), because it gives you something meaningful to focus on that's not work-related (whereas if you're watching TV, for instance, thoughts of work are liable to creep up while your mind is less active). I'm not arguing that you should necessarily avoid virtual communication in your free time, as you're likely to use it even when volunteering or engaging in other hobbies (e.g., online gaming). Instead, I'm suggesting that you should avoid *work-related* virtual communication during your recovery time. Even a single glance at your work messages during your personal time is enough to pull you out of your "vacation" mentality and reignite worries about your job.

Alanna Harvey cofounded the app Flipd to help users track how much time they spend focusing on specific tasks without being distracted by their phones (this was years before Apple launched Screen Time, which is used for the same purpose). With all the time she spent developing Flipd and thinking about productivity, Harvey has become an expert on finding a balance between virtual communication and unplugging. In a perspective that aligns with the Corporate Tortoise and the Hare moral we explored at the beginning of the chapter, she told me, "I'm a firm believer that the eighty-hour workweek, the hustle culture, can't be conducive to success long-term. If we are living to work, then we'll never disconnect. The work that you do doesn't need to be all-consuming. The more we allow ourselves the time and space to have hobbies and relationships, the better we will be at our jobs."

As busy as she is, Harvey manages to start out her workdays with a run, which she believes helps her tap into her creativity and gain a sense of accomplishment. After her daily runs, Harvey feels like she can "seize the day." There's science to back this sentiment. According to research, engaging in physical activity before the start of your workday can reduce emotional exhaustion and improve focus and overall well-being. While many of us might groan at the idea of waking up even earlier to get a workout in (right there with you groaners), engaging in physical activity changes your outlook on your work. All things considered, taking twenty minutes in the morning to set yourself up for a positive mental framework that will potentially last for the entire day seems like a reasonable trade-off—especially when you add in the ancillary benefits of working out, like lower weight and increased longevity.

One of the problems that many of us face is that we're so burned out by the end of the workday, we just want to be mindless in our relaxation. If you're like me, the last thing you want to do at the end of a hectic day is something active. But when it comes to detaching yourself from work and the endless stream of work-related virtual communication, sometimes it's not enough to just veg out on the couch until bedtime (or, dare I say, fill your after-work hours with house chores). Taking the extra effort to be thoughtful about how we're switching off is—counterintuitively—necessary to actually disconnect and rejuvenate on a daily basis.

As shown by research led by Sabine Sonnentag from the University of Mannheim, the most successful work detachers, who unplug from work at the end of the day and come back in the morning revitalized and reset, engage in not one but four different types of detachment every day. The first is *psychological detachment*, which means deliberately switching off your work mindset and communication tools in order to focus on personal time. The second is *relaxation*, which includes activities that have low levels of stimulation (e.g., reading a nonwork book or communicating with fellow hobby enthusiasts on an online forum). The third is *mastery*, which involves learning something new or improving a skill (e.g., growing a garden, building a shelf, learning a new language). And the fourth is *control*, which is when individuals define for themselves how they'll spend nonwork time rather than passively allowing it to be dictated for them. While you might think the effort required to allocate free time into these four categories would be at odds with relaxing, research shows it's actually the opposite. Not only will you be able to more effectively disconnect after each day, but this proactive attitude will carry over to your work and help you be more productive as well.

Thinking about your outside-of-work time in terms of these four buckets—psychological detachment, relaxation, mastery, and control— will help you to separate from your work-related virtual communication and replenish your mental resources more effectively. Even better, these methods of detaching aren't just helpful for individual employees— they also benefit organizations. Rejuvenated employees are less likely to burn out, which means less attrition for companies. Further, employees who are happier and less stressed are more likely to be proactive and help others in their jobs.

I want to make it clear that even the most rejuvenating leisure activities won't fully be able to make up for an inordinately stressful job situation that won't allow you time away from your work virtual communication. Sometimes the only path toward a better quality of life is seeking employment at an organization that more closely aligns with your priorities.

When it comes to achieving maximum rejuvenation, a little experimentation may be needed to find the right balance for you. With so many distractions vying for our attention, it's not enough to step away from our devices. Finding ways to mentally disengage and rejuvenate takes effort, but it's an investment that will improve your mental well-being and could even extend your career.

Fake It Till You Make It

Vincent van Gogh said, "If you hear a voice within you say 'you cannot paint,' then by all means paint, and that voice will be silenced." This sentiment applies to more than just painting. A group of researchers set out to determine which characteristics make us most successful at work. They discovered that an employee's previous job experience, which many organizations rely on to make hiring decisions, is a mediocre predictor of future performance and turnover. Rather, self-efficacy, or a belief that you're capable of performing in a way that's necessary to achieve your desired outcomes, is often a better indicator of how well someone will perform in their job. It turns out that success at your job is about more than actual ability; confidence is a major predictor of work communication outcomes. The idea here is that confidence (or a lack thereof) is a bit of a self-fulfilling prophecy. If you're worrying that your email is going to come off the wrong way and make you look bad, that lack of confidence can seep into your message and undermine your communication. This sentiment also applies to thriving. If you have convinced yourself there is no way to separate from your work communication, it widens the divide between your goals and how attainable those goals are. Simply put, when we don't have experience with something—whether it's using a new collaboration tool at work or learning how to ice-skate—we are often inclined to expect failure. When you find yourself in this precarious position, self-efficacy can help bridge that gap and increase psychological well-being.

Many people undervalue how great a role self-efficacy plays in workplace virtual communication. More broadly, higher self-efficacy also improves overall job performance, job satisfaction, strength of relationships, and ability to cope with challenges. Professors from the University of South Carolina found that remote workers' success with using new web platforms was mostly driven by self-efficacy, enjoyment, and learning goal orientation (as opposed to intelligence or raw skill). When workers have high degrees of self-efficacy, they report increased feelings of organizational commitment and more positive judgments about their ability to complete tasks (and their subsequent satisfaction with their task performance). A study of computer users in Finland showed that those with a heightened sense of self-efficacy found new technology programs easier to use (and also believed them to be more useful) than participants lower on self-efficacy, despite the program having an identical difficulty level for both groups. Thus, a strategy here is to reframe your thinking from *I'm stressed that this interaction is going to make me look bad* to *I'm going to make my best effort and then put this interaction out of my head.* Easier said than done, I know, but you can be confident that the knowledge and tools you've gained throughout this book will enable you to be more successful in any communication challenge. Once you internalize this confident mindset, there are ancillary benefits. For instance, you may find that when you do make a mistake in your virtual communication, it doesn't keep you up at night. So, the next time you accidentally click a confetti party reaction on a video call . . . or accidentally turn your face into a sad kitten . . . or spill coffee on yourself on camera . . . rather than ducking away from your screen in shame, own it. Because you're a virtual communication pro.

Beyond making you better at your job and reducing the anxiety that comes with being constantly plugged in to virtual communication, self-efficacy has broader health benefits. Honing self-efficacy has been shown to reduce social anxiety and depression, enhance relationships, lower the impact of social pressures, and even help people come to terms with chronic illnesses. Self-efficacy and confidence are also related to life satisfaction and an ability to plan for (and deal with consequences relating to) the future. Not only will confidence help you in your job and work relationships, but it will also lead to a more satisfying life. And, like any tool worth developing, the better you cultivate your sense of virtual communication self-efficacy, the more positive the results will be on your work and life.

You've Got Hologram

Similar to the tortoise and the hare (or Peter Hopper and Shelldon Terrapin, if you prefer), making the most of your virtual communication is about finding the right balance. Like all good things, achieving your *just-right* virtual communication balance will depend on you defining your goal and having enough self-efficacy to believe it's achievable.

As much as I tried, there just wasn't enough room in this book to address every virtual communication scenario you might encounter. And as you've discovered, identifying the optimal virtual communication approach in any given situation depends on your goals and interaction partner. Further, our style of communicating (both in and out of work) has changed dramatically in the last decade. I can only speculate, therefore, how different it will look in another ten years. One of my goals for this book is to provide you with tools that will apply to a broad range of communication platforms so that, as communication trends come and go, you'll have a blueprint to analytically and mindfully tackle any interaction. Blurring lines between work and home—and virtual and in-person—will only get more nebulous with continued advances in virtual reality, holographic interactions, and augmented reality. Learning how to use new communication modes will become a necessity for your continued success both in and out of the office. If you can approach these new tools strategically and with confidence rather than trepidation, you'll already have won 90 percent of the battle.

On the whole, virtual communication self-efficacy isn't just a learned skill—it's an attitude that will enable you to surprise even yourself with your ability to gracefully keep pace with the ever-changing workplace communication technology landscape. With so many of our jobs relying on a degree of agility in adapting to new virtual communication trends, honing your digital self-efficacy will allow you to thrive in your career in the long term. My hope is that the confidence you've gained through learning the science-based communication tools presented throughout this book will help you expertly navigate a world that is increasingly ruled by technology.

KEY LESSONS
Perspective Taking
+ Remember that others generally aren't thinking about what we wrote or said as much as we assume (spotlight effect). Take solace in the knowledge that most one-off virtual communication errors are unlikely to impact your relationships or career in the longer term, and thus aren't worth dwelling on.

Initiative

✦ Take the initiative to talk with your manager and team about expectations for after-hours communication. It may seem counterproductive to communicate about communication, but it's necessary to maintain work engagement and avoid burnout.

✦ Making an effort to spend time in nature can help you feel more energized. Ditto for volunteering. Both allow you to disconnect from work better than a more passive activity (e.g., watching TV).

✦ If you want to get that feeling of deep relaxation without ever leaving your house, take the initiative to conceptualize your weekends as a vacation. Think and behave in ways that will make the weekend feel more special and vacation-like. The result will be greater job success and less chance of burnout.

✦ The best work detachers make an effort to engage in four types of behavior: 1) psychological detachment (intentionally switching off your work mindset to focus on personal time), 2) relaxation (engaging in activities that have low stimulation levels), 3) mastery (learning something new), and 4) control (actively deciding for yourself how you'll spend your nonwork time).

Nonverbal

✦ To reduce stress and avoid videoconferencing fatigue during video calls, turn off your camera so you don't have to worry about your nonverbal behavior.

✦ During video calls, look at the other person instead of yourself to increase happiness and engagement. Focusing on the other person's nonverbal behavior rather than your own will reduce stress.

Goals

✦ Is your goal to maximize performance or mental well-being? Low-richness communication (e.g., cameras-off) is often less beneficial in terms of impression management, but it's also less stressful.

✦ Some degree of after-hours communication decreases stress and strengthens social capital by helping to build your network. Too much will lead to burnout, undermine your relationships, and worsen your job performance. By setting goals and boundaries for when and how often you'll respond to after-hours work communication, you'll be able to quickly identify when you're out of sync so you can recalibrate.

✦ Self-efficacy (believing you're capable of meeting your own goals) is a major predictor of thriving, both at work and in your personal life. Reframe your thinking from *I can't because* to a specific blueprint you can follow to achieve your goals.

Conclusion

To AI and Beyond

I paced around the house, traveling the same worn path in the carpet, while I checked my phone for the thousandth time . . . in the last five minutes. Still no messages or missed calls, even though I had my volume all the way up. My dogs, convinced we were playing some new game, ran around me in circles barking.

"Stop pacing," my wife called from the other room. "You're making everyone nervous!"

The dogs barked in agreement.

At that moment, my phone started to ring.

"Hello?"

"I've got good news for you, Andrew."

My literary agent, Sylvie Carr, knowing I was too much on pins and needles for pleasantries, got right into it.

"We got a response?" I asked.

"We got *three* responses," Sylvie replied, her smile radiating through the phone. "I don't want to jinx it, but the odds are excellent that *PING* is going to become a book! I'd like to start setting up some calls. . . ."

Being in the fortunate position of choosing between three reputable publishing houses, I needed to decide where *PING* would find its permanent home. Over the next week, I engaged in myriad conversations across various communication modes with each prospective publisher.

How did I manage to secure a deal that everyone was happy with? I used the virtual communication toolkit I'd developed based on research and experience, and which was the very subject of the book I wanted to share with the world.

The problem, as I so often hear from executives and my students, is that there are too many kinds of virtual communication (and too many incoming messages) to know the right way to handle them. While I acknowledge there's no blanket *email good, meetings bad* answer to virtual communication, there is a way to set yourself up for success in any digital interaction. I have distilled these principles into the PING framework I reference throughout this book.

To round things off, I'm going to put my money where my mouth is and show you the entire framework in action. And I figured there would be no better way to illustrate how it works than to describe how it enabled this book to become a reality. A meta-analysis, if you will.

PING at Play

PING: perspective taking, initiative, nonverbal, goals

Perspective taking: Knowing that we'd be interacting virtually, and thus I'd likely be more self-focused, I made an effort to shift my thinking from what I wanted (the best possible book deal) to what they wanted (à la Chapter 7's lesson to avoid egocentrism and enhance perspective taking, without tipping over into empathy) before my first conversation with each publisher. I realized that a publisher wants to feel confident in their investment of both time and money. The problem is that the publisher doesn't know if a first-time author has the ability and wherewithal to write a popular-press book that would be of interest to a broad diversity of people across myriad industries. I realized that if I wanted to convince a publishing house to believe in my book and, by extension, me, I needed to quickly develop a high-trust relationship with them.

For my first meeting with each publishing team, I made a conscious decision to choose the best virtual communication mode to fit my goals (Chapter 1). Therefore, Sylvie and I suggested a video meeting rather than defaulting to phone calls for our first conversation with each publishing group. After reading this book, you know there are several reasons why choosing video for a first meeting is beneficial (e.g., Chapter 4: richer communication modes help the other party feel more familiar with you). Instead of a faceless person, the publishers would be able to see a professionally dressed (but not overly formal) academic who was highly engaged in the call (Chapter 3). I made sure there was also a good amount of small talk that began what might otherwise have been a dry book pitch. In fact, one of the editors at the publishing house I later signed with jokingly noted, "I feel like this is a free therapy session where I get to talk about everything that bothers me with virtual communication." By the end of the conversation, the team didn't just have a face to put with my name—they had a sense of who I am (Chapter 5), and how that personality would be woven into the book I planned to write.

Initiative: Before meeting with each of the publishers, I made a point of looking up each team member and incorporating that knowledge into our conversation. By making it clear I was familiar with the other authors they represented (some of whom I knew personally), as well as the types of books they preferred to put their resources behind, I demonstrated that I cared about them in particular. In other words, I hadn't just sent my book proposal out into the ether and hoped for the best. My agent and I had chosen these publishing groups because we did our research and knew they would be the best fit for my project. This step was especially necessary for showing my interest (Chapter 3), as this process can feel cold and impersonal in virtual interactions compared to bygone days, when authors would fly out to meet publishers in person.

Once we got into the more serious part of the conversation, I didn't simply launch into a summary of my book and explanation about why I thought it needed to be published (which I'd already done electronically via my proposal). Instead, I made a point of telling the team some personal anecdotes. This tactic did double duty by clarifying *why* I was interested in virtual communication and helping the team to feel like they knew me (recall Chapter 6's lesson of using virtual communication to establish trust, strengthen relationships, and close the physical distance).

Based on my earlier perspective taking, I also took the initiative to alleviate concerns I suspected the other party might have. Specifically, I made a point of demonstrating my productivity and noting that, even though this would be my first book, I wasn't new to the process of writing and publishing (this is related to Chapter 5's lesson of using video to demonstrate authenticity and manage impressions). I even got some relieved laughs when I assured the teams that, if they worked with me, they wouldn't be in a situation where they were waiting for the next *Game of Thrones* book for years at a time (not that I expect *PING* to have the same waiting-for-the-sequel-with-bated-breath effect, but hey, you never know).

Nonverbal: Having my introduction conversations via video enabled my interaction partners to see my enthusiasm as I talked about the book. They could tell from my facial expressions that I was authentically excited (Chapter 5). That mode choice helped me to see their reactions, as well. If people's eyes started to glaze over or dart away from the screen, I knew it was time to pivot and steer the conversation to topics that would be more interesting to my audience. I used their nonverbal cues to direct me as I led the conversation, rather than sticking to an inflexible script.

Goals: While you'd rightly suspect that my ultimate goal was to secure a book deal, I had micro-goals for each interaction. For the first conversation I had with each group, my goal was to lay the foundations of a strong relationship in which the publishing house could feel confident in me. Once I signed a deal, I wanted to ensure that the editing team would trust in my expertise and conscientiousness enough to let me determine the approach to the book's topics. I was also conscious of maintaining a good relationship even with the publishers I didn't sign with, as we could bolster each other's networks and make useful connections to other experts in our respective fields. And virtual communication has made it possible to stay in touch every so often (recall Chapter 4's lessons about the value of reconnecting and maintaining relationships with lukewarm contacts). With these goals in mind, I framed conversations less around the book's intended subject and more about how my personal experiences, career, and research knowledge would enable me to create a product they'd be proud to support.

After multiple rounds of conversations with each of the three publishing groups, I took one final step to meet my goal of establishing trust (Chapter 6). Taking advantage of email's permanence, and to signal my appreciation for everyone's time, I sent personalized thank-you emails after each call. In these emails, I noted specific topics we'd discussed during the call (rather than defaulting to generic *it was great talking more about my project* kinds of platitudes). I chose email—the least interruptive mode (Chapter 2)—since calling to thank them could have come at an inconvenient time for the other people and undermined any positive impact of the conversation. Additionally, I took advantage of the tendency of explicit emotions to appear stronger when conveyed via permanent modes, so my email recipients could process my message later without distractions, as well as forward it to any other stakeholders in their company as they saw fit (Chapter 7).

Let's take a step back from the individual PING components and apply the framework as a whole to finish up the story. After meeting with each of the publishers, an interesting situation ensued. All three publishing houses wanted my book. They participated in a closed auction, which meant they each submitted a bid without knowing anything about what the other bidders were offering. As the deadline approached, the bids were communicated to Sylvie via email or text message—both for productivity's sake and due to the straightforward nature of the information. I also communicated with Sylvie via asynchronous communication during this period, but for different reasons. Since we were conversing so much (about which bids had been received, what the offers were, and our plan going forward), texting was useful so that we could both work around our family obligations (Chapter 8)—whether that involved Sylvie voice-messaging me while she was driving her child to school, or me texting her while helping my father-in-law to recover his Netflix password (I am the resident technology expert, after all). Being flexible in our communication style helped with balance, as well as creating boundaries that enabled us to thrive both at work and home during a high-stakes situation (Chapter 9).

Once the bids were in, Sylvie and I met via video to come up with a strategy. We chose this mode because we were exchanging more complex information at this point (Chapter 2). She was the expert on the publishing process and had knowledge of each of the specific individuals we were considering working with, whereas my background in both research and corporate consulting gave me strong expertise on negotiation strategies. So together we made a good team.

The final stage of the deal was a phone call between my agent and our top-choice publishing group. We chose phone rather than video or email so that Sylvie could hear the other participants' tone (and convey our own excitement) without letting any unintentional signals leak through her facial expressions (Chapter 5). We made a big ask, knowing we would likely settle somewhere in the middle, which we did. In this way, everyone walked away from the negotiation happy.

In each stage of this process, I relied on the PING framework. I put myself in the other people's shoes and considered what was most important to them. I made deliberate choices about which communication mode to select, and ensured I had a plan for how I wanted the conversation to go (rather than leaving it up to chance). I was attuned to the nonverbal cues my communication partners were giving off across modes. And I weighed potential outcome trade-offs with my clearly defined objectives.

My goal in sharing this analysis is that the PING framework will help you to achieve your intended outcomes in all your virtual communication, whether you're exchanging casual messages with a longtime client or negotiating the terms of your dream job.

A New [Digital] Dawn

This book has been about what you can do to make your virtual communication work for you. In recent years, there has been an increasing number of predictions that artificial intelligence (AI) will soon be doing all of our communication for us. If that's the case, then wouldn't this entire book be rendered irrelevant? In a word: no.

At the time of this book's publication, there is a major focus on AI interactive tools and chatbots derived from large language models (LLMs); however, this topic is not new. Even years before the public introduction of these more recent AI tools, there were chatbots of high enough quality that their messages were nearly indistinguishable from human customer service employees. I recall chatting with SmarterChild, one of the most popular early conversational chatbots, on AOL Instant Messenger (AIM) in the early 2000s (if that doesn't date me, I don't know what will). Beyond just the words themselves, both researchers and businesses have implemented a number of creative approaches to making these chatbots seems more "human" to their unaware interaction partners, including having the chatbots purposely lag messages (so it seems like a real human is spending time thinking or typing), referring to the person by name, and intentionally using typos or slang. Researchers have even directed chatbots to ask a human they're conversing with if the human is "real," thereby preempting the actual human's use of this same question and making the chatbot seem more like a person in the process.

There are times when using AI to fully take over your virtual communication can be both practical and efficient. Specifically, the interactions that are ripest for AI assistance are one-off, straightforward customer service interactions in which relationships don't matter. For instance, an AI chatbot can effectively walk customers through the download process of an app they just purchased or facilitate the return process for a recently purchased item. It's beneficial to use AI for these types of interactions because they're generally resolved without much effort, and most people don't care whether they're interacting with another human or a bot. In these scenarios, using AI tools as a replacement for human communication can enhance productivity.

However, even in the most AI-friendly situations, there is still a tricky conundrum as to whether the companies or individuals leveraging AI should reveal to the people they're interacting with that they are using AI or chatbots to assist with—or fully take over—communication. The issue is that in long and complex enough interactions, many people will eventually realize they are communicating with a chatbot rather than a real human, and research shows that people generally view chatbots (and the organizations that use them) as less authentic, sincere, and trustworthy, especially in high-importance contexts. When people know they're interacting with a chatbot, they are less cooperative and less likely to make a purchase. Thus, the decision of whether to use AI should come down to your goals: Is productivity and reducing costs most important, or are you trying to build up your reputation and goodwill with others? Answering this question and defining your priorities will help guide your usage of AI as a replacement for a human touch.

Regardless of how good AI tools are (or might become) at communicating on your behalf, there will still only be a narrow set of circumstances in which these tools might be able to fully take over for you, as opposed to acting more as an assistant by providing suggested text and editing. Why is this so? Because there is—and always will be—an inherently human component to our communication.

Have you ever gone to a restaurant because they boasted of making the best "hand-cut" fries? Or purchased a "hand-blown" glass ornament that was twice the price of another one that looked almost identical but was mass-produced? We're attracted to things that require a human to put in effort, because it makes them seem higher-quality and more personalized. Adding that human touch just makes everything seem better.

Let's say you're a manager at a financial firm. You ask a new employee to give you their view on an investment, and instead of engaging in a deep conversation on the topic, they simply give you a paragraph copied directly from an AI tool. They are up front about the fact that they used AI, and they proudly explain that letting AI do the work will allow them to spend more time on other projects. It seems like the right choice for efficiency's sake, and yet, you may start to wonder if you even need that employee.

Looking forward, the future of work can be broadly divided into two categories: a) jobs/tasks that are completely replaced by AI, and b) jobs/tasks that require a human or seem better with human involvement. In the latter case, those interacting with you will want *you* to be the one communicating—whether because they want your expertise/opinion/input or because the relational component is important to the role. For example, would you feel satisfied simply venting your anger about a bad hotel stay to an AI algorithm? Think back to the strategies I discussed about building trust (Chapter 6), like self-disclosing and bonding over similarities. If you want to be effective at establishing trust even when using AI tools to help generate responses, you still need to put effort into communicating the more "human" components yourself (i.e., an AI tool won't be able to self-disclose for you or discuss your hobbies without you first providing it with that information). Additionally, as I highlighted across chapters, your goals are going to vary from one context to the next (e.g., writing an efficient message or building a relationship over time), and the ideal communication choices will depend on what's most important to you in each interaction. Even if it's a situation where the other person won't be offended that you used AI rather than personally writing the whole message yourself,* humans will still be needed to provide prompts to the communication tools about objectives, personal preferences, and information about what/how to communicate.

These complexities are magnified in richer communication interactions. While it might technically be possible to use an AI version of yourself during video meetings, your coworkers, managers, and customers aren't going to get that warm and fuzzy feeling from an algorithm with your appearance telling them about your child's birthday party. That won't endear your communication partners to you, establish trust (Chapter 6), or make the other person feel more comfortable (Chapter 8). Imagine receiving a sympathy email from one of your colleagues after the loss of a loved one that was generated by AI. No matter how "right" the words sound, the message would feel much lower effort than even a one-sentence condolence delivered via phone without AI assistance. At the end of the day, the most valuable interactions will never be able to fully remove humans from the equation.

All that said, technology has the benefit of making each of us more productive. It can generate ideas, reduce typos, resolve grammatical errors, and decrease editing time. An AI model that processed this book (or any of the research it's based on) may even be able to offer virtual communication strategies as you are writing (e.g., "You should consider adding more positive words so your message isn't misinterpreted as negative") or post hoc (e.g., by analyzing meeting transcripts) about how you could communicate better. As new communication assistants emerge (AI-based or otherwise), we'll have more tools at our disposal

---

* Note: there is a reason why handwritten letters are so impactful.

for improving communication productivity and performance. These tools will be especially valuable for the "middle" parts of communication, where you provide the initial information or parameters of the communication, and the AI assistant will save time by crafting a message that you can then tweak and personalize as needed. Those who rely solely on these tools to meet all their communication needs will find less success despite their increased productivity, however. As AI and other automation tools continue to gain popularity, adding a human touch to your communication is likely to become even more valuable, as it will uniquely signal how much you care about the interaction. No matter how good AI becomes, it can't independently engage in the elements of PING (e.g., AI is unable to act on information only you have access to in your mind, fully interpret people's nonverbal behaviors by utilizing your personal knowledge of how they normally act outside of virtual communication, or innately identify your personal goals).

That's where you come in.

The nature of virtual communication (and indeed every element of our digital lives) is that it will continue to shift. With each change, there will be a concurrent need to adapt how we approach our communication and choose strategies that will be most effective. The knowledge you've gained throughout this book will imbue you with the digital self-efficacy needed to handle each of these changes strategically and confidently. While your company may favor new platforms—and even potentially new modes altogether—your plan of attack is going to follow the same path. By using the PING approach, you'll be positioned to keep up with the shifting technological landscape and ensure you're leveraging communication tools to enhance your job without being overwhelmed by them.

In a world where our physical presence is no longer a prerequisite for engaging in most conversations and developing relationships, honing our virtual communication toolkit is inextricably linked with career satisfaction and success. Now that you are aware of the science behind virtual communication strategies, I have every confidence you'll be able to leverage these tools to make the most out of your interactions. If you want to keep up to date on the latest research and strategies on the topics discussed in this book, you can check out the Ping Group website (www.PingGroup.org/Resources) for free resources.

Before you close this book and venture forth into your virtual interactions, let's bring everything together with one final piece of advice. Sometimes, having the biggest impact requires only sending a short email, a voice message, or—dare I say—a quick ping.

Appendix

Virtual Communication Styles Tool
Overview
Understanding your virtual communication style is useful for improving your interaction outcomes in both professional and personal environments. This tool will not only help you identify your virtual communication style, but will also help you adapt your communication approach to facilitate clearer exchanges, forge stronger connections in virtual settings, and achieve your communication goals.

Follow the instructions below to gain insight into your virtual communication style. To get the best results, answer each question honestly based on your instincts and typical behavior when engaging in virtual communication.

Step 1: Communication Style Assessment
Directions: For each question, select a score of 1–5 without overthinking your answer:

1= Strongly Disagree
2= Disagree
3= Neither Agree nor Disagree
4= Agree
5= Strongly Agree

Note: The term *messages* in the questions below refers broadly to any kind of text-based virtual message (email, instant messages, phone text messages, etc.).

1. I often choose to temporarily ignore work messages during the workday so I can get my work tasks done.
   My score _____
2. I often send a single-sentence or few-word response to work emails.
   My score _____
3. I ignore any work messages outside of normal work hours.
   My score _____
4. I find it more efficient to discuss tasks and issues in real-time meetings with coworkers rather than via email.
   My score _____
5. During the workday, I use notifications (e.g., sound or vibrate) on my phone to alert me to incoming messages.
   My score _____
6. I regularly send messages that are multiple paragraphs long.
   My score _____
7. I find using text-based communication (e.g., email and instant messages) to be much more efficient for handling work matters than meetings.
   My score _____
8. I regularly check my work messages outside of normal work hours to see if there is anything I need to deal with.
   My score _____
9. I often find it difficult to get my point across via text-based communication (e.g., email and instant messages).
   My score _____

10. I only respond to messages in predetermined, confined time periods during the workday.

    My score _____

11. Long messages are a waste of time.

    My score _____

12. Any work messages that are sent to me outside of normal work hours can wait until the next workday for me to respond to them.

    My score _____

13. During the workday, I frequently check my inbox and/or phone to see what messages have come in.

    My score _____

14. When responding to work messages, my goal is to finish them as quickly as possible.

    My score _____

15. When I'm focused on a work task, I don't let incoming messages interrupt my focus.

    My score _____

16. I'm concerned I'll miss out on important information if I don't check my work messages outside of work hours.

    My score _____

17. Real-time meetings almost always feel like a waste of time.

    My score _____

18. I believe it's important to be thorough in responding to work messages to make sure I didn't miss anything.

    My score _____

19. I set boundaries to ensure my work communication doesn't interrupt my life outside of work.

    My score _____

20. During the workday, I aim to be responsive and answer work messages as soon as I get them.

    My score _____

21. I have trouble gauging my work colleagues' intended meaning over text-based communication (e.g., email and instant messages).
My score _____

22. It's more important to provide all potentially necessary information in a message rather than keep it brief.
My score _____

23. I often find myself responding to work messages outside of normal work hours.
My score _____

24. I find that nearly anything my coworkers or I need to relay can be done over text-based communication (e.g., email or instant messaging).
My score _____

Step 2: Style Analysis

This tool is intended to help you begin to understand your communication strengths and weaknesses, as well as to help you gain a deeper perspective of how others might approach their virtual communication differently from you. This tool is by no means exhaustive, but it can help you to focus on some of the core differences between virtual communication styles.

Directions: Follow the guidance below to calculate your scores for each of the following:

✦ Communication Responders vs. Concentrators
✦ Communication Efficients vs. Deep-divers
✦ Communication Boundary-drawers vs. Boundary-crossers
✦ Communication Talkers vs. Texters

For each category, a score of 0 places you directly in the center of the continuum. The closer to +12 your score is, the more strongly you fit into the right-hand category. The closer your score is to –12, the more strongly you fit into the left-hand category.

Communication Responders vs. Concentrators

–12	0	+12
Concentrators		*Responders*

1. Add up your scores for Questions #5, 13, and 20:
   Subtotal #1_____
2. Add up your scores for Questions #1, 10, and 15:
   Subtotal #2_____
3. Subtract Subtotal #2 from Subtotal #1 (Subtotal #1 – Subtotal #2):
   Final Score _____

Communication Responders

Individuals who are inclined toward the *Communication Responders* category tend to frequently check their messages and send prompt replies. Communication Responders are more likely to have audio or vibration message notifications set on their mobile devices so they are more aware of information as it arrives. Their fast communication style keeps them informed—especially when it comes to time-sensitive information—because they see messages quickly. This approach enables Communication Responders to capitalize on opportunities more often than others, as they can volunteer and/or set the tone of conversation chains before others even realize the potential to do so. Similarly, Communication Responders' rapid responses can help increase their team's overall productivity by pushing tasks forward in a timely manner. However, because Communication Responders regularly interrupt their work tasks to read and respond to messages, it can be challenging for them to find long periods of focus time. This type of multitasking and reduced focus can lead to increased error rates and decreased individual productivity, as frequently switching between tasks can be very mentally taxing. Those who rate high in this category can benefit from setting aside a few blocks of time each day solely for deep work, during which you close out of all your communication tools and turn off all notifications.

Communication Concentrators

Those who are predisposed to the *Communication Concentrators* category tend to intentionally and temporarily ignore messages during certain periods of the workday so they can more fully focus on other tasks. They set aside specific blocks of time to read and respond to communication, and beyond those times, they limit the degree to which they attend to incoming messages. Concentrators excel in maintaining greater focus, both on their non-communication-related work tasks and their communication itself, by limiting communication multitasking. By minimizing distractions and maintaining their attention on key tasks, Communication Concentrators are more likely to produce high-quality work with fewer mistakes. Further, Communication Concentrators can be more individually productive, as they spend less time needing to catch back up on where they left off on work tasks after responding to messages. However, while immersed in their work, Concentrators may miss out on spontaneous opportunities or time-sensitive requests that require immediate attention, potentially impacting team collaboration and their longer-term goals. Those who rate high in this category can benefit from briefly connecting with colleagues to set expectations about when messages will be read and responded to, and how others can get in touch with you for time-sensitive issues.

Communication Efficients vs. Deep-divers

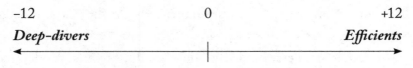

–12	0	+12
Deep-divers		*Efficients*

1. Add up your scores for Questions #2, 11, and 14:
   Subtotal #1_____

2. Add up your scores for Questions #6, 18, and 22:
   Subtotal #2_____
3. Subtract Subtotal #2 from Subtotal #1 (Subtotal #1 – Subtotal #2):
   Final Score _____

Communication Efficients

Individuals who are inclined toward the *Communication Efficients* category tend to provide very brief and concise responses to work communication. Their goal is to be as succinct with their communication as possible to save time for themselves and others, and avoid feeling "buried" by their inboxes. This approach can minimize communication burnout. Their efficiency also gives them more time to advance other work tasks rather than dedicating a significant portion of their day to their messages. Communication Efficients can face challenges when it comes to the apparent brevity of their communication style; while some people will appreciate not receiving overly long messages, others will view these abrupt responses as a signal that the message sender doesn't care. Efficients excel at identifying core communication points, but they can sometimes unintentionally miss responding to message components that their communication recipient deemed important. Further, the lack of detail Efficients provide in their responses can sometimes result in misinterpretations. Those who rate high in this category can benefit from inviting follow-up questions to their messages to address any potential gaps in understanding and prevent them from appearing abrupt.

Communication Deep-divers

Individuals who are predisposed to the *Communication Deep-divers* category take a comprehensive, detailed approach to all work communication. They respond to each point of a colleague's message, prioritizing the completeness of their communication over saving time. Communication Deep-divers excel at conveying engagement and interest in their work through their communication practices. By taking the time to send lengthier, well-crafted messages, they demonstrate conscientious-ness and ensure that message receivers feel like they were truly "heard." Additionally, this thorough approach to communication can have the added benefit of reducing misunderstandings. However, Communi-cation Deep-divers can struggle to get through all of their messages in a timely fashion due to the amount of time and energy they ded-icate to each one. Without a strict means of prioritizing, all commu-nication becomes important, which results in less time for completing non-communication-related work tasks and can lead to communication burnout. Deep-divers' detailed messages can sometimes frustrate Com-munication Efficients and put added pressure on others to respond with a similarly lengthy response. Those who rank high in this category can benefit by leading their longer communications with bullet points or summaries to focus on key points and practice conciseness.

Communication Boundary-drawers vs. Boundary-crossers

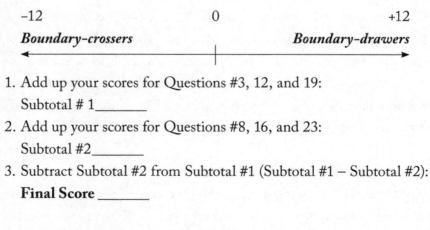

-12   0   +12

Boundary-crossers   *Boundary-drawers*

1. Add up your scores for Questions #3, 12, and 19:
   Subtotal # 1_____
2. Add up your scores for Questions #8, 16, and 23:
   Subtotal #2_____
3. Subtract Subtotal #2 from Subtotal #1 (Subtotal #1 – Subtotal #2):
   Final Score _____

Communication Boundary-drawers

Individuals who are inclined toward the *Communication Boundary-drawers* category adeptly differentiate between their professional communi-cation during work hours and personal communication during leisure time. They tend to protect their "off the clock" time with tactics such as shutting off their work devices, ignoring incoming work messages, and being fully mentally engaged when they're not at work. Communication Boundary-drawers are often skilled at disconnecting and taking advantage of their time away from the office. As a result, they return to work the next day (or following a weekend) feeling more refreshed and rejuvenated, which can lead to better work output and reduced risk of burnout. Conversely, Boundary-drawers can miss out on relational opportunities, such as communicating with their coworkers and supervisors in less formal message contexts outside of normal work hours. Their clear boundaries can make them seem less engaged and dedicated to their work compared to those who respond to messages more frequently outside of work hours. Those who rank high in this category can benefit from making a greater effort to engage in strengthening work relationships and being communicative during the workday to help offset any negative impressions stemming from being unavailable after work hours.

Communication Boundary-crossers

Individuals who tend toward the *Communication Boundary-crossers* category often find themselves blurring the lines between work and home by responding to work-related communication outside of normal work hours. Boundary-crossers are often perceived as dedicated, critical team members because of their willingness to stay "plugged in" outside of the traditional workday. They can develop stronger relationships with supervisors and team members because of their engagement in work communication outside of their contracted hours. Another benefit of being one of the first to respond to after-hours communication is that, in certain contexts, Communication Boundary-crossers are able to set the tone and proactively direct conversations. Because of their lack of clear lines between work and their lives outside of work, however, Boundary-crossers can often feel an inability to escape from work. Their time off can be less rejuvenating because they are either engaging in—or thinking about—their work communication. This constant connectivity can be distracting during time off, making it more difficult to fully recharge, and can potentially lead to burnout. Those who rank high in this category can benefit from setting aside time after work purely for rejuvenation, during which work devices and notifications are turned off.

Communication Talkers vs. Texters

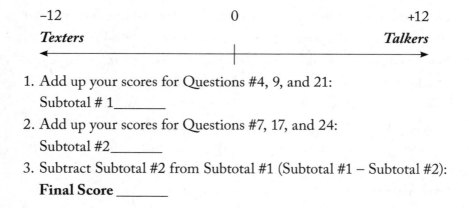

1. Add up your scores for Questions #4, 9, and 21:
   Subtotal # 1_____
2. Add up your scores for Questions #7, 17, and 24:
   Subtotal #2_____
3. Subtract Subtotal #2 from Subtotal #1 (Subtotal #1 − Subtotal #2):
   Final Score _____

Communication Talkers

Individuals who are inclined toward the *Communication Talkers* category tend to prefer conversations that are held in real time and face-to-face (either in person or via video calls), and they find that text-based communication can often be limiting and frustrating. They find it more effective to see and hear the person (or people) they're communicating with, as doing so can strengthen relationships and expedite certain communication by eliminating the time lags that occur with text-based communication, such as email. When complicated information is involved in an interaction, Talkers are less likely to overlook important details because of their ability to ask follow-up questions and better gauge nonverbal behavior due to interacting synchronously. They can face challenges due to feeling a need to constantly be "on" and self-monitor during their interactions, as their communication partner(s) can see their body language and hear any mistakes in real time. As a result, Talkers can become fatigued because of their communication practices. Talkers can also face slower work progress due to time spent engaging in "small talk" and scheduling difficulties that arise when trying to coordinate synchronous meetings. Those who rank high in this category can benefit from more regularly leveraging text-based communication (e.g., email, instant message, and texting) rather than video or in-person meetings to reduce the number of time- and socially-intensive interactions for themselves (and their collaborators).

Communication Texters

Individuals who are predisposed to the *Communication Texters* category feel that real-time meetings are generally a poor use of time, and that most interactions can be dealt with more effectively via text-based communication (e.g., email or instant messaging). Texters benefit from being able to communicate at their own pace and in a format that doesn't require them to monitor their physical presence (e.g., facial expressions, video backgrounds, and clothing). They are more often able to avoid the hassle and time commitment of needing to schedule synchronous meetings—and sometimes avoid meetings altogether—which can give them more time to complete non-communication work tasks sooner. Texters also benefit from the "delayed" nature of text-based communication, whereby they can plan out what they intend to relay and avoid being caught off guard by an unexpected question or comment. Texters can face challenges because their preference for text-based communication can reduce their efficiency when many back-and-forth messages are required to complete a task or project. Further, Texters' propensity to avoid richer interactions can lead to more misinterpretations during interactions due to a lack of nonverbal behavior (tone of voice, facial expressions, etc.). Texters may have reduced opportunities for building trust and increasing relational strength with the people they are interacting with, especially with colleagues who prefer to connect face-to-face. Those who rank high in this category can benefit from more regularly incorporating phone, video, or in-person meetings to strengthen their connections with others and better show their "effort."

Acknowledgments

This book never would have happened without my amazing partner and wife, Stephanie Fazio. It was her journey as a fantasy author that motivated me to pursue a book of my own. Thanks to her expertise and creative insights, instead of being just another dry academic article, this book transformed into a captivating story of how to master virtual communication. Her brilliant ideas, dedication, and love inspire me every day.

I am immensely grateful to Adam Grant for his mentorship and for opening the door to writing (and publishing) this book. And for making sure it had a title that would make people want to read it. Throughout my career, he has challenged me and helped make me a better researcher, writer, and thinker.

My literary agent, Sylvie Carr, has been with me through every step of this journey as both a guide and supporter. Without her, this book would still be several dozen notebooks' worth of chicken scratch and disorganized chaos. I'm more grateful than words can express for the countless hours she's dedicated to helping me fine-tune the wording of this book and find it a home.

Ronnie Alvarado, Maria Espinosa, Stephanie Hitchcock, and Richard Rhorer, the team at Simon Acumen, have believed in me from the beginning. Their tireless efforts to bring my ideas into reality—and transform my vague design concepts into a stunning cover—are deeply appreciated.

I am grateful to Riya Singh for her diligent research, as well as discovery of quotes and stories. Her efforts breathed life into the pages of this book.

A special thanks to Hayley Blunden, who provided invaluable ideas and feedback not only for this book, but for many research projects we've worked on together. I couldn't ask for a better collaborator.

Teresa Amabile has been one of my biggest champions since I was a starry-eyed (and stumbling) PhD student. Her mentorship has been instrumental in shaping my journey as an author.

Norm and Elaine Brodsky were the ones who first introduced me to the world of business and taught me countless important lessons (such as the difference between cc and bcc). I am inspired by their boundless energy and desire to make the world a better place. Bob Brodsky, Randi Brodsky, and Rhoda Schneider have always supported and encouraged me, and never doubted I would be successful wherever life took me.

John Fazio and Ellen Schaeffer are the extra set of parents I never thought I'd be lucky enough to have. Their presence in my life has been a source of love, strength, and humility every time they beat me at Wordle.

I'm grateful to Brinden Chand, Jacqueline Holloway, Jennifer Hutcheson, Elaine Richards, Jason Fried, David Heinemeier Hansson, Alanna Harvey, Brian Lo, Everett Spain, Alfredo Ramirez, and Ana Schomaker for generously offering their time for interviews or facilitating them for this book. Their contributions gave this book personality and dimension that I couldn't have done without.

Aside from the small detail of saving my life, Justin Ginsburgh has been a constant supporter and source of career advice. I'm always astonished by his accomplishments and can't wait to see what transformative project he works on next.

The remarkable work and dedication of Drs. Ivan Fuss, Farid Boulad, Nancy Kernan, and Peter Steinherz are the reason why I am healthy and able to do all the things I love. I've worked with many medical professionals throughout my life, and their commitment to going above and beyond—as well as their extraordinary knowledge and compassion—is a source of inspiration.

Ting Zhang, Paige Dangerfield, Yasaswini Konthala, Saahari Kumar, Aryan Bhalla, and Avi Meher provided invaluable assistance and contributions to the ideas presented in this book. Their collective encouragement, suggestions, and insights have made this book a million times better than it would have been without them.

There are countless others who helped get me to where I am both personally and professionally, and I'm grateful to all those who have imparted valuable lessons, stories, and advice.

Image Sources

Page 67: "Ace Hotel New York," Revinate, https://marketing.revinate.com/public/promotion/view-in-browser/message-log/bbc7c2ee-48fc-4272-ba31-6cdebc7aeeb1.

Page 67: Kath Pay, "How to create an effective apology email: 7 examples," Martech, October 12, 2022, https://martech.org/how-to-create-an-effective-apology-email-7-examples/.

Pages 68: Paper Planes, "6 Email Disaster Stories to read before you hit send," *Medium*, December 28, 2016, https://blog.newtonhq.com/6-email-disaster-stories-to-read-before-you-hit-send-8207d9b5dd4e.

Page 69: Karen R. Chinander and Maurice E. Schweitzer, "The Input Bias: The Misuse of Input Information in Judgments of Outcomes," *Organizational Behavior and Human Decision Processes* 91, no. 2 (2003): 243–53.

Page 86: Abi Cook, Meg Thompson, and Paddy Ross, "Virtual First Impressions: Zoom Backgrounds Affect Judgements of Trust and Competence," *PLoS ONE* (2023).

Page 95: Thomas Gilovich, Victoria Husted Medvec, and Kenneth Savitsky, "The Spotlight Effect in Social Judgment: An Egocentric Bias in Estimates of the Salience of One's Own Actions and Appearance," *Journal of Personality and Social Psychology* 78, no. 2 (2000): 211–22.

Pages 104, 105: Andrew Brodsky and Mike Tolliver, "No, Remote Employees Aren't Becoming Less Engaged," *Harvard Business Review*, December 22, 2022, https://hbr.org/2022/12/no-remote-employees-arent-becoming-less-engaged.

Page 131: "This is the actual end of the #lawyercat video, with the filter removed and our faces revealed!," 394th District Court of Texas - Live Stream, March 30, 2022, YouTube video, 0:32, https://www.youtube.com/ watch?v=AzWFEF267jk.

Page 131: "Congressman Tom Emmer appears upside down on Zoom hearing," Reuters, February 11, 2021, YouTube video, https://www.youtube.com/watch?v=dsMSWmF3DJc.

Page 147: "Children interrupt BBC News interview - BBC News," BBC News, March 10, 2017, YouTube video, https://www.youtube.com/ watch?v=Mh4f9AYRCZY.

Page 154: Kate Muir, Adam Joinson, Emily Collins, Rachel Cotterill, and Nigel Dewdney, "When Asking 'What' and 'How' Helps You Win: Mimicry of

Interrogative Terms Facilitates Successful Online Negotiations," *Negotiation and Conflict Management Research* (2020).

Page 157: "Rock Center Directors' Discussion with Roz Brewer," Stanford Law School, July 27, 2020, YouTube video, https://www.youtube.com/ watch?v=E523uDvVTok.

Page 158: "Walgreens CEO Roz Brewer to Leaders: Put Your Phones Away and Listen to Employees," Harvard Business Review, December 9, 2021, YouTube Video, https://www.youtube.com/ watch?v=Rk1y7Yahtic.

Page 158: "Littles Q&A with Roz Brewer, CEO of Walgreens - Iconic Mentor Auction 2022," Big Brothers Big Sisters of Metro Atlanta, January 21, 2022, YouTube video, https://www.youtube.com/ watch?v=FxCt7nx24Dw.

Page 159: "How to foster true diversity and inclusion at work (and in your community) | Rosalind G. Brewer," TED, December 23, 2020, YouTube video, https://www .youtube.com/ watch?v=klXVQsbhFsE.

Page 160: Francis J. Flynn and Chelsea R. Lide, "Communication Miscalibration: The Price Leaders Pay for Not Sharing Enough," *Academy of Management Journal* 66, no. 4 (2023): 1102–22.

Page 171: Adam Nagourney, David E. Sanger, and Johanna Barr, "Hawaii Panics After Alert About Incoming Missile Is Sent in Error," *The New York Times*, January 13, 2018, https://www.nytimes.com/2018/01/13/us/hawaii-missile.html.

Page 182: Adam D. Galinsky, William W. Maddux, Debra Gilin, and Judith B. White,"Why It Pays to Get Inside the Head of Your Opponent: The Differential Effects of Perspective Taking and Empathy in Negotiations," *Psychological Science* 19, no. 4 (2008): 378–84.

Pages 194–95: "Email exchange between Steve Jobs and James Murdoch," Zach Seward, https://www.documentcloud.org/ documents/ 702951-email-exchange -between-steve-jobs-and-james.html.

Pages 194–95: Zachary M. Seward, "The Steve Jobs emails that show how to win a hard-nosed negotiation," Quartz, May 22, 2013, https://qz.com/ 87184/ the-steve -jobs-emails-that-show-how-to-win-a-hard-nosed-negotiation.

Page 208: Peter Steiner, "On the Internet, nobody knows you're a dog," August 24, 2018, Licensed by Andrew Brodsky from CartoonStock, https://www.cartoonstock .com/cartoon?searchID=CC22230.

Page 231: Shuang Ren, Jia Hu, Guiyao Tang, and Doren Chadee, "Digital Connectivity for Work After Hours: Its Curvilinear Relationship with Employee Job Performance," *Personnel Psychology* 76, no. 3 (2023): 731–57.

Page 235: Talia Ariss et al., "Where to Look? Alcohol, Affect, and Gaze Behavior during a Virtual Social Interaction," *Clinical Psychological Science* 11, no. 2 (2023): 239–52.

Page 236-237: OutHorse Your Email," Visit Island, https://www.visiticeland .com/outhorse-your-email/.

Page 239: "Sisyphus," OpenClipArt, April 10, 2019, https://openclipart.org/detail /318206/sisyphus.

Notes

Chapter 1: The PING Approach

1 Stewart Brand and R. E. Crandall, "The Media Lab: Inventing the Future at MIT," *Computers in Physics* 2, no. 1 (1988): 91–92.

3 Bin Wang, Yukun Liu, and Sharon K. Parker, "How Does the Use of Information Communication Technology Affect Individuals? A Work Design Perspective," *Academy of Management Annals* 14, no. 2 (2020): 695–725.

3 Cristina B. Gibson, Laura Huang, Bradley L. Kirkman, and Debra L. Shapiro, "Where Global and Virtual Meet: The Value of Examining the Intersection of These Elements in Twenty-First-Century Teams," *Annual Review of Organizational Psychology and Organizational Behavior* 1, no. 1 (2014): 217–44.

3 Luis L. Martins, Lucy L. Gilson, and M. Travis Maynard, "Virtual Teams: What Do We Know and Where Do We Go from Here?," *Journal of Management* 30, no. 6 (2004): 805–35.

3 Hayley Blunden and Andrew Brodsky, "A Review of Virtual Impression Management Behaviors and Outcomes," *Journal of Management* (2024).

4 Likoebe M. Maruping and Ritu Agarwal, "Managing Team Interpersonal Processes Through Technology: A Task-Technology Fit Perspective," *Journal of Applied Psychology* 89, no. 6 (2004): 975–90.

5 "'The Times They Are A-Changin': The Official Bob Dylan Site," https://www.bobdylan.com/songs/times-they-are-changin/.

5 Emma Goldberg, "ChatFished: How to Lose Friends and Alienate People with A.I.," *New York Times*, May 7, 2023, https://www.nytimes.com/2023/05/07/business/ai-chatbot-messaging-work.html/.

6 Ravi S. Gajendran and David A. Harrison, "The Good, the Bad, and the Unknown About Telecommuting: Meta-Analysis of Psychological Mediators and Individual Consequences," *Journal of Applied Psychology* 92, no. 6 (2007): 1524–41.

6 Sumita Raghuram, N. Sharon Hill, Jennifer L. Gibbs, and Likoebe M. Maruping, "Virtual Work: Bridging Research Clusters," *Academy of Management Annals* 13, no. 1 (2019): 308–41.

6 Maria Charalampous, Christine A. Grant, Carlo Tramontano, and Evie Michailidis, "Systematically Reviewing Remote E-workers' Well-Being at Work:

A Multidimensional Approach," *European Journal of Work and Organizational Psychology* 28, no. 1 (2019): 51–73.

6 Tsedal Neeley, *Remote Work Revolution: Succeeding from Anywhere* (New York: Harper Business, 2021).

6 Jason Fried and David Heinemeier Hansson, *Remote: Office Not Required* (Currency, 2013).

6 Ethan Bernstein, Hayley Blunden, Andrew Brodsky, Wonbin Sohn, and Ben Waber, "The Implications of Working Without an Office," *Harvard Business Review* 15 (2020).

10 Alice Park, "Avandia Stays on the Market, but for How Long?," *Time*, July 14, 2010, https://time.com/archive/6934534/avandia-stays-on-the-market-but-for-how-long/.

11 Gardiner Harris, "Diabetes Drug Maker HID Test Data, Files Indicate," *New York Times*, July 13, 2010, https://www.nytimes.com/2010/07/13/health/policy/13avandia.html/.

11 Turner, Terry, "Avandia," Drugwatch, March 21, 2024, https://www.drugwatch.com/avandia/.

12 Matthew Zeitlin, "Scott Rudin on Obama's Favorite Movies: 'I Bet He Likes Kevin Hart,'" BuzzFeed News, December 11, 2014, https://www.buzzfeednews.com/article/matthewzeitlin/scott-rudin-on-obama-i-bet-he-likes-kevin-hart/.

12 Karlee Weinmann, "11 Cringeworthy 'Reply-All' Email Disasters," Business Insider, November 4, 2011, https://www.businessinsider.com/11-cringe-worthy-reply-all-email-disasters-2011-11?op=1#we-owe-him-nothing-1/.

15 Alan R. Dennis, Robert M. Fuller, and Joseph S. Valacich, "Media, Tasks, and Communication Processes: A Theory of Media Synchronicity," *MIS Quarterly* (2008): 575–600.

16 Roderick I. Swaab, Adam D. Galinsky, Victoria Medvec, and Daniel A. Diermeier, "The Communication Orientation Model: Explaining the Diverse Effects of Sight, Sound, and Synchronicity on Negotiation and Group Decision-Making Outcomes," *Personality and Social Psychology Review* 16, no. 1 (2012): 25–53.

17 Julie E. Boland, Pedro Fonseca, Ilana Mermelstein, and Myles Williamson, "Zoom Disrupts the Rhythm of Conversation," *Journal of Experimental Psychology: General* 151, no. 6 (2022): 1272–82.

17 Jesper Aagaard, "On the Dynamics of Zoom Fatigue," *Convergence* 28, no. 6 (2022): 1878–91.

17 "Coworkers on Zoom Trapped in Infinite Loop of Telling Each Other 'Oh Sorry, No, Go Ahead,'" The Onion, May 18, 2020, https://www.theonion.com/coworkers-on-zoom-trapped-in-infinite-loop-of-telling-e-1843523932/.

18 Amit Kumar and Nicholas Epley, "It's Surprisingly Nice to Hear You: Misunderstanding the Impact of Communication Media Can Lead to Suboptimal Choices of How to Connect With Others," *Journal of Experimental Psychology: General* 150, no. 3 (2021): 595–607.

19 Mike Trudell, "Quinn Cook Used an Example from Their Group Text About Lebron's Leadership: 'Bron Sent a Text After 2 Weeks or so When We All Hadn't Been Together: Miss You Guys,' Just Something Uplifting like, 'Can't Wait to Get

Back on the Floor with You Guys, Finish What We Started,'" Twitter, July 11, 2020, https://twitter.com/LakersReporter/status/1282063745930326016/.

19 Brad Sullivan, "Quinn Cook Reveals 'Uplifting' Text LeBron James Sent Lakers After NBA Halted Season," Lakers Daily, July 11, 2020, https://lakersdaily.com /quinn-cook-reveals-uplifting-text-lebron-james-sent-lakers-after-nba-halted-sea son/.

19 Hayley Blunden and Andrew Brodsky, "Beyond the Emoticon: Are There Unintentional Cues of Emotion in Email?" *Personality and Social Psychology Bulletin* 47, no. 4 (2021): 565–79.

Chapter 2: To Meet or Not to Meet . . . That Is the Question

25 David Allen, "Meetings Handled Well Reduce Email. Email Handled Well Reduces Meetings," Twitter, January 18, 2012, https://twitter.com/gtdguy/status /159780367153373184/.

25 "Cat," Wikipedia, Wikimedia Foundation, January 23, 2024, https://en.wikipedia .org/wiki/Cat/.

25 "Death from Laughter," Wikipedia, Wikimedia Foundation, January 26, 2024, https://en.wikipedia.org/wiki/Death_from_laughter/.

25 Michael Levy, Donald E. Stewart, and Christopher Hardy Wise Kent, "Encyclopædia Britannica," Britannica, accessed March 18, 2024, https://www.britan nica.com/topic/Encyclopaedia-Britannica-English-language-reference-work.

26 "History of Wikipedia," Wikipedia, Wikimedia Foundation, January 30, 2024, https://en.wikipedia.org/wiki/History_of_Wikipedia/.

26 Lily Rothman, "Wikipedia at 15: How the Concept of a Wiki Was Invented," *Time*, January 15, 2016, https://time.com/4177280/wiki-history-wikipedia/.

26 Michael Aaron Dennis, "Wiki | Definition & Facts," *Encyclopaedia Britannica*, January 21, 2024, https://www.britannica.com/topic/wiki/.

26 "WikiWikiWeb," Wikipedia, Wikimedia Foundation, January 26, 2024, https:// en.wikipedia.org/wiki/WikiWikiWeb/.

26 "Wikipedia | Definition, History, & Facts," *Encyclopaedia Britannica*, January 21, 2024, https://www.britannica.com/topic/Wikipedia/.

26 "History of Wikipedia," Wikipedia, Wikimedia Foundation, January 30, 2024, https://en.wikipedia.org/wiki/History_of_Wikipedia/.

26 "Wikipedia | Definition, History, & Facts," *Encyclopaedia Britannica*, January 21, 2024, https://www.britannica.com/topic/Wikipedia/.

27 "Wikipedia | Definition, History, & Facts"; "History of Wikipedia," Wikipedia, January 30, 2024, https://en.wikipedia.org/wiki/History_of_Wikipedia/.

27 Jim Giles, "Special Report Internet Encyclopaedias Go Head to Head," *Nature* 438, no. 15 (2005): 900–901.

27 Dan Fletcher, "Wikipedia," *Time*, August 18, 2009, https://time.com/archive /6906347/wikipedia/.

27 Jennifer Still, "How to Create a Wikipedia Page for a Person, Place, Company, or Any Notable Topic," Business Insider, August 23, 2022, https://www.business insider.com/guides/tech/how-to-create-a-wikipedia-page.

28 Rails Foundation, "Ruby on Rails," Ruby on Rails, accessed March 18, 2024, https://rubyonrails.org/.

29 Adley, "How to Make Cotton Candy in Your Dryer," TikTok, August 23, 2021, https://www.tiktok.com/@theadleyshow/video/6999826319995440390.

30 "Will AI Fix Work?" Microsoft, May 9, 2023, https://www.microsoft.com/en -us/worklab/work-trend-index/will-ai-fix-work.

30 Emma Goldberg, "ChatFished: How to Lose Friends and Alienate People with AI," *New York Times*, May 7, 2023, https://www.nytimes.com/2023/05/07 /business/ai-chatbot-messaging-work.html/.

30 Likoebe M. Maruping and Ritu Agarwal, "Managing Team Interpersonal Pro- cesses through Technology: A Task-Technology Fit Perspective," *Journal of Applied Psychology* 89, no. 6 (2004): 975–90.

30 Andrea B. Hollingshead, Joseph E. McGrath, and Kathleen M. O'Connor, "Group Task Performance and Communication Technology: A Longitudinal Study of Computer-Mediated Versus Face-to-Face Work Groups," *Small Group Research* 24, no. 3 (1993): 307–33.

30 "Instagram," accessed March 18, 2024, https://www.instagram.com/explore/tags /productivityhack/.

30 "TikTok—Make Your Day," accessed March 18, 2024, https://www.tiktok.com /tag/productivityhack.

30 Lydia Dishman, "These Are the Weirdest Productivity Hacks That Really Work," *Fast Company*, October 4, 2017, https://www.fastcompany.com/40475389/these -are-the-weirdest-productivity-hacks-that-really-work/.

31 Charissa Cheong, "MrBeast Said He Has a 'Mental Breakdown Every Other Week' Because He Is So Focused on Making YouTube Videos," Business Insider, June 29, 2023, https://www.insider.com/mrbeast-youtube-mental-breakdown -videos-work-life-balance-2023-6/.

31 Joe Pinsker, "'Ugh, I'm So Busy': A Status Symbol for Our Time," *Atlantic*, March 1, 2017, https://www.theatlantic.com/business/archive/2017/03/busyness -status-symbol/518178/.

31 Silvia Bellezza, Neeru Paharia, and Anat Keinan, "Conspicuous Consumption of Time: When Busyness and Lack of Leisure Time Become a Status Symbol," *Jour- nal of Consumer Research* 44, no. 1 (2017): 118–38.

31 Ravi S. Kudesia, Ashish Pandey, and Christopher S. Reina, "Doing More with Less: Interactive Effects of Cognitive Resources and Mindfulness Training in Coping with Mental Fatigue from Multitasking," *Journal of Management* 48, no. 2 (2022): 410–39.

31 Rachel F. Adler and Raquel Benbunan-Fich, "Juggling on a High Wire: Multi- tasking Effects on Performance," *International Journal of Human-Computer Studies* 70, no. 2 (2012): 156–68.

31 Hope King, "Here's Why You Can't Get Any Work Done," Axios, May 9, 2023, https://www.axios.com/2023/05/09/work-productivity-distractions-email-chat/.

32 "Shopify," Yahoo Finance, accessed March 18, 2024, https://finance.yahoo.com /quote/SHOP/profile.

32 Jena McGregor, "This Company Is Canceling All Meetings with More Than Two Employees to Free Up Workers' Time," *Forbes*, January 3, 2023, https://www

.forbes.com/sites/jenamcgregor/2023/01/03/shopify-is-canceling-all-meetings -with-more-than-two-people-from-workers-calendars-and-urging-few-to-be -added-back/?sh=b3fbd8a6fe8a/.

32 Harley Finkelstein, "Yesterday, Shopify Got Rid of ALL Recurring Meetings of More than Three People. Approx 10,000 Calendar Events Were Deleted Yesterday . . . ," LinkedIn, January 4, 2023, https://www.linkedin.com/posts/harleyf_this-company -is-canceling-all-meetings-with-activity-7016494558817525761-hMcY/.

32 Ivana Saric, "The Glaring Cost of Meetings," Axios, July 13, 2023, https://www .axios.com/2023/07/13/meetings-productivity-cost-cut/.

32 Saric, "Glaring Cost of Meetings."

33 Megan Cerullo, "Unnecessary Meetings Can Cost Big Companies $100 Million a Year, Report Finds," CBS News, September 30, 2022, https://www.cbsnews.com /news/unnecessary-meetings-cost-big-companies-100-million-annually/.

33 Finkelstein, "Yesterday."

33 Lindsey Wilkinson, "Shopify Expects Productivity Boost from Meeting Ban," CIODive, March 24, 2023, https://www.ciodive.com/news/Shopify-meeting -ban-productivity-remote-work/645969/.

33 Leslie A. Perlow, Constance Noonan Hadley, and Eunice Eun, "Stop the Meeting Madness," *Harvard Business Review*, June 26, 2017, https://hbr.org/2017/07/stop -the-meeting-madness/.

33 Ashley Whillans, Dave Feldman, and Damian Wisniewski, "The Psychology Behind Meeting Overload," *Harvard Business Review*, December 13, 2023, https:// hbr.org/2021/11/the-psychology-behind-meeting-overload.

33 Maria Aspan, "Why Mark Cuban Hates Public Speaking, Phone Calls—and Lunches," *Inc.*, January 5, 2021, https://www.inc.com/maria-aspan/mark-cuban -disses-public-speaking-and-business-lunches.html/.

33 Nina Zipkin, "Why Elon Musk Hates Meetings," *Entrepreneur*, April 19, 2018, https://www.entrepreneur.com/living/why-elon-musk-hates-meetings/312247/.

33 Courtney Connley, "Jeff Bezos' 'Two Pizza Rule' Can Help You Hold More Productive Meetings," CNBC, April 30, 2018, https://www.cnbc.com/2018/04/30 /jeff-bezos-2-pizza-rule-can-help-you-hold-more-productive-meetings.html/.

34 Ruth Umoh, "Jeff Bezos, Mark Cuban and Elon Musk Avoid This Productivity Killer—and You Should Too," CNBC, June 13, 2018, https://www.cnbc .com/2018/06/13/jeff-bezos-mark-cuban-and-elon-musk-all-avoid-meetings.html/.

34 Christopher C. Rosen, Lauren S. Simon, Ravi S. Gajendran, Russell E. Johnson, Hun Whee Lee, and Szu-Han Joanna Lin, "Boxed In by Your Inbox: Implications of Daily E-mail Demands for Managers' Leadership Behaviors," *Journal of Applied Psychology* 104, no. 1 (2019): 19–33.

34 Rosen et al.

34 Mark Muraven and Roy F. Baumeister, "Self-Regulation and Depletion of Limited Resources: Does Self-Control Resemble a Muscle?" *Psychological Bulletin* 126, no. 2 (2000): 247–59.

36 Joseph B. Walther, "Selective Self-Presentation in Computer-Mediated Communication: Hyperpersonal Dimensions of Technology, Language, and Cognition," *Computers in Human Behavior* 23, no. 5 (2007): 2538–57.

37 Ellen J. Langer, Arthur Blank, and Benzion Chanowitz, "The Mindlessness of Ostensibly Thoughtful Action: The Role of 'Placebic' Information in Interpersonal Interaction," *Journal of Personality and Social Psychology* 36, no. 6 (1978): 635–42.

38 David Larcker, "How Netflix Redesigned Board Meetings," *Harvard Business Review*, August 30, 2021, https://hbr.org/2018/05/how-netflix-redesigned-board-meetings/.

39 Larcker, "How Netflix Redesigned."

39 Joseph A. Allen and Nale Lehmann-Willenbrock, "The Key Features of Workplace Meetings: Conceptualizing the Why, How, and What of Meetings at Work," *Organizational Psychology Review* 13, no. 4 (2023): 355–78.

39 Ethan Bernstein, Hayley Blunden, Andrew Brodsky, Wonbin Sohn, and Ben Waber, "The Implications of Working Without an Office," *Harvard Business Review* 15 (2020).

39 Alyson Krueger, "Fewer Work Meetings? Corporate America Is Trying," *New York Times*, April 10, 2023, https://www.nytimes.com/2023/04/07/business/office-meetings-time.html/.

39 Steven G. Rogelberg, Cliff Scott, and John Kello, "The Science and Fiction of Meetings," *MIT Sloan Management Review* 48, no. 2 (2007): 18–21.

39 Nale Lehmann-Willenbrock, Joseph A. Allen, and Dain Belyeu, "Our Love/Hate Relationship with Meetings: Relating Good and Bad Meeting Behaviors to Meeting Outcomes, Engagement, and Exhaustion," *Management Research Review* 39, no. 10 (2016): 1293–1312.

40 Leslie A. Perlow, Constance Noonan Hadley, and Eunice Eun, "Stop the Meeting Madness," *Harvard Business Review*, June 26, 2017, https://hbr.org/2017/07/stop-the-meeting-madness/.

40 Melissa A. Cohen, Steven G. Rogelberg, Joseph A. Allen, and Alexandra Luong, "Meeting Design Characteristics and Attendee Perceptions of Staff/Team Meeting Quality," *Group Dynamics: Theory, Research, and Practice* 15, no. 1 (2011): 90–104.

40 Simone Kauffeld and Nale Lehmann-Willenbrock, "Meetings Matter: Effects of Team Meetings on Team and Organizational Success," *Small Group Research* 43, no. 2 (2012): 130–58.

41 W. H. Cooper, R. B. Gallupe, S. Pollard, and J. Cadsby, "Some Liberating Effects of Anonymous Electronic Brainstorming," *Small Group Research* 29, no. 2 (1998): 147–78.

41 Melanie S. Brucks and Jonathan Levav, "Virtual Communication Curbs Creative Idea Generation," *Nature* 605, no. 7908 (2022): 108–12.

41 Julie E. Boland, Pedro Fonseca, Ilana Mermelstein, and Myles Williamson, "Zoom Disrupts the Rhythm of Conversation," *Journal of Experimental Psychology: General* 151, no. 6 (2022): 1272–82.

42 Boland, Fonseca, Mermelstein, and Williamson, "Zoom Disrupts the Rhythm of Conversation."

42 Cooper et al., "Some Liberating Effects."

42 Gleb Tsipursky, "Why Virtual Brainstorming Is Better for Innovation," *Harvard Business Review*, July 27, 2023, https://hbr.org/2022/02/why-virtual-brainstorming-is-better-for-innovation/.

42 David S. Kerr and Uday S. Murthy, "Divergent and Convergent Idea Generation in Teams: A Comparison of Computer-Mediated and Face-to-Face Communication," *Group Decision and Negotiation* 13 (2004): 381–99.

43 Richard L. Daft and Robert H. Lengel, "Organizational Information Requirements, Media Richness and Structural Design," *Management Science* 32, no. 5 (1986): 554–71.

46 Thomas Jackson, Ray Dawson, and Darren Wilson, "The Cost of Email Interruption," *Journal of Systems and Information Technology* 5, no. 1 (2001): 81–92.

46 Gloria Mark, Shamsi T. Iqbal, Mary Czerwinski, Paul Johns, Akane Sano, and Yuliya Lutchyn, "Email Duration, Batching and Self-Interruption: Patterns of Email Use on Productivity and Stress," in *Proceedings of the 2016 CHI Conference on Human Factors in Computing Systems* (2016), 1717–28.

46 Indy Wijngaards, Florie R. Pronk, and Martijn J. Burger. "For whom and under what circumstances does email message batching work?." *Internet Interventions* 27, (2022), https://doi.org/10.1016/j.invent.2022.100494.

46 Stephen Monsell, "Task Switching," *Trends in Cognitive Sciences* 7, no. 3 (2003): 134–40.

47 Kimberly D. Elsbach and Andrew B. Hargadon, "Enhancing Creativity through 'Mindless' Work: A Framework of Workday Design," *Organization Science* 17, no. 4 (2006): 470–83; John P. Trougakos, Ivona Hideg, Bonnie Hayden Cheng, and Daniel J. Beal, "Lunch Breaks Unpacked: The Role of Autonomy as a Moderator of Recovery during Lunch," *Academy of Management Journal* 57, no. 2 (2014): 405–21.

47 Quintus R. Jett and Jennifer M. George, "Work Interrupted: A Closer Look at the Role of Interruptions in Organizational Life," *Academy of Management Review* 28, no. 3 (2003): 494–507.

47 Sooyeol Kim, YoungAh Park, and Lucille Headrick, "Daily Micro-Breaks and Job Performance: General Work Engagement as a Cross-Level Moderator," *Journal of Applied Psychology* 103, no. 7 (2018): 772–86.

47 Kimberly D. Elsbach, Dan M. Cable, and Jeffrey W. Sherman, "How Passive 'Face Time' Affects Perceptions of Employees: Evidence of Spontaneous Trait Inference," *Human Relations* 63, no. 6 (2010): 735–60.

48 Adrian F. Ward, Kristen Duke, Ayelet Gneezy, and Maarten W. Bos, "Brain Drain: The Mere Presence of One's Own Smartphone Reduces Available Cognitive Capacity," *Journal of the Association for Consumer Research* 2, no. 2 (2017): 140–54.

48 Thomas Jackson, Ray Dawson, and Darren Wilson, "The Cost of Email Interruption," *Journal of Systems and Information Technology* 5, no. 1 (2001): 81–92.

49 Tim Ferriss, "How to Check E-Mail Twice a Day . . . and Have Your Boss Accept It," *The Blog of Author Tim Ferriss*, March 22, 2007, https://tim.blog/2007/03/22/how-to-check-e-mail-twice-a-day-or-once-every-10-days/.

49 Langer, Blank, Chanowitz, "Mindlessness."

49 Arvind Malhotra, Ann Majchrzak, and Benson Rosen, "Leading Virtual Teams," *Academy of Management Perspectives* 21, no. 1 (2007): 60–70; Nuzul Azam Haron, Law Teik Hua, Salihudin Hassim, Fathollah Eftekhari, Muhammad Tahir

Muhammad, and Aizul Nahar Harun, "Strategies to Improve Communication Management within Virtual Project Teams," *Science and Technology* 27, no. 3 (2019): 2015–30.

50 Laura M. Giurge and Vanessa K. Bohns, "You Don't Need to Answer Right Away! Receivers Overestimate How Quickly Senders Expect Responses to Non-Urgent Work Emails," *Organizational Behavior and Human Decision Processes* 167 (2021): 114–28.

51 Karina Schumann and Michael Ross, "Why Women Apologize More Than Men: Gender Differences in Thresholds for Perceiving Offensive Behavior," *Psychological Science* 21, no. 11 (2010): 1649–55.

51 Spencer Kornhaber, "How Beyonce's 'Lemonade' Event on HBO Saturday Night Might Rewrite the Pop-Star Playbook," *Atlantic*, April 20, 2016, https://www.the atlantic.com/entertainment/archive/2016/04/beyonce-marketing-lemonade-specu lation/478968/.

51 Joseph B. Walther and Lisa C. Tidwell, "Nonverbal Cues in Computer-Mediated Communication, and the Effect of Chronemics on Relational Communication," *Journal of Organizational Computing and Electronic Commerce* 5, no. 4 (1995): 355–78.

52 Hayley Blunden and Andrew Brodsky, "A Review of Virtual Impression Management Behaviors and Outcomes," *Journal of Management* (2024).

52 Sun Young Hwang, Negar Khojasteh, and Susan R. Fussell, "When Delayed in a Hurry: Interpretations of Response Delays in Time-Sensitive Instant Messaging," *Proceedings of the ACM on Human-Computer Interaction* 3, no. GROUP (2019): 1–20.

52 Blunden and Brodsky, "Review."

53 "Close Calls with Nuclear Weapons," Union of Concerned Scientists, archived from the original July 24, 2023, retrieved April 5, 2016.

53 Eric Schlosser, *Command and Control: Nuclear Weapons, the Damascus Accident, and the Illusion of Safety* (New York: Penguin, 2013).

53 Adam Grant, "Your Email Does Not Constitute My Emergency," *New York Times*, April 13, 2023, https://www.nytimes.com/2023/04/13/opinion/email -time-work-stress.html/.

54 Jeremy Birnholtz, Graham Dixon, and Jeffrey Hancock, "Distance, Ambiguity and Appropriation: Structures Affording Impression Management in a Collocated Organization," *Computers in Human Behavior* 28, no. 3 (2012): 1028–35.

55 R. Dennis Middlemist, Eric S. Knowles, and Charles F. Matter, "Personal Space Invasions in the Lavatory: Suggestive Evidence for Arousal," *Journal of Personality and Social Psychology* 33, no. 5 (1976): 541–46.

56 Kareem Fahim, "Slap to a Man's Pride Set Off Tumult in Tunisia," *New York Times*, January 22, 2011, https://www.nytimes.com/2011/01/22/world/africa/22sidi.html/.

56 Philip N. Howard, Aiden Duffy, Deen Freelon, Muzammil M. Hussain, Will Mari, and Marwa Maziad, "Opening Closed Regimes: What Was the Role of Social Media During the Arab Spring?," available at SSRN 2595096 (2011).

56 Gadi Wolfsfeld, Elad Segev, and Tamir Sheafer, "Social Media and the Arab Spring: Politics Comes First," *International Journal of Press/Politics* 18, no. 2 (2013): 115–37.

57 Fahim, "Slap to a Man's Pride."

57 "Arab Spring | History, Revolution, Causes, Effects, & Facts," *Encyclopaedia Britannica*, December 8, 2023, https://www.britannica.com/event/Arab-Spring/.

58 Microsoft Outlook, "Stop Playing Calendar Tetris and Ask Cortana to Schedule Your Meetings with Scheduler in #microsoft365:Https://T.Co/Fiqnbpqpxu Pic .Twitter.Com/Iwikh85jzo," Twitter, August 25, 2021, https://twitter.com/Outlook /status/1430530422518296584/.

Chapter 3: Seeing Is Believing. Or Is It?

61 Bill Vaughan, quoted in "April 2, 1969," Free Lance-Star, Senator Soaper (Fredericksburg, VA), April 2, 1969, p. 1, col. 2, accessed October 27, 2023, from Google News Archive.

61 Nick Bilton, "EXCLUSIVE: The Leaked Fyre Festival Pitch Deck Is Beyond Parody," *Vanity Fair*, May 1, 2017, https://www.vanityfair.com/news/2017/05/fyre -festival-pitch-deck/.

61 Gil Kaufman, "Fyre Festival Fiasco: Timeline of a Disaster," *Billboard*, May 12, 2017, https://www.billboard.com/culture/events/fyre-festival-timeline-fiasco-7777047/.

62 Jennifer Lynn, "Fyre Festival, the Biggest FOMO-Inducing Event of 2017, Turned Out to Be a Disaster," Grazia, December 13, 2016, https://graziadaily.co.uk/celeb rity/news/fyre-festival-2017/.

62 Amelia Tait, "The Full Story of the Legendary Fyre Festival Cheese Sandwich," Vice, April 29, 2019, https://www.vice.com/en/article/mb8va8/the-full-story-of -the-legendary-fyre-festival-cheese-sandwich/.

62 Chloe Gordon, "I worked at Fyre Festival. It Was Always Going to Be a Disaster," *The Cut*, April 28, 2017, https://www.thecut.com/2017/04/fyre-festival -exumas-bahamas-disaster.html.

62 Jeva Lange, "The 17 Most Insane Moments from the Fyre Festival Documentaries," Theweek, January 18, 2019, https://theweek.com/articles/818330/17-most -insane-moments-from-fyre-festival-documentaries/.

63 Lange, "17 Most Insane Moments."

63 Chris Smith, director, *Fyre* (Netflix, 2019), 1 hour, 37 minutes, https://www.net flix.com/watch/81035279.

63 Danni Button, "Fyre Fest II Is Really Happening—Here's Everything That Went Wrong at the First One," TheStreet, August 30, 2023, https://www.thestreet.com /travel/fyre-fest-2-tickets/.

63 Jenner Furst and Julia Willoughby Nason, directors, *Fyre Fraud* (Hulu, 2019), 1 hour, 36 minutes, https://www.hulu.com/movie/fyre-fraud-e47078f3-1c0e-49a8 -9da9-c571a7a20fec.

63 Bilton, "EXCLUSIVE."

64 Paul M. Leonardi, Sienna Helena Parker, and Roni Shen, "How Remote Work Changes the World of Work," *Annual Review of Organizational Psychology and Organizational Behavior* 11 (2024): 193–219.

65 Tony Long, "July 22, 1962: Mariner 1 Done in by a Typo," *Wired*, July 22, 2009, https://www.wired.com/2009/07/dayintech-0722/.

65 NASA, "Mariner 1—NASA Science," accessed March 18, 2024, https://science .nasa.gov/mission/mariner-1/.

65 Charles Fishman, "The Most Expensive Hyphen in History," *Fast Company*, June 18, 2019, https://www.fastcompany.com/90365077/the-most-expensive -hyphen-in-history/.

65 Naaman Zhou, "Australian $50 Note Typo: Spelling Mistake Printed 46 Million Times," *Guardian*, May 14, 2019, https://www.theguardian.com/australia-news /2019/may/09/australian-50-note-typo-spelling-mistake-printed-46-million-times/.

66 Hayley Blunden and Andrew Brodsky, "Beyond the Emoticon: Are There Unintentional Cues of Emotion in Email?" *Personality and Social Psychology Bulletin* 47, no. 4 (2021): 565–79.

66 Lee Ross, "The Intuitive Psychologist and His Shortcomings: Distortions in the Attribution Process," *Advances in Experimental Social Psychology* 10 (1977): 173–220.

66 Paul Harvey, Kristen Madison, Mark Martinko, T. Russell Crook, and Tamara A. Crook, "Attribution Theory in the Organizational Sciences: The Road Traveled and the Path Ahead," *Academy of Management Perspectives* 28, no. 2 (2014): 128–46.

66 Blunden and Brodsky, "Beyond the Emoticon."

66 Jane A. Vignovic and Lori Foster Thompson, "Computer-Mediated Cross-Cultural Collaboration: Attributing Communication Errors to the Person versus the Situation," *Journal of Applied Psychology* 95, no. 2 (2010): 265–76.

67 Harold H. Kelley and John L. Michela, "Attribution Theory and Research," *Annual Review of Psychology* 31, no. 1 (1980): 457–501; Caleb T. Carr and Chad Stefaniak, "Sent from My iPhone: The Medium and Message as Cues of Sender Professionalism in Mobile Telephony," *Journal of Applied Communication Research* 40, no. 4 (2012): 403–24.

67 Vignovic and Thompson, "Computer-Mediated Cross-Cultural Collaboration."

67 Kath Pay, "How to create an effective apology email: 7 examples," Martech, October 12, 2022, https://martech.org/how-to-create-an-effective-apology-email-7 -examples/.

68 Ruth Reader, "A Brief History of Fab, from Mega-Hype to Crash and Burn," VentureBeat, March 5, 2015, https://venturebeat.com/business/a-brief-history-of-fab -from-mega-hype-to-crash-and-burn/.

68 Paper Planes, "6 Email Disaster Stories to read before you hit send," Medium, December 28, 2016, https://blog.newtonhq.com/6-email-disaster-stories-to-read -before-you-hit-send-8207d9b5dd4e.

69 Karen R. Chinander and Maurice E. Schweitzer, "The Input Bias: The Misuse of Input Information in Judgments of Outcomes," *Organizational Behavior and Human Decision Processes* 91, no. 2 (2003): 243–53.

70 Chinander and Schweitzer, "Input Bias."

71 Chinander and Schweitzer, "Input Bias."

71 Kimberly D. Elsbach, Dan M. Cable, and Jeffrey W. Sherman, "How Passive 'Face Time' Affects Perceptions of Employees: Evidence of Spontaneous Trait Inference," *Human Relations* 63, no. 6 (2010): 735–60.

72 Elsbach, Cable, and Sherman, "How Passive 'Face Time' Affects Perceptions."

72 Joshua J. Fenton, Anthony F. Jerant, Klea D. Bertakis, and Peter Franks, "The Cost of Satisfaction: A National Study of Patient Satisfaction, Health Care Uti-

lization, Expenditures, and Mortality," *Archives of Internal Medicine* 172, no. 5 (2012): 405–11.

72 Barak D. Richman and Kevin A. Schulman, "Are Patient Satisfaction Instruments Harming Both Patients and Physicians?" *JAMA* 328, no. 22 (2022): 2209–10.

74 Mike Isaac, "Inside Uber's Aggressive, Unrestrained Workplace Culture," *New York Times*, February 23, 2017, https://www.nytimes.com/2017/02/22/technology/uber-workplace-culture.html/.

74 Lauren Goode and Dieter Bohn, "Here's Arianna Huffington's Memo to Uber Employees About the Investigation She's Helping Lead," *The Verge*, February 22, 2017, https://www.theverge.com/2017/2/22/14705636/arianna-huffington-uber-memo-investigation.

75 Ioana C. Cristea and Paul M. Leonardi, "Get Noticed and Die Trying: Signals, Sacrifice, and the Production of Face Time in Distributed Work," *Organization Science* 30, no. 3 (2019): 552–72.

76 Cristea and Leonardi, "Get Noticed and Die Trying."

77 Deepak Malhotra and Max H. Bazerman, "Psychological Influence in Negotiation: An Introduction Long Overdue," *Journal of Management* 34, no. 3 (March 7, 2008): 509–31.

77 Robert B. Cialdini, Wilhelmina Wosinska, Daniel W. Barrett, Jonathan Butner, and Malgorzata Gornik-Durose, "Compliance with a Request in Two Cultures: The Differential Influence of Social Proof and Commitment/Consistency on Collectivists and Individualists," *Personality and Social Psychology Bulletin* 25, no. 10 (1999): 1242–53.

77 Robert B. Cialdini and Noah J. Goldstein, "Social Influence: Compliance and Conformity," *Annual Review Psychology* 55 (2004): 591–621.

77 Michael Lynn, "Scarcity Effects on Value: A Quantitative Review of the Commodity Theory Literature," *Psychology & Marketing* 8, no. 1 (1991): 43–57.

76 Kai Ryssdal and Nicholas Guiang, "Raising the Curtain on 'Productivity Theater,'" Marketplace, October 4, 2022, https://www.marketplace.org/2022/10/04/productivity-theater-home-office-remote-work/.

81 Youngjin Yoo and Maryam Alavi, "Media and Group Cohesion: Relative Influences on Social Presence, Task Participation, and Group Consensus," *MIS Quarterly* (2001): 371–90.

82 Chris L. Kleinke, "Gaze and Eye Contact: A Research Review," *Psychological Bulletin* 100, no. 1 (1986): 78–100.

83 Géraldine Fauville, Anna C. M. Queiroz, Mufan Luo, Jeffrey Hancock, and Jeremy N. Bailenson, "Impression Formation from Video Conference Screenshots: The Role of Gaze, Camera Distance, and Angle," *Technology, Mind, and Behavior* 3, no. 1 (2022).

83 Laura K. Guerrero and Tammy A. Miller, "Associations between Nonverbal Behaviors and Initial Impressions of Instructor Competence and Course Content in Videotaped Distance Education Courses," *Communication Education* 47, no. 1 (1998): 30–42.

83 Samar Helou, Elie El Helou, Naoko Evans, Taiki Shigematsu, Jeanine El Helou, Miki Kaneko, and Ken Kiyono, "Physician Eye Contact in Telemedicine Video

Consultations: A Cross-Cultural Experiment," *International Journal of Medical Informatics* 165 (2022): 1–11.

83 Emily Pfender and Scott Caplan, "Nonverbal Immediacy Cues and Impression Formation in Video Therapy," *Counselling Psychology Quarterly* 36, no. 3 (2023): 395–407.

83 Angelo Cafaro, Hannes Högni Vilhjálmsson, and Timothy Bickmore, "First Impressions in Human–Agent Virtual Encounters," *ACM Transactions on Computer-Human Interaction (TOCHI)* 23, no. 4 (2016): 1–40.

83 Atsushi Fukayama, Takehiko Ohno, Naoki Mukawa, Minako Sawaki, and Norihiro Hagita, "Messages Embedded in Gaze of Interface Agents—Impression Management with Agent's Gaze," in *Proceedings of the SIGCHI Conference on Human Factors in Computing Systems* (2002), 41–48.

84 Gerardo Delgado, "NVIDIA Broadcast 1.4 Adds Eye Contact and Vignette Effects with Virtual Background Enhancements," NVIDIA, January 12, 2023, https://www.nvidia.com/en-us/geforce/news/jan-2023-nvidia-broadcast-update.

84 "AMC," Yahoo Finance, accessed March 18, 2024, https://finance.yahoo.com/quote/AMC/financials/.

84 Isaiah Richard, "AMC CEO Becomes a Viral Meme after 'Pantsless Interview' with a YouTuber About Company's Stock Trading," Tech Times, June 7, 2021, https://www.techtimes.com/articles/261150/20210606/amc-ceo-becomes-viral-meme-pantsless-interview-youtuber-companys-stock.htm/.

85 Neil Hester and Eric Hehman, "Dress Is a Fundamental Component of Person Perception," *Personality and Social Psychology Review* 27, no. 4 (2023): 414–33.

85 Anat Rafaeli and Michael G. Pratt, "Tailored Meanings: On the Meaning and Impact of Organizational Dress," *Academy of Management Review* 18, no. 1 (1993): 32–55.

85 Erica R. Bailey, C. Blaine Horton, and Adam D. Galinsky, "Enclothed Harmony or Enclothed Dissonance? The Effect of Attire on the Authenticity, Power, and Engagement of Remote Workers," *Academy of Management Discoveries* 8, no. 3 (2022): 341–56.

86 Abi Cook, Meg Thompson, and Paddy Ross, "Virtual First Impressions: Zoom Backgrounds Affect Judgements of Trust and Competence," *PLoS ONE* (2023).

86 Christina D. Scott, "You Can Record an Asynchronous Video Interview Anywhere! . . . but Should You?" (Master's thesis, Saint Mary's University, 2022), https://library2.smu.ca/handle/01/30958/.

86 Noah Zandan and Hallie Lynch, "Dress for the (Remote) Job You Want," *Harvard Business Review*, February 1, 2021, https://hbr.org/2020/06/dress-for-the-remote-job-you-want.

87 Judee K. Burgoon, "Interpersonal Expectations, Expectancy Violations, and Emotional Communication," *Journal of Language and Social Psychology* 12, no. 1–2 (1993): 30–48.

87 V. H. Vroom, *Work and Motivation* (New York: Wiley, 1964).

87 Sun-Young Park, Moonhee Cho, and Soojin Kim, "The Effect of CSR Expectancy Violation: Value from Expectancy Violation Theory and Confirmation Bias," *Journal of Marketing Communications* 27, no. 4 (2021): 365–88.

125 Brodsky, "Virtual Surface Acting in Workplace Interactions."

125 Groth, Hennig-Thurau, and Walsh, "Customer Reactions to Emotional Labor."

125 Grandey, "When 'the Show Must Go On.'"

126 Brodsky, "Virtual Surface Acting in Workplace Interactions."

126 Juliana Schroeder and Nicholas Epley, "The Sound of Intellect: Speech Reveals a Thoughtful Mind, Increasing a Job Candidate's Appeal," *Psychological Science* 26, no. 6 (2015): 877–91.

127 Juliana Schroeder, Michael Kardas, and Nicholas Epley, "The Humanizing Voice: Speech Reveals, and Text Conceals, a More Thoughtful Mind in the Midst of Disagreement," *Psychological Science* 28, no. 12 (2017): 1745–62.

127 Bryson Taylor and Gross, "Better.com CEO."

128 Stacy Fernandez, "'I Prefer to Be Demeaned in the Way That I Choose To': Laid-off Worker Wonders Why Amazon Insists on Doing It Via Zoom," Daily Dot, January 28, 2024, https://www.dailydot.com/news/laid-off-amazon-worker-forced-to-zoom/.

128 Nicole James, "Nicole James," TikTok, accessed March 18, 2024, https://www.tiktok.com/@nrjwriter/video/7323297907686247722.

129 Tony Hsieh, "CEO Letter," Internet Archive, July 22, 2009, https://web.archive.org/web/20230720062445/https://www.zappos.com/ceoletter/.

130 Brodsky, "Virtual Surface Acting in Workplace Interactions."

130 Alicia A. Grandey and Allison S. Gabriel, "Emotional Labor at a Crossroads: Where Do We Go from Here?" *Annual Review of Organizational Psychology Organizational Behavior* 2, no. 1 (2015): 323–49.

130 "'I'm not a cat': lawyer gets stuck on Zoom kitten filter during court case," Guardian News, February 9, 2021, YouTube video, https://www.youtube.com/watch?v=lGOofzZOyl8.

130 Christina Zdanowicz, "Lawyer tells judge 'I'm not a cat' after a Zoom filter mishap in virtual court hearing," CNN, February 10, 2021, https://www.cnn.com/2021/02/09/us/cat-filter-lawyer-zoom-court-trnd/index.html

131 Caroline Kelly, "'You're Upside Down, Tom': Congressman Appears Upside-down on Video During Hearing," CNN, February 10, 2021, https://www.cnn.com/2021/02/10/politics/congress-tom-emmer-upside-down/index.html/.

132 Elliot Aronson, Ben Willerman, and Joanne Floyd, "The Effect of a Pratfall on Increasing Interpersonal Attractiveness," *Psychonomic Science* 4, no. 6 (1966): 227–28.

132 Aronson, Willerman, and Floyd, "Effect of a Pratfall."

133 Aronson, Willerman, and Floyd.

134 Aronson, Willerman, and Floyd.

135 Jeanine Warisse Turner, Jean A. Grube, Catherine H. Tinsley, Cynthia Lee, and Cheryl O'Pell, "Exploring the Dominant Media: How Does Media Use Reflect Organizational Norms and Affect Performance?" *Journal of Business Communication* (1973) 43, no. 3 (2006): 220–25.

Chapter 6: Building Bridges, Not Firewalls

137 Stephen R. Covey, *The 7 Habits of Highly Effective People* (New York: Simon & Schuster, 2020), 188.

137 Kristen Bell (@kristenanniebell), "This Is a Picture of Both the Floor of My House and the Interior of My Brain," Instagram, November 12, 2017, https://www.insta gram.com/p/Bbaq9aYFJSL/.

138 "Kristen Bell's Sloth Meltdown," TheEllenShow, January 30, 2012, YouTube video, https://www.youtube.com/watch?v=t5jw3T3Jy70.

138 Kristen Bell (@kristenanniebell), "Instagram Profile," Instagram, accessed September 5, 2024, https://www.instagram.com/kristenanniebell/.

138 "Kristen Bell," IMDb, accessed March 18, 2024, https://www.imdb.com/name /nm0068338/.

138 "Dunshire Productions," accessed March 18, 2024, https://www.dunshireproduc tions.com/.

139 "Dunshire Productions."

140 Richard Currie, "Zoom CEO Reportedly Tells Staff: Workers Can't Build Trust or Collaborate . . . on Zoom," Microsoft Start, August 24, 2023, https://www.msn .com/en-us/money/companies/zoom-ceo-reportedly-tells-staff-workers-cant-build -trust-or-collaborate-on-zoom/ar-AA1fJ9uO.

140 John K. Butler Jr., "Trust Expectations, Information Sharing, Climate of Trust, and Negotiation Effectiveness and Efficiency," *Group & Organization Management* 24, no. 2 (1999): 217–38.

140 Vithya Leninkumar, "The Relationship between Customer Satisfaction and Customer Trust on Customer Loyalty," *International Journal of Academic Research in Business and Social Sciences* 7, no. 4 (2017): 450–65.

140 Ana Cristina Costa, C. Ashley Fulmer, and Neil R. Anderson, "Trust in Work Teams: An Integrative Review, Multilevel Model, and Future Directions," *Journal of Organizational Behavior* 39, no. 2 (2018): 169–84.

140 R. J. Deluga, "The Relation between Trust in the Supervisor and Subordinate Organizational Citizenship Behavior," *Military Psychology* 7, no. 1 (1995): 1–16.

140 Serap Altuntas and Ulku Baykal, "Relationship between Nurses' Organizational Trust Levels and Their Organizational Citizenship Behaviors," *Journal of Nursing Scholarship* 42, no. 2 (2010): 186–94.

140 Elizabeth W. Morrison, "Employee Voice and Silence," *Annual Review of Organizational Psychology and Organizational Behavior* 1, no. 1 (2014): 173–97.

140 Peter Holland, Brian Cooper, and Cathy Sheehan, "Employee Voice, Supervisor Support, and Engagement: The Mediating Role of Trust," *Human Resource Management* 56, no. 6 (2017): 915–29.

141 Caroline A. Bartel, Amy Wrzesniewski, and Batia M. Wiesenfeld, "Knowing Where You Stand: Physical Isolation, Perceived Respect, and Organizational Identification among Virtual Employees," *Organization Science* 23, no. 3 (2012): 743–57.

141 Sirkka L. Jarvenpaa and Dorothy E. Leidner, "Communication and Trust in Global Virtual Teams," *Organization Science* 10, no. 6 (1999): 791–815.

142 DaJung Woo, Camille G. Endacott, and Karen K. Myers, "Navigating Water Cooler Talks Without the Water Cooler: Uncertainty and Information Seeking during Remote Socialization," *Management Communication Quarterly* 37, no. 2 (2023): 251–80.

142 Marie-Line Germain, "Developing Trust in Virtual Teams," *Performance Improvement Quarterly* 24, no. 3 (2011): 29–54.

142 Penelope Sue Greenberg, Ralph H. Greenberg, and Yvonne Lederer Antonucci, "Creating and Sustaining Trust in Virtual Teams," *Business Horizons* 50, no. 4 (2007): 325–33.

142 Jeanne M. Wilson, Susan G. Straus, and Bill McEvily, "All in Due Time: The Development of Trust in Computer-Mediated and Face-to-Face Teams," *Organizational Behavior and Human Decision Processes* 99, no. 1 (2006): 16–33.

142 "Trials and Prisons Chronology," Nelson Mandela Foundation, accessed March 18, 2024, https://www.nelsonmandela.org/content/page/trials-and-prison-chronology/.

142 "Mandela Death: How a Prisoner Became a Legend," BBC News, December 7, 2013, https://www.bbc.com/news/magazine-25256818/.

142 Richard Stengel, "How Nelson Mandela Came to Work with F. W. de Klerk to End Apartheid," *Time*, November 12, 2021, https://time.com/6116963/nelson-mandela-fw-de-klerk/.

142 "Trials and Prisons Chronology," Nelson Mandela Foundation, accessed March 18, 2024, https://www.nelsonmandela.org/content/page/trials-and-prison-chronology/.

142 Tom Cohen, "Nelson Mandela: Man of Many Handshakes," CNN, December 5, 2013, https://www.cnn.com/2013/12/05/world/africa/nelson-mandela-handshakes/index.html/.

143 Cohen, "Nelson Mandela."

143 Greg L. Stewart, Susan L. Dustin, Murray R. Barrick, and Todd C. Darnold, "Exploring the Handshake in Employment Interviews," *Journal of Applied Psychology* 93, no. 5 (2008): 1139–46.

143 Michael Morris, Janice Nadler, Terri Kurtzberg, and Leigh Thompson, "Schmooze or Lose: Social Friction and Lubrication in E-mail Negotiations," *Group Dynamics: Theory, Research, and Practice* 6, no. 1 (2002): 89–100.

144 Jessica R. Methot, Emily H. Rosado-Solomon, Patrick E. Downes, and Allison S. Gabriel, "Office Chitchat as a Social Ritual: The Uplifting Yet Distracting Effects of Daily Small Talk at Work," *Academy of Management Journal* 64, no. 5 (2021): 1445–71.

145 Deborah A. Small, George Loewenstein, and Paul Slovic, "Sympathy and Callousness: The Impact of Deliberative Thought on Donations to Identifiable and Statistical Victims," *Organizational Behavior and Human Decision Processes* 102, no. 2 (2007): 143–53.

146 Small, Loewenstein, and Slovic, "Sympathy and Callousness."

146 Curtis Puryear and Joseph A. Vandello, "Inflammatory Comments Elicit Less Outrage When Made in Anonymous Online Contexts," *Social Psychological and Personality Science* 10, no. 7 (2019): 895–902.

146 Mei Alonzo and Milam Aiken, "Flaming in Electronic Communication," *Decision Support Systems* 36, no. 3 (2004): 205–13.

147 ABC News, "Kids Crash Their Parent's Teleconference Call," YouTube, March 11, 2017, https://www.youtube.com/watch?v=zC9GYxrBZ2Q/.

147 *The Ellen Show*, "Ellen Dissects the Kid-Interrupted BBC Interview," YouTube, March 15, 2017, https://www.youtube.com/watch?v=dmeBMvGhf1g/.

149 Morris et al., "Schmooze or Lose."

149 John R. Carlson and Robert W. Zmud, "Channel Expansion Theory and the Experiential Nature of Media Richness Perceptions," *Academy of Management Journal* 42, no. 2 (1999): 153–70.

149 Youngjin Yoo and Maryam Alavi, "Media and Group Cohesion: Relative Influences on Social Presence, Task Participation, and Group Consensus," *MIS Quarterly* (2001): 371–90.

150 Li Jiang, Leslie K. John, Reihane Boghrati, and Maryam Kouchaki, "Fostering Perceptions of Authenticity via Sensitive Self-Disclosure," *Journal of Experimental Psychology: Applied* 28, no. 4 (2022): 898–915.

150 David M. Sloan, "Self-Disclosure and Psychological Well-Being," in *Social Psychological Foundations of Clinical Psychology*, ed. James E. Maddux and June P. Tangney (New York: Guilford Press, 2010), 212–225.

150 Fariborz Rahimnia and Mohammad Sadegh Sharifirad, "Authentic Leadership and Employee Well-Being: The Mediating Role of Attachment Insecurity," *Journal of Business Ethics* 132 (2015): 363–77.

150 David W. Lehman, Kieran O'Connor, Balázs Kovács, and George E. Newman, "Authenticity," *Academy of Management Annals* 13, no. 1 (2019): 1–42.

150 Don A. Moore, Terri R. Kurtzberg, Leigh L. Thompson, and Michael W. Morris, "Long and Short Routes to Success in Electronically Mediated Negotiations: Group Affiliations and Good Vibrations," *Organizational Behavior and Human Decision Processes* 77, no. 1 (1999): 22–43.

150 Karen Huang, Michael Yeomans, Alison Wood Brooks, Julia Minson, and Francesca Gino, "It Doesn't Hurt to Ask: Question-Asking Increases Liking," *Journal of Personality and Social Psychology* 113, no. 3 (2017): 430–52.

151 Huang et al., "It Doesn't Hurt to Ask."

152 Mark Levine, Amy Prosser, David Evans, and Stephen Reicher, "Identity and Emergency Intervention: How Social Group Membership and Inclusiveness of Group Boundaries Shape Helping Behavior," *Personality and Social Psychology Bulletin* 31, no. 4 (2005): 443–53.

153 Levine et al.

153 Richard L. Moreland and Robert B. Zajonc, "Exposure Effects in Person Perception: Familiarity, Similarity, and Attraction," *Journal of Experimental Social Psychology* 18, no. 5 (1982): 395–415.

153 Susan Sprecher, "Effects of Actual (Manipulated) and Perceived Similarity on Liking in Get-Acquainted Interactions: The Role of Communication," *Communication Monographs* 81, no. 1 (2014): 4–27.

153 Feyzan Karabulut, Sarah G. Moore, and Paul R. Messinger, "Choosing Backgrounds for Success: The Role of Videoconference Backgrounds in Self-Presentation," *Journal of the Association for Consumer Research* 8, no. 2 (2023): 153–64.

153 Nicolas Roulin, Eden-Raye Lukacik, Joshua S. Bourdage, Lindsey Clow, Hayam Bakour, and Pedro Diaz, "Bias in the Background? The Role of Background In-

formation in Asynchronous Video Interviews," *Journal of Organizational Behavior* 44, no. 3 (2023): 458–75.

153 Roulin et al., "Bias in the Background?"

154 Kate Muir, Adam Joinson, Emily Collins, Rachel Cotterill, and Nigel Dewdney, "When Asking 'What' and 'How' Helps You Win: Mimicry of Interrogative Terms Facilitates Successful Online Negotiations," *Negotiation and Conflict Management Research* (2020): 1–17.

155 Roderick I. Swaab, William W. Maddux, and Marwan Sinaceur, "Early Words That Work: When and How Virtual Linguistic Mimicry Facilitates Negotiation Outcomes," *Journal of Experimental Social Psychology* 47, no. 3 (2011): 616–21.

155 Alice Kotlyarenko, "Emoticon vs. Emoji: The Key Differences Explained," MUO, May 20, 2022, https://www.makeuseof.com/tag/emoticon-vs-emoji-differences/.

155 "COL Everett Spain," United States Military Academy West Point, https://www.westpoint.edu/behavioral-sciences-and-leadership/profile/everett_spain.

156 Swaab, Maddux, and Sinaceur, "Early Words That Work."

156 T. L. Chartrand and R. van Baaren, "Human Mimicry," *Advances in Experimental Social Psychology* 41 (2009): 219–74.

158 Devon Johnson and Kent Grayson, "Cognitive and Affective Trust in Service Relationships," *Journal of Business Research* 58, no. 4 (2005): 500–507.

158 J. David Lewis and Andrew Weigert, "Trust as a Social Reality," *Social Forces* 63, no. 4 (1985): 967–85.

160 Francis J. Flynn and Chelsea R. Lide, "Communication Miscalibration: The Price Leaders Pay for Not Sharing Enough," *Academy of Management Journal* (2022): 1102–1122.

161 Mark Powell, "Quinn Cook Reveals Text LeBron James Sent Teammates During Hiatus," FanSided, July 12, 2020, https://fansided.com/2020/07/12/quinn-cook-reveals-text-lebron-james-sent-teammates/.

161 Mike Trudell, "Quinn Cook Used an Example from Their Group Text About Lebron's Leadership: 'Bron Sent a Text After 2 Weeks or so When We All Hadn't Been Together:' miss You Guys,' Just Something Uplifting like, 'Can't Wait to Get Back on the Floor with You Guys, Finish What We Started,'" Twitter, July 11, 2020, https://twitter.com/LakersReporter/status/1282063745930326016/.

162 Jonah Berger, Alan T. Sorensen, and Scott J. Rasmussen, "Positive Effects of Negative Publicity: When Negative Reviews Increase Sales," *Marketing Science* 29, no. 5 (2010): 815–27.

163 Tessa Haesevoets, David De Cremer, Leander De Schutter, Jack McGuire, Yu Yang, Xie Jian, and Alain Van Hiel, "Transparency and Control in Email Communication: The More the Supervisor Is Put in CC the Less Trust Is Felt," *Journal of Business Ethics* 168 (2021): 733–53.

166 Steven Perlberg, "Reuters Employees Bombarded with Reply-All Email Catastrophe," *Wall Street Journal*, August 26, 2015, https://www.wsj.com/articles/BL-DGB-43205/.

166 "Email Storm," Wikipedia, Wikimedia Foundation, January 26, 2024, https://en.wikipedia.org/wiki/Email_storm/.

166 Matt Weinberger, "As Many as 11,543 Microsoft Employees Got Swept Up in a Reply-All Email Apocalypse," Business Insider, January 28, 2019, https://www .businessinsider.com/microsoft-employee-github-reply-all-email-storm-2019-1/.

Chapter 7: The Virtual Wrecking Ball

171 John C. Maxwell, *Everyone Communicates, Few Connect: What the Most Effective People Do Differently* (New York: HarperCollins, 2010), 65.

171 Adam Nagourney, David E. Sanger, and Johanna Barr, "Hawaii Panics after Alert About Incoming Missile Is Sent in Error," *New York Times*, January 13, 2018, https://www.nytimes.com/2018/01/13/us/hawaii-missile.html/.

171 "Fear. Panic. And Tears. For 38 Minutes, Hawaii Thought It Was Under Attack," Hawaii News Now, January 15, 2018, https://www.hawaiinewsnow.com/story /37259815/biggest-fright-of-my-life-many-scramble-for-shelter-after-false-alarm -missile-warning/.

172 Ashley Nagaoka, "After missile alert mistake, UH students ran for cover and hid in classrooms," Hawaii News Now, January 13, 2018, https://www.hawaiinewsnow .com/story/37260525/after-missile-alert-mistake-uh-students-ran-for-cover-and -hid-in-classrooms/.

172 "Hawaii Officials Mistakenly Warn Islanders of Inbound Missile," Oregonlive, January 13, 2018, https://www.oregonlive.com/today/2018/01/hawaii_officials _mistakenly_wa.html/.

172 Extra Spin Staff, "Hawaiian Man Prepares to Live Final Minutes on Golf Course after Rumored Missile Launch," *Golf*, December 31, 2018, https://golf .com/news/hawaiian-man-prepares-to-live-final-minutes-on-golf-course-after -rumored-missile-launch/.

172 Juergen T. Steinmetz, "Ballistic Missile Threat Inbound for Hawaii—Take Im- mediate Shelter! A 50-Minute Panic for Tourists and Residents," eTurboNews, January 14, 2018, https://eturbonews.com/ballistic-missile-threat-inbound -hawaii-take-immediate-shelter-50-minute-panic-tourists-residents/.

172 "'The Whole State Was Terrified': How Hawaii Reacted to False Missile Alert," BBC News, January 13, 2018, https://www.bbc.com/news/world-us-canada -42675666/.

172 Doug Criss and Jeremy Grisham, "Man Sues Hawaii, Saying the False Missile Alert Caused His Heart Attack," CNN, November 28, 2018, https://www.cnn .com/2018/11/28/health/hawaii-false-alert-lawsuit-trnd/index.html/.

172 Nagourney, Sanger, and Barr, "Hawaii Panics."

173 Daantje Derks, Agneta H. Fischer, and Arjan E. R. Bos, "The Role of Emotion in Computer-Mediated Communication: A Review," *Computers in Human Behavior* 24, no. 3 (2008): 766–85.

174 Skye Schooley, "Lost in Translation: 13 International Marketing Fails," Business News Daily, February 21, 2023, https://www.businessnewsdaily.com/5241-interna tional-marketing-fails.htm.

174 Melanie Curtin, "7 of the Biggest Business Translation Fails in History (and What You Can Learn from Them)," *Inc.*, July 18, 2019, https://www.inc.com/melanie

-curtin/7-of-biggest-business-translation-fails-and-what-you-can-learn-from-them.html/.

174 Schooley, "Lost in Translation."

174 Jordan Novet, "Marc Benioff Tells Salesforce Workers That New Employees Are 'Facing Lower Productivity,'" CNBC, December 17, 2022, https://www.cnbc.com/2022/12/16/marc-benioff-says-newer-salesforce-employees-are-less-productive.html/.

174 Don, "Asking for a Friend," Know Your Meme, December 30, 2023, https://knowyourmeme.com/memes/asking-for-a-friend/.

174 Ashley Stewart, "Salesforce's Marc Benioff causes an uproar by suggesting in a leaked internal Slack message that new employees are less productive," Business Insider, December 16, 2022, https://www.businessinsider.com/marc-benioff-salesforce-new-employees-less-productive-uproar-2022-12?op=1.

175 L. Newton, "Overconfidence in the Communication of Intent: Heard and Unheard Melodies" (PhD diss., Stanford University, 1990), 1.

176 Justin Kruger, Nicholas Epley, Jason Parker, and Zhi-Wen Ng, "Egocentrism Over E-mail: Can We Communicate as Well as We Think?" *Journal of Personality and Social Psychology* 89, no. 6 (2005): 925–36.

177 David D. Dawley and William P. Anthony, "User Perceptions of E-mail at Work," *Journal of Business and Technical Communication* 17, no. 2 (2003): 170–200.

178 Kristin Byron, "Carrying Too Heavy a Load? The Communication and Miscommunication of Emotion by Email," *Academy of Management Review* 33, no. 2 (2008): 309–27.

179 Dominic Thompson and Ruth Filik, "Sarcasm in Written Communication: Emoticons Are Efficient Markers of Intention," *Journal of Computer-Mediated Communication* 21, no. 2 (2016): 105–20.

180 Jeff Weiner, "LinkedIn Login, Sign In," LinkedIn, June 13, 2016, https://www.linkedin.com/pulse/linkedin-microsoft-changing-way-world-works-jeff-weiner/.

180 Adam D. Galinsky, William W. Maddux, Debra Gilin, and Judith B. White, "Why It Pays to Get Inside the Head of Your Opponent: The Differential Effects of Perspective Taking and Empathy in Negotiations," *Psychological Science* 19, no. 4 (2008): 378–84.

182 Mark H. Davis, "Measuring Individual Differences in Empathy: Evidence for a Multidimensional Approach," *Journal of Personality and Social Psychology* 44, no. 1 (1983): 113–26.

182 C. Daniel Batson, Jim Fultz, and Patricia A. Schoenrade, "Distress and Empathy: Two Qualitatively Distinct Vicarious Emotions with Different Motivational Consequences," *Journal of Personality* 55, no. 1 (1987): 19–39.

182 Nicholas Epley, Eugene M. Caruso, and Max H. Bazerman, "When Perspective Taking Increases Taking: Reactive Egoism in Social Interaction," *Journal of Personality and Social Psychology* 91, no. 5 (2006): 872–89.

183 C. Daniel Batson and Tecia Moran, "Empathy-Induced Altruism in a Prisoner's Dilemma," *European Journal of Social Psychology* 29, no. 7 (1999): 909–24.

183 C. Daniel Batson and Nadia Ahmad, "Empathy-Induced Altruism in a Prisoner's

Dilemma II: What If the Target of Empathy Has Defected?" *European Journal of Social Psychology* 31, no. 1 (2001): 25–36.

184 John R. Carlson and Robert W. Zmud, "Channel Expansion Theory and the Experiential Nature of Media Richness Perceptions," *Academy of Management Journal* 42, no. 2 (1999): 153–70.

184 Scott C. D'Urso and Stephen A. Rains, "Examining the Scope of Channel Expansion: A Test of Channel Expansion Theory with New and Traditional Communication Media," *Management Communication Quarterly* 21, no. 4 (2008): 486–507.

185 Ismail Shakil, "Canadian Farmer's Thumbs-up Emoji Leads to $62,000 Fine for Undelivered Flax," Reuters, July 8, 2023, https://www.reuters.com/world/americas /canadian-farmers-thumbs-up-emoji-leads-62000-fine-undelivered-flax-2023-07-07/.

185 "South West Terminal Ltd. V Achter Land, 2023 SKKB 116 (CanLII)," CanLII, June 6, 2023. https://www.canlii.org/en/sk/skkb/doc/2023/2023skkb116 /2023skkb116.html/.

185 Tileah Dobson, "Emojis Can Cost You Thousands of Dollars or Land You in Jail— Here's Why," *New York Post*, September 8, 2023, https://nypost.com/2023/09/08 /emojis-can-cost-you-thousands-of-dollars-or-land-you-in-jail-heres-why/.

186 Thomas Holtgraves, "Emoji, Speech Acts, and Perceived Communicative Success," *Journal of Language and Social Psychology* 43, no. 1 (2024): 83–103.

186 J. Richard Hackman and Ruth Wageman, "When and How Team Leaders Matter," *Research in Organizational Behavior* 26 (2004): 37–74.

186 Ella Glikson, Arik Cheshin, and Gerben A. van Kleef, "The Dark Side of a Smiley: Effects of Smiling Emoticons on Virtual First Impressions," *Social Psychological and Personality Science* 9, no. 5 (2018): 614–25.

187 Philippe Naughton, "'Ketchupgate' E-Mail Lawyer Resigns," *Times* (London), March 31, 2010, https://www.thetimes.co.uk/article/ketchupgate-e-mail-lawyer -resigns-w0bxsqbzxs2/.

187 Matthew Held, "Five Ways to Keep Your Tone in Check When Writing Business Emails," HuffPost, December 9, 2014, https://www.huffpost.com/archive/ca/entry /business-emails_b_5955124/.

189 sonsofmaxwell, "United Breaks Guitars," YouTube, July 7, 2009, https://www.you tube.com/watch?v=5YGc4zOqozo.

190 Ravi Sawhney, "Broken Guitar Has United Playing the Blues to the Tune of $180 Million," *Fast Company*, July 30, 2009, https://www.fastcompany.com/1320152 /broken-guitar-has-united-playing-blues-tune-180-million/.

190 "'United Breaks Guitars': Did It *Really* Cost the Airline $180 Million?" HuffPost, December 7, 2017, https://www.huffpost.com/entry/united-breaks-guitars -did_n_244357/.

190 Taylor Dunn, Rebecca Jarvis, and Catherine Thorbecke, "How Reddit Users Sent GameStop Stock Soaring, Upending the Market," ABC News, January 28, 2021, https://abcnews.go.com/Business/reddit-users-gamestop-stock-soaring-upending -market/story?id=75513249/.

190 "R/Wallstreetbets," Reddit, accessed March 18, 2024, https://www.reddit.com/r /wallstreetbets/.

191 Roger Cheng, "Reddit's AMC, GameStop Surge Happened Because of Anger

Over Wall Street," CNET, February 1, 2021, https://www.cnet.com/culture/red dits-amc-gamestop-surge-happened-because-of-anger-over-wall-street/.

191 Yun Li, "GameStop, Reddit and Robinhood: A Full Recap of the Historic Retail Trading Mania on Wall Street," CNBC, January 30, 2021, https://www.cnbc.com/2021/01/30/gamestop-reddit-and-robinhood-a-full-recap-of -the-historic-retail-trading-mania-on-wall-street.html/.

191 Hillary Hoffower and Dominic-Madori Davis, "GameStop Is the Latest Example of Reddit Rage Going Mainstream," Business Insider, February 6, 2021, https://www.businessinsider.com/gamestop-example-of-internet-rage-going -mainstream-gamergate-qanon-2021-2/.

191 Arik Cheshin, Anat Rafaeli, and Nathan Bos, "Anger and Happiness in Virtual Teams: Emotional Influences of Text and Behavior on Others' Affect in the Absence of Non-Verbal Cues," Organizational Behavior and Human Decision Processes 116, no. 1 (2011): 2–16.

191 Roland Neumann and Fritz Strack, "'Mood Contagion': The Automatic Transfer of Mood between Persons," Journal of Personality and Social Psychology 79, no. 2 (2000): 211–23.

191 Elaine Hatfield, John T. Cacioppo, and Richard L. Rapson, "Primitive Emotional Contagion," 1992.

192 Mike Sager, "What I've Learned: Carrie Fisher," Esquire, January 29, 2007, https://www.esquire.com/entertainment/interviews/a2053/esq0102-jan-fisher/.

193 Alice F. Stuhlmacher and Maryalice Citera, "Hostile Behavior and Profit in Virtual Negotiation: A Meta-Analysis," Journal of Business and Psychology 20 (2005): 69–93.

193 "Should I Ask Over Zoom, Phone, Email, or In-Person? Communication Channel and Predicted versus Actual Compliance."

194 Zachary M. Seward, "The Steve Jobs Emails That Show How to Win a Hard-Nosed Negotiation," Quartz, July 21, 2022, https://qz.com/87184/the-steve-jobs -emails-that-show-how-to-win-a-hard-nosed-negotiation/.

196 Deepak Malhotra and Max H. Bazerman, "Psychological Influence in Negotiation: An Introduction Long Overdue," Journal of Management 34, no. 3 (2008): 509–31.

196 Jason Fried, "Basecamp: Where We Came From," Basecamp, accessed March 18, 2024, https://basecamp.com/about/.

197 Ping Dong, Xun Huang, and Robert S. Wyer Jr., "The Illusion of Saving Face: How People Symbolically Cope with Embarrassment," Psychological Science 24, no. 10 (2013): 2005–12.

197 Bert R. Brown, "The Effects of Need to Maintain Face on Interpersonal Bargaining," Journal of Experimental Social Psychology 4, no. 1 (1968): 107–22.

197 Judith B. White, Renée Tynan, Adam D. Galinsky, and Leigh Thompson, "Face Threat Sensitivity in Negotiation: Roadblock to Agreement and Joint Gain," Organizational Behavior and Human Decision Processes 94, no. 2 (2004): 102–24.

197 Marwan Sinaceur, William W. Maddux, Dimitri Vasiljevic, Ricardo Perez Nückel, and Adam D. Galinsky, "Good Things Come to Those Who Wait: Late First Offers Facilitate Creative Agreements in Negotiation," Personality and Social Psychology Bulletin 39, no. 6 (2013): 814–25.

197 Roderick I. Swaab, Adam D. Galinsky, Victoria Medvec, and Daniel A. Diermeier,

"The Communication Orientation Model: Explaining the Diverse Effects of Sight, Sound, and Synchronicity on Negotiation and Group Decision-Making Outcomes," *Personality and Social Psychology Review* 16, no. 1 (2012): 25–53.

197 W. Richard Walker, Rodney J. Vogl, and Charles P. Thompson, "Autobiographical Memory: Unpleasantness Fades Faster Than Pleasantness Over Time," *Applied Cognitive Psychology* 11, no. 5 (1997): 399–413.

197 Andrew M. Lane, Chris Beedie, and Peter C. Terry, "Distinctions between Emotion and Mood," 2007.

198 Daniel Goleman, *Working with Emotional Intelligence* (New York: Bantam, 1998), 3.

Chapter 8: We All Know What Happens When You Assume . . .

203 Office of DEI Education and Learning Initiatives, Brandeis University, "Quotes Related to DEI," accessed March 18, 2024, https://www.brandeis.edu/diversity /learning/resources/dei-quotes.html/.

204 Susan Rigetti, "Reflecting on One Very, Very Strange Year at Uber," May 22, 2017, https://www.susanjfowler.com/blog/2017/2/19/reflecting-on-one-very-strange -year-at-uber/.

204 Amelia Tait, "Susan Fowler: 'When the Time Came to Blow the Whistle on Uber, I Was Ready,'" *Guardian*, March 4, 2020, https://www.theguardian.com/world /2020/mar/01/susan-fowler-uber-whistleblower-interview-travis-kalanick/.

204 Stephanie Zacharek, Eliana Dockterman, and Haley Sweetland Edwards, "The Silence Breakers," *Time*, accessed March 18, 2024, https://time.com/time-person -of-the-year-2017-silence-breakers/.

204 Dave Lee, "Uber Fires 20 Staff After Harassment Investigation," BBC News, June 6, 2017, https://www.bbc.com/news/business-40179472/.

204 Elizabeth Elkind, "Susan Fowler Details Fallout, Says She Was 'Followed' After Blog Post Exposing Uber Sexual Harassment," CBS News, February 18, 2020, https://www.cbsnews.com/news/susan-fowler-details-fallout-blog-post-exposing -uber-sexual-harassment-silicon-valley-culture/.

204 "Uber Overhauls Its Policies for Sex Assault Cases," CBS News, May 15, 2018, https://www.cbsnews.com/newyork/news/uber-sexual-assault-policy-change/.

205 Rob Price, "Uber Slammed for Promotion That Offered to 'Let Your Wife Take a Day Off From the Kitchen,'" Business Insider, September 17, 2017, https:// www.insider.com/uber-ubereats-promotion-let-your-wife-take-a-day-off-from -the-kitchen-2017-9/.

205 Hemanth.HM, "Sorry @uber but Why Do You Think That Only the 'Wife' Needs to Be at the Kitchen! Pic.Twitter.Com/Hzjlbsdt34," Twitter, September 16, 2017, https://twitter.com/GNUmanth/status/909131867093270528/.

205 Rashi, "Thank You @uber for Defining Gender Roles in India. of Course Women Are Meant to Slog It out in the Kitchen & the Men Need to Buy US Freedom Https://T.Co/Ew57zyxdng," Twitter, September 17, 2017, https://twitter.com /rashi_kakkar/status/909264601031823360/.

205 Uber Comms, "This Was Totally Inappropriate. We've Removed It and We Apologize," Twitter, September 17, 2017, https://twitter.com/Uber_Comms/sta tus/909273407287521280/.

205 Kleinman, By Zoe, "Uber Sorry for 'Wife Appreciation Day' Promotion," BBC News, September 18, 2017, https://www.bbc.com/news/technology-41306434/.

205 "Gender Attitudes in India: What's Changed and What Hasn't," India Development Review, January 27, 2023, https://idronline.org/article/gender/gender-att itudes-in-india-whats-changed-and-what-hasnt/.

205 Jeff Diamant, "In India and Many Other Countries, There Is Little Gap between Men and Women in Attitudes on Gender Issues," Pew Research Center, March 15, 2022, https://www.pewresearch.org/short-reads/2022/03/15/in-india -and-many-other-countries-there-is-little-gap-between-men-and-women-in-atti tudes-on-gender-issues/.

205 Zoe Kleinman, "Uber Sorry for 'Wife Appreciation Day' Promotion," BBC News, September 18, 2017, https://www.bbc.com/news/technology-41306434/.

206 John Suler, "The Online Disinhibition Effect," *Cyberpsychology & Behavior* 7, no. 3 (2004): 321–26.

206 Mei Alonzo and Milam Aiken, "Flaming in Electronic Communication," *Decision Support Systems* 36, no. 3 (2004): 205–13.

207 Jens Mazei, Joachim Hüffmeier, Philipp Alexander Freund, Alice F. Stuhlmacher, Lena Bilke, and Guido Hertel, "A Meta-Analysis on Gender Differences in Negotiation Outcomes and Their Moderators," *Psychological Bulletin* 141, no. 1 (2015): 85–104.

208 Michael Cavna, "'NOBODY KNOWS YOU'RE A DOG': As Iconic Internet Cartoon Turns 20, Creator Peter Steiner Knows the Joke Rings as Relevant as Ever," *Washington Post*, June 30, 2023, https://www.washingtonpost.com/blogs/comic-riffs /post/nobody-knows-youre-a-dog-as-iconic-internet-cartoon-turns-20-creator-peter -steiner-knows-the-joke-rings-as-relevant-as-ever/2013/07/31/73372600-f98d-11e2 -8e84-c56731a202fb_blog.html/.

208 Julia Binswanger, "'New Yorker' Cartoon About a Dog on the Internet Breaks Auction Records," *Smithsonian*, October 25, 2023, https://www.smithsonianmag .com/smart-news/the-most-reprinted-new-yorker-cartoon-breaks-record-at-auction -for-a-single-panel-comic-180983135/.

209 Becky Ka Ying Lau, Janet Geipel, Yanting Wu, and Boaz Keysar, "The Extreme Illusion of Understanding," *Journal of Experimental Psychology: General* (2022).

210 Sherry Turkle, *Life on the Screen: Identity in the Age of the Internet* (New York: Simon & Schuster, 1997), 184.

211 Markus M. Mobius and Tanya S. Rosenblat, "Why Beauty Matters," *American Economic Review* 96, no. 1 (2006): 222–35.

211 Eva Singhal Sierminska, "Does It Pay to Be Beautiful?" *IZA World of Labor* (2023).

211 Jens Agerström, "Why Does Height Matter in Hiring?" *Journal of Behavioral and Experimental Economics* 52 (2014): 35–38.

211 Timothy A. Judge and Daniel M. Cable, "The Effect of Physical Height on Workplace Success and Income: Preliminary Test of a Theoretical Model," *Journal of Applied Psychology* 89, no. 3 (2004): 428–41.

211 Vivek Kaul, "The Necktie Syndrome: Why CEOs Tend to Be Significantly Taller Than the Average Male," *Economic Times*, September 30, 2011, https://economic times.indiatimes.com/the-necktie-syndrome-why-ceos-tend-to-be-significantly -taller-than-the-average-male/articleshow/10178115.cms/.

211 Susan G. Straus, Jeffrey A. Miles, and Laurie L. Levesque, "The Effects of Video-conference, Telephone, and Face-to-Face Media on Interviewer and Applicant Judgments in Employment Interviews," *Journal of Management* 27, no. 3 (2001): 363–81.

211 Yair Amichai-Hamburger, "Potential and Promise of Online Volunteering," *Computers in Human Behavior* 24, no. 2 (2008): 544–62.

211 Jane A. Vignovic and Lori Foster Thompson, "Computer-Mediated Cross-Cultural Collaboration: Attributing Communication Errors to the Person versus the Situation," *Journal of Applied Psychology* 95, no. 2 (2010): 265–76.

211 Straus, Miles, and Levesque, "The Effects of Videoconference, Telephone, and Face-to-Face Media."

211 Neil Anderson, "Applicant and Recruiter Reactions to New Technology in Selection: A Critical Review and Agenda for Future Research," *International Journal of Selection and Assessment* 11, no. 2–3 (2003): 121–36.

212 Alice F. Stuhlmacher, Maryalice Citera, and Toni Willis, "Gender Differences in Virtual Negotiation: Theory and Research," *Sex Roles* 57 (2007): 329–39.

212 John Suler, "The Online Disinhibition Effect," *International Journal of Applied Psychoanalytic Studies* 2, no. 2 (2005): 184–88.

212 John Suler, "The Online Disinhibition Effect," *Cyberpsychology & Behavior* 7, no. 3 (2004): 321–26.

212 Adam N. Joinson, "Disinhibition and the Internet," *Psychology and the Internet*, no. 2 (2007): 75–92.

212 Nicholas Epley and Justin Kruger, "When What You Type Isn't What They Read: The Perseverance of Stereotypes and Expectancies Over E-mail," *Journal of Experimental Social Psychology* 41, no. 4 (2005): 414–22.

215 Vignovic and Thompson, "Computer-Mediated Cross-Cultural Collaboration."

215 Fiona Macdonald, "The Greatest Mistranslations Ever," BBC News, February 24, 2022, https://www.bbc.com/culture/article/20150202-the-greatest-mistranslations-ever/.

216 Philip E. Tetlock, "Accountability: A Social Check on the Fundamental Attribution Error," *Social Psychology Quarterly* (1985): 227–36.

216 Fritz Heider, "Social Perception and Phenomenal Causality," *Psychological Review* 51, no. 6 (1944): 358–74.

216 Edward E. Jones, and Richard E. Nisbett. "The Actor and the Observer: Divergent Perceptions of the Causes of Behavior" in *Attribution: Perceiving the Causes of Behavior*, ed. Edward E. Jones, David E. Kanouse, Harold H. Kelley, Richard E. Nisbett, Steven Valins, and Bernard Weiner (Morristown, NJ: General Learning, 1972), 79–94.

219 Jeanne Brett, Kristin Behfar, and Jeffrey Sanchez-Burks, "Managing Cross-Culture Conflicts: A Close Look at the Implication of Direct Versus Indirect Confrontation," in *Handbook of Conflict Management Research*, 136–54 (Cheltenham, UK: Edward Elgar, 2014).

219 Stella Ting-Toomey, Ge Gao, Paula Trubisky, Zhizhong Yang, Hak Soo Kim, Sung-Ling Lin, and Tsukasa Nishida, "Culture, Face Maintenance, and Styles of Handling Interpersonal Conflict: A Study in Five Cultures," *International Journal of Conflict Management* 2, no. 4 (1991): 275–96.

219 Kun Yang and Shuang Qian, "Your Smiling Face Is Impolite to Me: A Study of the Smiling Face Emoji in Chinese Computer-Mediated Communication," *Social Science Computer Review* (2023): 08944393231219481.

221 Phyllis Moen, Julie Robison, and Vivian Fields, "Women's Work and Caregiving Roles: A Life Course Approach," *Journal of Gerontology* 49, no. 4 (1994): S176–S186.

221 Michel Bédard, Rylee Kuzik, Lori Chambers, D. William Molloy, Sacha Dubois, and Judith A. Lever, "Understanding Burden Differences between Men and Women Caregivers: The Contribution of Care-Recipient Problem Behaviors," *International Psychogeriatrics* 17, no. 1 (2005): 99–118.

221 Maryam Navaie-Waliser, Aubrey Spriggs, and Penny H. Feldman, "Informal Caregiving: Differential Experiences by Gender," *Medical Care* (2002): 1249–59.

221 Yeonjung Lee and Fengyan Tang, "More Caregiving, Less Working: Caregiving Roles and Gender Difference," *Journal of Applied Gerontology* 34, no. 4 (2015): 465–83.

221 Joukje Swinkels, Theo van Tilburg, Ellen Verbakel, and Marjolein Broese van Groenou, "Explaining the Gender Gap in the Caregiving Burden of Partner Caregivers," *Journals of Gerontology: Series B 74*, no. 2 (2019): 309–317.

221 Gleb Tsipursky, "This CEO Gets It Wrong When He Claims Returning to the Office Will Help Diversity," *Fast Company*, September 1, 2022, https://www.fastcompany.com/90782337/ceo-gaslighting-return-office-help-diversity.

221 Naomi Nix, "Facebook's Workforce Grew More Diverse When It Embraced Remote Work," *Washington Post*, July 19, 2022, https://www.washingtonpost.com/technology/2022/07/19/facebook-diversity-report-2022/.

222 Sapna Maheshwari and Emily Flitter, "As Wayfair Workers Protest Migrant Detention, the Specter of a Consumer Boycott Rises," *New York Times*, June 26, 2019, https://www.nytimes.com/2019/06/26/business/wayfair-walkout.html/.

223 Ayanna Pressley, "We Must Actively #Resist Any & All Efforts By This Cruel, Incompetent Administration to Cage Children and Separate Families. I Proudly Stand in Solidarity W/ the Hardworking Individuals at #wayfair Who Are Walking Out in the Name of #Justice & Humanity, https://T.Co/Ufvczngetj," Twitter, June 25, 2019, https://twitter.com/RepPressley/status/1143604691181428736/.

223 Zacharek, Dockterman, and Edwards, "The Silence Breakers."

223 Elizabeth Elkind, "Uber Whistleblower Susan Fowler Claims She Was Followed After Making Allegations: 'It Was Terrifying,'" CBS News, February 18, 2020, https://www.cbsnews.com/news/susan-fowler-details-fallout-blog-post-exposing-uber-sexual-harassment-silicon-valley-culture/.

Chapter 9: Navigating the Noise

225 Contributors to Wikimedia projects, "Albert Einstein," Wikiquote, January 11, 2024, https://en.wikiquote.org/wiki/Albert_Einstein/.

225 "Library of Congress AESOP Fables," accessed March 18, 2024, https://www.read.gov/aesop/025.html/.

227 Melissa Mazmanian, Wanda J. Orlikowski, and JoAnne Yates, "The Autonomy

Paradox: The Implications of Mobile Email Devices for Knowledge Professionals," *Organization Science* 24, no. 5 (2013): 1337–13.

228 Stephen R. Barley, Debra E. Meyerson, and Stine Grodal, "E-mail as a Source and Symbol of Stress," *Organization Science* 22, no. 4 (2011): 887–906.

228 Wendy J. Casper, Hoda Vaziri, Julie Holliday Wayne, Sara DeHauw, and Jeffrey Greenhaus, "The Jingle-Jangle of Work–Nonwork Balance: A Comprehensive and Meta-Analytic Review of Its Meaning and Measurement," *Journal of Applied Psychology* 103, no. 2 (2018): 182–214.

228 Samuel Aryee, Ekkirala S. Srinivas, and Hwee Hoon Tan, "Rhythms of Life: Antecedents and Outcomes of Work-Family Balance in Employed Parents," *Journal of Applied Psychology* 90, no. 1 (2005): 132–46.

229 Zaria Gorvett, "Can You Work Yourself to Death?" BBC Worklife, February 25, 2022, https://www.bbc.com/worklife/article/20160912-is-there-such-thing-as -death-from-overwork.

230 Blake E. Ashforth and Yitzhak Fried, "The Mindlessness of Organizational Behaviors," *Human Relations* 41, no. 4 (1988): 305–29.

230 Stan De Spiegelaere, Guy Van Gyes, and Geert Van Hootegem, "Not All Autonomy Is the Same: Different Dimensions of Job Autonomy and Their Relation to Work Engagement & Innovative Work Behavior," *Human Factors and Ergonomics in Manufacturing & Service Industries* 26, no. 4 (2016): 515–27.

230 Jenna A. Van Fossen, Nathan M. Baker, Elizabeth A. Mack, Chu-Hsiang Chang, Shelia R. Cotten, and Isabella Catalano, "The Moderating Effect of Scheduling Autonomy on Smartphone Use and Stress among Older Workers," *Work, Aging and Retirement* 9, no. 4 (2023): 329–41.

230 Mazmanian, Orlikowski, and Yates, "Autonomy Paradox."

230 Paul M. Leonardi, Jeffrey W. Treem, and Michele H. Jackson, "The Connectivity Paradox: Using Technology to Both Decrease and Increase Perceptions of Distance in Distributed Work Arrangements," *Journal of Applied Communication Research* 38, no. 1 (2010): 85–105.

230 Larissa K. Barber and Alecia M. Santuzzi, "Please Respond ASAP: Workplace Telepressure and Employee Recovery," *Journal of Occupational Health Psychology* 20, no. 2 (2015): 172–89.

231 Shuang Ren, Jia Hu, Guiyao Tang, and Doren Chadee, "Digital Connectivity for Work After Hours: Its Curvilinear Relationship with Employee Job Performance," *Personnel Psychology* 76, no. 3 (2023): 731–57.

233 David Charter, "Even I've Got Zoom Fatigue, Says Eric Yuan, Founder of Zoom," *Times* (London), May 5, 2021, https://www.thetimes.co.uk/article/even -ive-got-zoom-fatigue-says-eric-yuan-founder-of-zoom-rwpr2thsf.

233 Chip Cutter, "Even the CEO of Zoom Says He Has Zoom Fatigue," *Wall Street Journal*, May 4, 2021, https://www.wsj.com/articles/even-the-ceo-of-zoom-says -he-has-zoom-fatigue-11620151459/.

233 "Tired of Zoom Calls? So Is Citigroup's Chief Executive," *New York Times*, May 25, 2021, https://www.nytimes.com/2021/03/25/business/tired-of-zoom -calls-so-is-citigroups-chief-executive.html/.

233 Kristen M. Shockley, Allison S. Gabriel, Daron Robertson, Christopher C. Rosen, Nitya Chawla, Mahira L. Ganster, and Maira E. Ezerins, "The Fatiguing Effects of Camera Use in Virtual Meetings: A Within-Person Field Experiment," *Journal of Applied Psychology* 106, no. 8 (2021): 1137–55.

234 Erica R. Bailey, C. Blaine Horton, and Adam D. Galinsky, "Enclothed Harmony or Enclothed Dissonance? The Effect of Attire on the Authenticity, Power, and Engagement of Remote Workers," *Academy of Management Discoveries* 8, no. 3 (2022): 341–56.

234 Talia Ariss, Catharine E. Fairbairn, Michael A. Sayette, Brynne A. Velia, Howard Berenbaum, and Sarah Brown-Schmidt, "Where to Look? Alcohol, Affect, and Gaze Behavior During a Virtual Social Interaction," *Clinical Psychological Science* 11, no. 2 (2023): 239–52.

236 "OutHorse Your Email," Visit Iceland, accessed March 18, 2024, https://www.visiticeland.com/outhorse-your-email/.

236 Jaime Kurtz, "Working to Live or Living to Work?" *Psychology Today*, December 8, 2016, https://www.psychologytoday.com/us/blog/happy-trails/201612/working-to-live-or-living-to-work/.

237 Loïc Lerouge and Francisco Trujillo Pons, "Contribution to the Study on the 'Right to Disconnect' from Work: Are France and Spain Examples for Other Countries and EU Law?" *European Labour Law Journal* 13, no. 3 (June 14, 2022): 450–65.

237 "ShowDoc," Senato, accessed March 18, 2024, https://www.senato.it/japp/bgt/showdoc/17/DDLMESS/0/1022243/index.html/.

237 Slov-Lex, "311/2001 Z.z. - Zákonník práce - SLOV-LEX," Slov-lex, July 2, 2001, https://www.slov-lex.sk/pravne-predpisy/SK/ZZ/2001/311/20210301.html/.

237 Radovan Pala, "Latest Changes in Employment Law in Slovakia," Taylor Wessing, February 23, 2021, https://www.taylorwessing.com/en/insights-and-events/insights/2021/02/latest-changes-in-employment-law-in-slovakia/.

237 Monte McNaughton, "Bill 27, Working for Workers Act, 2021," Legislative Assembly of Ontario, 2021, https://www.ola.org/en/legislative-business/bills/parliament-42/session-2/bill-27/.

237 "Republic of the Philippines MALACAÑANG," LawPhil Project, May 1, 1974, https://lawphil.net/statutes/presdecs/pd1974/pd_442_1974.html/.

237 Benedict Smith, "Escenic," *Telegraph*, August 30, 2013, https://www.telegraph.co.uk/news/worldnews/europe/germany/10276815/Out-of-hours-working-banned-by-German-labour-ministry.html/.

238 Milford Beagle Jr., "10th Mountain Division Commander to Leaders: Leave Soldiers Alone After Hours," 7 News, June 9, 2022, https://www.wwnytv.com/2022/06/09/10th-mountain-division-commander-leaders-leave-soldiers-alone-after-hours/.

238 "Sisyphus," Greek Mythology, November 30, 2023, https://www.greekmythology.com/Myths/Mortals/Sisyphus/sisyphus.html./.

239 Paul Raeburn, "Arianna Huffington: Collapse from Exhaustion Was 'Wake-up Call,'" *Today*, May 9, 2014, https://www.today.com/health/arianna-huffington-collapse-exhaustion-was-wake-call-2D79644042/.

239 Ruth Umoh, "Why Arianna Huffington Literally Tucks Her Phone into Bed Every

Night—and Why You Should Too," CNBC, November 28, 2017, https://www .cnbc.com/2017/11/28/why-arianna-huffington-literally-tucks-her-phone-into -bed-every-night.html/.

240 Steve Garbarino, "Why Some Power Dialers Still Flip for Flip Phones," *Wall Street Journal*, December 6, 2013, https://www.wsj.com/articles/SB100014240527 02304854804579236101787159602/.

240 Maya Kosoff and Alyson Shontell, "12 Wildly Successful People Who Still Use Flip Phones," Business Insider, January 3, 2015, https://www.businessinsider .com/successful-people-who-still-use-flip-phones-2014-12#warren-buffett-has -showed-off-his-nokia-flip-phone-on-cnn-12/.

240 Alison Coleman, "Six Business Leaders Share Their Digital Detox Strategies," Forbes, November 27, 2018, https://www.forbes.com/sites/alisoncoleman/2018 /11/27/six-business-leaders-share-their-digital-detox-strategies/?sh=3bf486 b01456/.

240 "Why Karlie Kloss Has a Weekly Digital Detox," *Mirror*, February 13, 2016, https://www.mirror.co.uk/3am/celebrity-news/karlie-kloss-weekly-digital-detox -7362723/.

240 Ryan Holmes, "Why Everyone Should Try Declaring Email Bankruptcy," Business Insider, February 12, 2015, https://www.businessinsider.com/why-you-should -stop-fighting-the-endless-onslaught-of-incoming-messages-and-declare-email -bankruptcy-2015-2/.

240 Rachel Gillett, "The Tricks Tim Cook, Bill Gates, and Other High-Powered Executives Use to Clear Their Inboxes," *Inc.*, November 18, 2015, https://www.inc .com/business-insider/email-habits-of-successful-executives.html/.

241 William J. Becker, Liuba Y. Belkin, Samantha A. Conroy, and Sarah Tuskey, "Killing Me Softly: Organizational E-mail Monitoring Expectations' Impact on Employee and Significant Other Well-Being," *Journal of Management* 47, no. 4 (2021): 1024–52.

241 Sandy J. Wayne, Grace Lemmon, Jenny M. Hoobler, Gordon W. Cheung, and Morgan S. Wilson, "The Ripple Effect: A Spillover Model of the Detrimental Impact of Work–Family Conflict on Job Success," *Journal of Organizational Behavior* 38, no. 6 (2017): 876–94.

242 Nicola von Allmen, Andreas Hirschi, Anne Burmeister, and Kristen M. Shockley, "The Effectiveness of Work–Nonwork Interventions: A Theoretical Synthesis and Meta-Analysis," *Journal of Applied Psychology* (2023): 1115–1131.

242 A. E. M. Hess, "On Holiday: Countries with the Most Vacation Days," *USA Today*, June 8, 2013, https://www.usatoday.com/story/money/business/2013/06/08 /countries-most-vacation-days/2400193/.

242 Robert Wood Johnson Foundation and Harvard School of Public Health, "The Workplace and Health," 2016, http://www.rwjf.org/content/dam/farm/reports /surveys_and_polls/2016/rwjf430330/.

242 Vincent Phan and James W. Beck, "Why Do People (Not) Take Breaks? An Investigation of Individuals' Reasons for Taking and for Not Taking Breaks at Work," *Journal of Business and Psychology* 38, no. 2 (2023): 259–82.

243 Colin West, Cassie Mogilner, and Sanford E. DeVoe, "Happiness from Treat-

ing the Weekend Like a Vacation," *Social Psychological and Personality Science* 12, no. 3 (2021): 346–56.

243 Anthony C. Klotz, Shawn T. McClean, Junhyok Yim, Joel Koopman, and Pok Man Tang, "Getting Outdoors after the Workday: The Affective and Cognitive Effects of Evening Nature Contact," *Journal of Management* 49, no. 7 (2023): 2254–87.

243 Eva J. Mojza, Christian Lorenz, Sabine Sonnentag, and Carmen Binnewies, "Daily Recovery Experiences: The Role of Volunteer Work during Leisure Time," *Journal of Occupational Health Psychology* 15, no. 1 (2010): 60–74.

244 Malte Roswag, Sascha Abdel Hadi, Jan A. Häusser, and Andreas Mojzisch, "Running Toward My Challenges: Day-Level Effects of Physical Activity before Work on Appraisal of the Upcoming Workday and Employee Well-Being," *Journal of Occupational Health Psychology* (2023).

244 John P. Trougakos, Daniel J. Beal, Stephen G. Green, and Howard M. Weiss, "Making the Break Count: An Episodic Examination of Recovery Activities, Emotional Experiences, and Positive Affective Displays," *Academy of Management Journal* 51, no. 1 (2008): 131–46.

244 Adelle X. Yang and Christopher K. Hsee, "Idleness versus Busyness," *Current Opinion in Psychology* 26 (2019): 15–18.

244 Andrew Brodsky and Teresa M. Amabile, "The Downside of Downtime: The Prevalence and Work Pacing Consequences of Idle Time at Work," *Journal of Applied Psychology* 103, no. 5 (2018): 496–512.

245 Sabine Sonnentag and Charlotte Fritz, "The Recovery Experience Questionnaire: Development and Validation of a Measure for Assessing Recuperation and Unwinding from Work," *Journal of Occupational Health Psychology* 12, no. 3 (2007): 204–221.

245 Nitya Chawla, Rebecca L. MacGowan, Allison S. Gabriel, and Nathan P. Podsakoff, "Unplugging or Staying Connected? Examining the Nature, Antecedents, and Consequences of Profiles of Daily Recovery Experiences," *Journal of Applied Psychology* 105, no. 1 (2020): 19–39.

245 Sabine Sonnentag, "Recovery, Work Engagement, and Proactive Behavior: A New Look at the Interface between Nonwork and Work," *Journal of Applied Psychology* 88, no. 3 (2003): 518–28.

245 Sabine Sonnentag, Carmen Binnewies, and Eva J. Mojza, "Staying Well and Engaged When Demands Are High: The Role of Psychological Detachment," *Journal of Applied Psychology* 95, no. 5 (2010): 965–76.

245 Ulla Kinnunen, Johanna Rantanen, Jessica de Bloom, Saija Mauno, Taru Feldt, and Kalevi Korpela, "The Role of Work–Nonwork Boundary Management in Work Stress Recovery," *International Journal of Stress Management* 23, no. 2 (2016): 99–123.

245 Lara B. Aknin, Julia W. Van de Vondervoort, and J. Kiley Hamlin, "Positive Feelings Reward and Promote Prosocial Behavior," *Current Opinion in Psychology* 20 (2018): 55–59.

245 Arménio Rego, Neuza Ribeiro, and Miguel P. Cunha, "Perceptions of Organizational Virtuousness and Happiness as Predictors of Organizational Citizenship Behaviors," *Journal of Business Ethics* 93 (2010): 215–35.

246 Sabine Sonnentag, "Work, Recovery Activities, and Individual Well-Being: A Diary Study," *Journal of Occupational Health Psychology* 6, no. 3 (2001): 196–210.

246 Cynthia L. Cordes and Thomas W. Dougherty, "A Review and an Integration of Research on Job Burnout," *Academy of Management Review* 18, no. 4 (1993): 621–56.

246 Vincent van Gogh, "Letter from Vincent van Gogh to Theo van Gogh," Web Exhibits, October, 28, 1883, https://www.webexhibits.org/vangogh/letter/13/336.htm.

246 Frank L. Schmidt and John E. Hunter, "The Validity and Utility of Selection Methods in Personnel Psychology: Practical and Theoretical Implications of 85 Years of Research Findings," *Psychological Bulletin* 124, no. 2 (1998): 262–274.

246 Chad H. Van Iddekinge, John D. Arnold, Rachel E. Frieder, and Philip L. Roth, "A Meta-Analysis of the Criterion-Related Validity of Prehire Work Experience," *Personnel Psychology* 72, no. 4 (2019): 571–98.

246 Timothy A. Judge and Joyce E. Bono, "Relationship of Core Self-Evaluations Traits—Self-Esteem, Generalized Self-Efficacy, Locus of Control, and Emotional Stability—with Job Satisfaction and Job Performance: A Meta-Analysis," *Journal of Applied Psychology* 86, no. 1 (2001): 80–92.

247 Albert Bandura and Sebastian Wessels, *Self-Efficacy*, vol. 4 (1994).

247 D. Sandy Staples, John S. Hulland, and Christopher A. Higgins, "A Self-Efficacy Theory Explanation for the Management of Remote Workers in Virtual Organizations," *Journal of Computer-Mediated Communication* 3, no. 4 (1998): JCMC342.

247 Y. Yi Mun and Yujong Hwang, "Predicting the Use of Web-Based Information Systems: Self-Efficacy, Enjoyment, Learning Goal Orientation, and the Technology Acceptance Model," *International Journal of Human-Computer Studies* 59, no. 4 (2003): 431–49.

247 Magid Igbaria and Juhani Iivari, "The Effects of Self-Efficacy on Computer Usage," *Omega* 23, no. 6 (1995): 587–605.

248 Gian Vittorio Caprara and Patrizia Steca, "Self-Efficacy Beliefs as Determinants of Prosocial Behavior Conducive to Life Satisfaction Across Ages," *Journal of Social and Clinical Psychology* 24, no. 2 (2005): 191–217.

248 Albert Bandura, Gian Vittorio Caprara, Claudio Barbaranelli, Maria Gerbino, and Concetta Pastorelli, "Role of Affective Self-Regulatory Efficacy in Diverse Spheres of Psychosocial Functioning," *Child Development* 74, no. 3 (2003): 769–82.

248 Zachary M. Shnek, Jane Irvine, Donna Stewart, and Susan Abbey, "Psychological Factors and Depressive Symptoms in Ischemic Heart Disease," *Health Psychology* 20, no. 2 (2001): 141–145.

248 Roeline G. Kuijer and Denise T. D. De Ridder, "Discrepancy in Illness-Related Goals and Quality of Life in Chronically Ill Patients: The Role of Self-Efficacy," *Psychology and Health* 18, no. 3 (2003): 313–30.

248 M. Isabella Bisschop, Didi M. W. Kriegsman, Aartjan T. F. Beekman, and Dorly J. H. Deeg, "Chronic Diseases and Depression: The Modifying Role of Psychosocial Resources," *Social Science & Medicine* 59, no. 4 (2004): 721–33.

248 Nicole Azizli, Breanna E. Atkinson, Holly M. Baughman, and Erica A. Giammarco, "Relationships between General Self-Efficacy, Planning for the Future, and Life Satisfaction," *Personality and Individual Differences* 82 (2015): 58–60.

248 Vittorio Caprara and Steca, "Self-Efficacy Beliefs."

249 Anna-Sophie Ulfert-Blank and Isabelle Schmidt, "Assessing Digital Self-Efficacy: Review and Scale Development," *Computers & Education* (2022): 1–23.

Conclusion: To AI and Beyond

259 Daniel Adiwardana, Daniel, Minh-Thang Luong, David R. So, Jamie Hall, Noah Fiedel, Romal Thoppilan, Zi Yang et al., "Towards a Human-Like Open-Domain Chatbot," arXiv Preprint arXiv:2001.09977 (2020).

259 Ashwin Rodrigues, "A History of SmarterChild," Vice, March 16, 2016, https://www.vice.com/en/article/jpgpey/a-history-of-smarterchild/.

260 Keith Leavitt, Feng Qiu, and Debra L. Shapiro, "Using Electronic Confederates for Experimental Research in Organizational Science," *Organizational Research Methods* 24, no. 1 (2021): 3–25.

260 Hayley Blunden and Andrew Brodsky, "A Review of Virtual Impression Management Behaviors and Outcomes," *Journal of Management* (2024): 2197–2236.

260 Arthur S. Jago, "Algorithms and Authenticity," *Academy of Management Discoveries* 5, no. 1 (2019): 38–56.

260 Nika Mozafari, Welf H. Weiger, and Maik Hammerschmidt, "Trust Me, I'm a Bot—Repercussions of Chatbot Disclosure in Different Service Frontline Settings," *Journal of Service Management* 33, no. 2 (2022): 221–45.

260 J. McGuire, D. De Cremer, Y. Hesselbarth, L. De Schutter, K. M. Mai, and A. Van Hiel, "The Reputational and Ethical Consequences of Deceptive Chatbot Use," *Scientific Reports* 13, no. 1 (2023): 16246.

260 Xueming Luo, Siliang Tong, Zheng Fang, and Zhe Qu, "Frontiers: Machines vs. Humans: The Impact of Artificial Intelligence Chatbot Disclosure on Customer Purchases," *Marketing Science* 38, no. 6 (2019): 937–47.

260 Fatimah Ishowo-Oloko, Jean-François Bonnefon, Zakariyah Soroye, Jacob Crandall, Iyad Rahwan, and Talal Rahwan, "Behavioural Evidence for a Transparency–Efficiency Tradeoff in Human–Machine Cooperation," *Nature Machine Intelligence* 1, no. 11 (2019): 517–21.

261 Adam Waytz, *The Power of Human: How Our Shared Humanity Can Help Us Create a Better World* (New York: Norton, 2019).

261 Christoph Fuchs, Martin Schreier, and Stijn MJ Van Osselaer, "The Handmade Effect: What's Love Got to Do with It?" *Journal of Marketing* 79, no. 2 (2015): 98–110.

Index